Wilmette Public Library
1242 Wilmette Ave.
Wilmette, IL 60091
847-256-5025

THE MURDER GANG

THE MURDER GANG

FLEET STREET'S ELITE
GROUP OF CRIME
REPORTERS IN THE
GOLDEN AGE OF
TABLOID CRIME

NEIL ROOT

For Trevor Dolby
That fine fellow

First published 2018

The History Press
The Mill, Brimscombe Port
Stroud, Gloucestershire, GL5 2QG
www.thehistorypress.co.uk

© Neil Root, 2018

British Library Cataloguing in Publication Data.
A catalogue record for this book is available from the British Library.

ISBN 978 0 7509 8371 6

Typesetting and origination by The History Press
Printed and bound in Great Britain by TJ International Ltd

070.
44
Ro

CONTENTS

FOREWORD

BY DUNCAN CAMPBELL

They were, as Neil Root so eloquently describes them:

> men in overcoats, camel-hair and Crombie, notepads out, in and out
> of shops, pubs and cafes, pressing for leads, scanning the street, getting
> a feel, a taste, led by instinct and experience. It's three o'clock in the
> afternoon and the Murder Gang are at the crime scene, response
> time: less than thirty minutes.

The Murder Gang was the name given to the crime reporters of the
national press by Hilde Marchant, herself a brave and distinguished
journalist, in an affectionate article she wrote for *Picture Post* in 1947.
That thirty-minute response time was to a murder in central London
of someone who would now be called a 'have-a-go hero': Alec de
Antiquis who fatally intervened in a jewellery robbery in London's
West End that year and was shot dead.

This was the heyday of the crime reporter and, indeed, of the tabloid
press. By 1956, the *News of the World* was selling more than 7 million
copies every Sunday and its rival, *The People*, more than 5 million. What
did readers want in those days? Not over-egged tittle-tattle about
'celebrities' but tales of crime and, especially, of murder. It was the
task of those men – and they were almost all men until the 1970s – to
provide the who, why, where, when and how of every homicide for a

fascinated public as enthralled by true crime as by the novels of Agatha Christie and Edgar Wallace.

In his earlier book, Frenzy! Heath, Haigh and Christie: The First Great Tabloid Murders, published in 2011, Neil Root examined the ways in which the press dealt with three of Britain's most notorious killers: Neville Heath, who sadistically murdered women; John George Haigh, who famously dissolved his victims in an acid bath; and John Christie of 10 Rillington Place who let another man hang for his murders before being caught himself. He also explored the sometimes symbiotic relationship between the crime reporter and the criminal.

While we may feel we know much about murderers and rather less about their victims, what about the people who described them and brought them to life? Root has now focussed on the time and the place where the crime reporter was in his pomp and those characters whose lives revolved around Scotland Yard's press room and Fleet Street's pubs, rural murder scenes and smoky newsrooms and the narrow press benches of the Old Bailey and Bow Street magistrates' court. It was a busy, exciting life if it often tended to be a short one: chain-smoking and beer-drinking were as much a part of the job as shorthand-writing and cultivating talkative mates in the Flying Squad.

There was no shortage of characters: Percy Hoskins of the Daily Express, who had a grace and favour house in Park Lane, courtesy of his admiring proprietor, Lord Beaverbook; Norman 'Jock' Rae of the News of the World who helped to unmask the murderer, Dr Buck Ruxton in the 1930s; Duncan Webb of The People, who exposed the Messina brothers and their Soho prostitution network; Tom Tullett of the Daily Mirror to whom a murderer confessed, even producing for inspection a gruesome parcel of body parts of one of his victims.

They were writing at a time when a murder could still be followed by a hanging, despite a growing public unease about capital punishment. It was the Daily Mirror commentator, Cassandra, writing in July 1955, who expressed that disquiet in a column about the execution of Ruth Ellis for shooting her lover in Hampstead: 'It's a fine day for haymaking,' he wrote. 'A fine day for fishing. A fine day for lolling in the sunshine. And if you feel that way – and I mourn to say that millions of you do – it's a fine day for a hanging.'

But once the death penalty was abolished in 1969, as the journalist Victor Davis noted in appropriately colourful prose:

> much of the buzz went out of crime reporting. The Swinging Sixties swung a little less. No more judge's black cap, no more execution date planted squarely on the home secretary's desk as a reminder that there is a yes-or-no decision to take, no more Albert Pierrepoint and Harry Allen, the deadly duo, overnighting with the prison governor while they tested the trap, rigged the rope and ate a dinner always described as hearty – just like the condemned man's breakfast.

There were certainly a few more good days for hangings to come after Ruth Ellis was executed and the Murder Gang made sure that their readers were informed about every detail of the killings, the investigations, the perpetrators and the trials. Those days are gone now. Newspapers with declining circulations can no longer afford to cover murder cases in great detail and, in the wake of the scandals of phone-hacking and paying for tip-offs that led to the Leveson inquiry and the closure of the *News of the World*, relations between police and crime reporters are no longer so chummy. In the meantime, in all their rumpled glory – the Gang's all here.

DUNCAN CAMPBELL is the author of *We'll All Be Murdered in Our Beds! The Shocking History of Crime Reporting in Britain* and a former Chairman of the Crime Reporters' Association.

INTRODUCTION

This book documents the incredible activities of the 'Murder Gang'– the elite group of renegade Fleet Street crime reporters who covered the most famous British murders between the mid-1930s and the mid-1960s, a period in which crime, especially murder, saturated the front and inside pages of the tabloid newspapers as never before or since.

The nefarious collusion of police and newspapers as witnessed over the last few years with phone hacking and bribery has given the impression that we live in a world where corruption is endemic in both the Fourth Estate and almost every part of the 'establishment'. The impression is that we live in an age of moral turpitude to outstrip anything in our murky history. Delve just fifty years into the past and that impression will be thoroughly disabused. Indeed, the arrogance and greed of the newspapers, along with the establishment that in part nourishes and in part ignores them as they go on their merry money-making way, has its origins in an extraordinary period of British crime journalism where anything went so long as the story landed on the front page and papers were sold.

For the first time and from first-hand accounts this book will explore how the public's fascination with murder was whipped up by a breed of journalists who would stop at nothing to get the story. If that meant becoming criminals in the process then that was part of the job. It was a hard-drinking, chain-smoking, stressful, highly competitive job with long and irregular hours, populated by larger-than-life characters, often using dubious and highly unethical methods. Many of these journalists were on first-name terms with a string of brutal murderers as well as well-placed contacts within the police and court system. They could get information quickly, and get things done. In extremis there was Percy Hoskins (*Daily Express*) of whom it was said, 'If you are in trouble you should call Percy before your lawyer.'

Members of the Murder Gang drank in the same Fleet Street pubs and repaired to the same bars and hotels when chasing a story, but they were also ruthlessly competitive against each other personally and any rival newspaper. It was said that when the *Daily Express* covered a big murder story they would send four cars: the first car containing their Murder Gang reporters, the other three cars to block the road at crime scenes to stop other rival Murder Gang members from getting through. As a matter of course Murder Gang members got the scoop by listening in to police radios, and it was part of the game to remove part of the earpiece of nearby public telephones so that rivals could not phone in a story from a rural location. And those potatoes in the boot of their cars were not for lunch, but for jamming into their rivals' car exhaust pipes so the vehicle would not start. Then there were far fewer regulatory rules on media reporting. Clandestine meetings with killers on the run from the police and huge payments to murderers and their families were just the tools of the trade.

Revel Barker, who worked on the *Sunday Mirror* at the end of the period covered in this book, remembers today how Murder Gang reporters dressed and how they operated:

Crime reporters aped the dress of CID detectives – three piece suits, usually a trilby, and raincoats or trench coats, or heavy overcoats in winter. They also adopted copper slang – for instance, referring to suspects as 'Chummy'. They learnt to talk in pubs without moving their lips. The crime reporters were in the streets and in the pubs; then there were 'Scotland Yard reporters' who spent most of their time in the Yard Press Bureau, transmitting information, and sometimes trying to wheedle it out of the police.

TOP OF FORM

This era was undoubtedly the 'golden age' of tabloid crime coverage in Britain. There was a huge explosion of violent crime after the war, the whys and wherefores of which will be explored in this book. And not coincidentally did newspaper circulation reach its peak; the *News of the World* had 8 million regular Sunday readers in the 1950s, with the other papers not far behind. They were fed an unsavoury diet of mayhem and murder. In his famous late 1940s essay *The Decline of the English Murder*, George Orwell lamented that the 'quality' of British crime and its reporting had deteriorated from what he remembered of the 1920s.

The period covered by this book will detail how crime became the tabloid press's main focus in its quest to sell newspapers. The amount of grisly detail about murders at the time – especially after the Second World War when the British public was desensitised to criminal horrors – would shock even twenty-first-century tabloid readers. As the crime and social historian Donald Thomas has pointed out, this was the time when lurid and violent pulp crime writers such as Mickey Spillane and Hank Janson (both of whom had books banned, even then) were No.1 bestsellers. The threshold of conservative prudery shown by the 1961 *Lady Chatterley's Lover* trial, towards the end of the period covered in this book, was much lower than that shown to crime writing: sex was far more heavily censured than violence.

The stirrings of what became the Murder Gang can be traced to the mid-1930s, and the pack mentality grew from then. Crime reporting became more hazardous after the Second World War, largely due to the risk of new libel laws and the latent fear of contravening the Official Secrets Act. These new libel laws feature in some of the murder cases in this book, and we will see how the Murder Gang sometimes found ingenious ways to circumvent them.

As the reader turns the final page of this book, hopefully they will understand how the reporting of crime in the tabloids developed, and how it is linked to the tabloid press we have today. With many tabloid journalists arrested in the recent phone-hacking furore and the Leveson Report into press regulation that followed, many might have wondered how we descended to this low point of ethics in our free press.

This book attempts to tell the incredible, atmospheric and sometimes jaw-dropping story of how Fleet Street tabloid crime reporting developed from 1935 to 1965, by which time the modern tabloid template we know today came into being. Readers will meet the irrepressible and eccentric larger-than life characters who manned the phones in smoke-filled newsrooms, knocked on unwelcoming doors and walked smog-filled streets and country lanes in pursuit of dangerous killers. At the time some Murder Gang members were household names, as famous as some of the criminals they exposed were infamous.

The core members of the Murder Gang were the legendary Percy Hoskins, Montague Lacey and Len Hunter of the *Daily Express*; Norman 'Jock' Rae, James Howie Milligan and, later, Ronald Mount of the *News of the World*; Harry Procter of the *Daily Mirror*, *Daily Mail* and *Sunday Pictorial*; Victor Sims and Fred Redman of the *Sunday Pictorial* (the latter ironically later the *Sunday Mirror*'s 'Happy Homes' expert); Arthur Tietjen, Sid Brock, Hugh Brady of the *Daily Mail*, along with Rodney Hallworth, who would later join the *Daily Express*; Duncan 'Tommy' Webb of *The People*, who actually specialised more in organised crime than murder but was certainly 'one of the chaps'; Charles 'Tich' Leach of the Exchange Telegraph Co.; Jimmy Reid of the *Sunday Dispatch*; Cecil Catling of *The Star*; E.V. (Tom) Tullett of the *Sunday Express* and then *Daily Mirror*; Gerald Byrne of *Empire News*; Reginald 'Fireman' Foster of the *Daily Mail*, *News Chronicle* and *Sunday Express;* Sam Jackett of the *Evening News*, formerly of Reuters; Victor Toddington of the *Evening Standard*; William 'Bill' Ashenden of the *Daily Sketch* and the *Daily Graphic*; Owen Summers of the *Daily Sketch*; the veteran Stanley Bishop, Robert 'Bob' Traini and W.A.E. 'Billy' Jones of the *Daily Herald*; W.G. Finch of the Press Association; and Harold Whittall of the *Daily Mirror*.

Most members of the Murder Gang will feature at some point, but it has been decided for reasons of narrative symmetry to focus on some key members to take us from 1935 to 1965, from the first cases on which this group reported to the last murderers to be hanged, by which time the Murder Gang was fragmenting and times changing.

There are no women; the Murder Gang was an exclusively male 'club', an echo of the times. Conversely, although absent from the crime beat, women were already distinguishing themselves as foreign and war correspondents in this period: Hilde Marchant, who would immortalise the Murder Gang in her 1947 *Picture Post* article, had earlier been sent by the *Daily Express*'s editor Arthur Christiansen to cover the Siege of Madrid from a female perspective; the American journalist Martha Gellhorn covered several wars, of course; and Claire Hollingworth, a young British correspondent, got what has been called 'the scoop of the century', breaking the outbreak of the Second World War as Hitler mobilised his tank regiments in Poland, to name but three. It wouldn't be until much later that Fleet Street gained its first female crime reporters, such as the *Daily Mirror*'s Sylvia Jones – and even then she had a tough time at first in that still testosterone-soaked world.

The skill set and working methods of Murder Gang members also became increasingly sophisticated over time. Percy Hoskins, the most powerful and well-connected member of the Murder Gang, stalwart of the *Daily Express* from the mid-1920s right through to the early 1980s, summed this up in a speech he gave to the Medico-Legal Society in London on 8 January 1959, towards the end of the period of the active Murder Gang covered by this book:

When I first came to Fleet Street, the crime reporter was what our American colleagues call a 'leg man'. In other words, his job was to hang around police stations and to telephone his office with tips of murder, fire or sudden death. Then he could sit back with the confident assurance that someone else would be sent out to cover the story. His responsibility was at an end … Today, despite the doubt that may still persist in the minds of our critics, all this, with very few exceptions, has changed. The 'leg man' has disappeared. He has been replaced by the specialist, a man with a much higher degree of education, who by hard experience has acquired a sound grasp of his subject; a man who has sufficient knowledge of the law to know what he can or cannot print; a man who looks upon reporting as a stimulating and socially useful profession in which he is eager to rise as far as opportunity and native ability permit.

It is hoped that this book manages to capture a sense of that development. In the same speech, Hoskins admitted, 'Like every other profession, we have our black sheep.' This was certainly true, so underhand and unethical methods employed to get scoops are also documented in the following pages. The murders covered by this pack of Fleet Street journalists are of course often macabre and shocking – the very reason why these cases sold newspapers and the ruthless chase for scoops was on. It was a different world, and definitely a harder, less sensitive one. These journalists operated in that milieu, in those times, under different rules, and sometimes outside the laws of their own era. This is the story of the Murder Gang of Fleet Street.

I

A GRISLY JIGSAW

It was late summer for an optimist, and early autumn for a realist. The sedate landscape of the Scottish Borders, a healthy walk in the fresh air – just what Miss Susan Haines Johnson, a young woman visiting her family from Edinburgh, needed. Little did she know that her gentle stroll that day would soon set the Fleet Street crime sheets ablaze and that what she saw would make a marked entry into criminological history.

While millions all over Britain were wetting fingers and thumbs and rustling the crinkled pages of the *Sunday Pictorial*, *News of the World* and *Sunday Graphic*, Susan had walked alone about 2 miles north from where she was staying with family in the town of Moffat. She rested, leaning on the edge of a bridge overrunning a densely wooded valley with a stream called Gardenholme Linn. The British public would soon come to know this place, below where Susan had stopped, as 'a ravine'. Susan looked over the bridge at the view. Peace, tranquillity; she'd escaped from the city, seduced by nature. But what then suddenly drew her gaze was most unnatural.

Susan wasn't far from the Devil's Beef Tub, which lies a further three miles north, a deep valley surrounded by four hills, a favourite for walkers. The Scottish novelist Sir Walter Scott, author of *Rob Roy* and

Ivanhoe, romanticised this area in his writing, but the Scottish freedom fighter William Wallace had made it famous by his actions more than five centuries earlier, when he launched his first attack against the English by gathering the clans in the Devil's Beef Tub in 1297. Now, in 1935, the very bridge on which Susan Haines Johnson was standing was known locally as the Devil's Bridge.

It was a sort of package she saw, pushed against a rock in the stream that runs into the River Annan. Her eyes zoomed in on this object so strange to its surroundings, and her easy solitude was destroyed, though Susan could hardly believe her eyes. Poking out of the package was a human arm. Susan ran the 2 miles back to Moffat, to the hotel where her family was staying. Her brother Alfred did his best to calm her down and called the police.

The terrible and unexpected find made the local Scottish newspapers in coming days, and as always Fleet Street's Murder Gang of crime reporters wasn't far behind. Exactly a week later, the crime covered half of page 13 of the *News of the World*. By this time, an extensive search of the area in and around the stream under Devil's Bridge, under the aegis of Inspector Strath and his right-hand man Sergeant Sloane of the Dumfriesshire Police, had uncovered further dumped bundles, containing various body parts, and this was undoubtedly the catalyst for the crime reporter Norman Rae and his news editor sniffing out the chrysalis of a major murder story.

NEW MOVES IN RAVINE MURDERS RIDDLE
Police Confident Of Solving Gruesome Crime
News of the World, Sunday 6 October 1935

'Certified Net Sale Exceeds 3,350,000 Copies', the *News of the World* then proudly announced under its masthead every Sunday. This was nothing compared to the circulations that this and other British national newspapers would achieve in coming years, for which substantial credit was due to the Murder Gang. These hard-living, intuitive, cunning, manipulative and sometimes unethical or, by twenty-first-century standards, immoral hacks were already building close contacts with the police all over Britain, and especially with London's Metropolitan Police, and that of course meant Scotland Yard.

Incredibly, until the mid-1930s Scotland Yard had no Press Bureau, and therefore no official conduit between it and Fleet Street. Before the Press Bureau was established in 1936, the year after Susan Haines Johnson saw that arm protruding from that bridge in the Scottish Borders, informal 'press conferences' would be held in smoke-filled pubs, often with the Murder Squad detective in charge of the case tipping off favoured hacks. This lack of official channels meant that personal police contacts were imperative.

The early Press Bureau of the late 1930s was also not very helpful to the public. When the first telephone was installed in the Press Bureau in 1936, the duty police officer was incredulous: 'we will be expected to take calls from the public next!' In fact, a separate department known as the Information Room had been set up two years earlier, in 1934, to receive calls from the public on Whitehall 1212.

Early stalwarts of the Murder Gang such as Norman 'Jock' Rae, Percy Hoskins, Hugh Brady and Stanley Bishop would wait in their respective newspaper offices late into the night drinking Scotch waiting for the notorious Back Hall Inspector to do his rounds. He was a Metropolitan Police inspector who went around Fleet Street at night selling tip-offs. He was never identified by the hacks.

The police, within whose ranks corruption was endemic, did not trust Fleet Street, and members of the Murder Gang had to build individual relationships with key detectives of the time such as Ted Greeno, Reg Spooner, Jack Capstick, Robert Fabian, Bill Chapman and Peter Beveridge. If the hacks betrayed these policemen in any way, the channel would be immediately closed; information given 'off the record' had to stay 'off the record'.

But as the 1940s progressed and gave way to the 1950s, Scotland Yard, provincial police forces and Fleet Street became more professional. When Scotland Yard was based on the Embankment from 1890 to 1967 – where it returned in 2015 – the whole building only had two telephones, but after moving to The Broadway in 1967 there were numerous telephones and contact became easier. Still, some Murder Gang members would spend hours a day working at spare desks at Scotland Yard, so as to be on the spot for a tip-off if something came in.

It was almost definitely a police tip-off that led the *News of the World* Murder Gang reporters to chase the story of the body parts in 'the ravine' at the end of September and into October 1935. Norman 'Jock' Rae was first on the case, leading where the rest of Fleet Street would follow. The 'Sundays' usually had more resources to follow a case, and of course more time, as the reporters only had to file once a week, although, of course, they would sometimes be making multiple filings when covering several cases at once. Not that the 'Dailies' and the evening papers were in any way slouches with regard to workload: the members of the Murder Gang just had to gather sources and leads on a story, go deeper and do interviews, write it up and file to make the next day's or that evening's edition.

Rae, working closely with his *News of the World* colleague James Howie Milligan, would use the extra time they had incredibly well and get the biggest scoop of the case, at that early stage still referred to amongst the Murder Gang as the Ravine Murder. It was to become one of the biggest British murder cases of the 1930s, and in particular was to make Rae's name amongst the Murder Gang and all over Fleet Street. By the late 1940s he was almost a household name.

Norman Rae, known by most who knew him as 'Jock', was a Scot, being born in Aberdeen in 1896. He fabricated his age to serve in the Highland Division in the First World War, and after that conflict moved into journalism and to London. Rae's tough and bloody-mindedness masked a compassionate nature, his intellect mixed with streetwise instincts, his huge capacity for hard work, real tenacity and staying-power on a story, and his shrewd understanding of human nature and literary ability, made him a natural-born journalist – just as he himself must have sometimes wondered if some of the murderers he came to know over a long Fleet Street career were natural-born killers. Rae was also 'nobody's fool' as they used to say. Ravenously driven, adept at fighting his corner and defending his story by any means, he would sometimes go to extraordinary, near-illegal lengths to get his scoop. And this was of course a time when there was far less press regulation.

An early incident in Rae's Fleet Street career is enlightening as to his character and working methods. Rae himself had made the newspapers, for once the subject of the story, on 29 September 1927 – exactly eight years to the day before Susan Haines Johnson saw the package with the human arm on Devil's Bridge in the Scottish Borders, precipitating the rush of 'Jock' Rae and James Howie Milligan to Moffat. He had been arrested whilst chasing a story, a fire in Redhill Street in the Marylebone district of London, on 9 September that year, which claimed four lives. The headline, which ran twenty days later in the north-eastern regional paper the *Shields Daily News*, read, 'Wrongful Arrest: Police Fail In Case Against Journalist'. Rae was then aged 30, living in Clapham, South London and working in Fleet Street.

Appearing at Marylebone Police Court, Rae was defended by the King's Counsel barrister Mr J.D. Cassels, a noted brief who had already unsuccessfully defended the brutal 'ladykiller' Patrick Mahon, who had murdered and dismembered the tragic Emily Kaye in a cottage on the Crumbles, a stretch of beach close to Eastbourne, Sussex, three years earlier. (Interestingly, Cassels had also defended the culprits in the unconnected murder of Irene Munro in 1920, also on the Crumbles.) Patrick Mahon was hanged, but the prosecution case against him had been extremely formidable, almost watertight. The Mahon case was also forensically very important, as the painstaking work done by the legendary Home Office pathologist Sir Bernard Spilsbury on Emily Kaye's remains was ground-breaking, and led to the introduction of the 'Murder Bag' set of implements by Scotland Yard, which all detectives from then on had to take to murder scenes to preserve vital evidence. The Ravine Murder case, which Rae covered in 1935, would also prove to be forensically highly innovative.

Rae was facing a charge of obstructing the police on the day of the fatal fire, and he had been arrested by an Inspector Simpkin of the Metropolitan Police. Simpkin had testified at an earlier hearing that when he closed the street Rae had been asked to leave the vicinity but had refused. However, the presiding magistrate found that the prosecution had 'failed to satisfy him that Rae had obstructed the Inspector, or that his arrest was justified'. Rae was acquitted, and awarded 20 guineas for costs, a not insignificant sum then. The magistrate, Mr H.A.C. Bingley, said, 'The police always ask me to give them costs if they win. Whether my decision is right or wrong this defendant has been put to vast trouble and expense. He was arrested, I think, wrongfully.' It was a victory for Rae, but he would certainly have to develop far better relationships with the police in the future if he was to get what the 1920s American humourist and sports journalist Ring Lardner called 'the inside dope'. Above all, though, this incident shows how fiercely determined Norman Rae was in pursuit of a story, a quality which would help make him a leading member of the Murder Gang in coming years.

The *News of the World* in 1935 was a heady mixture of politics, sport, humour, 'charming bounder' love rat stories, household features, advertising and of course crime stories. It was then a broadsheet newspaper, and would remain so until Rupert Murdoch changed it into a tabloid when he bought it thirty-four years later. The Italian dictator Mussolini dominated headlines in the *News of the World* that summer and autumn, as he threatened to and eventually did march into Abyssinia. Recurring weekly features included the 'Great Men of Our Time' series by the Right Honourable Winston Churchill MP, then in the political wilderness without high office, but soon to warn about Hitler's massive rearmament programme and nefarious intentions, before becoming wartime Prime Minister in 1940.

The heavyweight British boxing champ Jack Petersen, a Welshman who had held the title for some months in 1932–33, relinquished it, but regained and held it between June 1934 and August 1936, told his story 'Fighting the Big Fellows' on consecutive Sundays, and Hugh Gallacher, the Scottish footballer of the 1920s and 1930s, a prolific goal-scorer for Scotland who also played for Newcastle United, Chelsea and other top league clubs, had his serial 'Inside the Football Game'.

A typical love-sex interest story of that year was headlined 'Pose of a Married Man: eloped with girl and ran up bills.' Humour also crept headlong into tabloid advertising. 'Public Enemy No.1 (Stomach Trouble)' with Maclean Brand Stomach Powder being the tonic, was a sardonic nod to the obsession on both sides of the Atlantic with the successive small-time gangsters thus named by J. Edgar Hoover's fledgling FBI – most famously the bank robber and killer John Dillinger and his gang, who were all over the front and crime pages in 1934 and 1935. Far more dangerous organised crime figures such as Al Capone (already in prison for tax evasion), Dutch Schultz (murdered by rival gangsters), and Lucky Luciano (about to be arrested for pimping and imprisoned, before later being deported) were off the radar.

Back in Britain, on Sunday 22 September 1935, a week before the discovery of the body part in a package beneath the bridge in Moffat, the *News of the World* reported that Tony Mancini had received three months' hard labour for stealing a wristwatch from a jewellery shop in Trowbridge, Wiltshire. Just ten months earlier, in December 1934, Mancini, whose real name was Cecil England and whose aliases as a petty criminal were the more exotic Hyman Gold and Jack Notyre, had been sensationally acquitted of the second Brighton Trunk Murder, after the body of his lover, the dancer and prostitute Violet Kaye, was found in a trunk at his Brighton lodgings. This terrible discovery was a direct result of a house-to-house search after a dismembered torso of a woman was found in a trunk at Brighton train station in July 1934, known as the first Brighton Trunk murder. Her legs were soon found in another trunk at Kings Cross station in London. She was never identified, her killer was never caught, and no link to Tony Mancini was ever established. The unknown tragic victim had been given the moniker 'The Girl with the Pretty Feet' by the Murder Gang. Coincidentally, Mancini was unsuccessfully prosecuted for the murder of Violet Kaye by J.D. Cassels KC, who had defended Norman Rae against his obstruction of a police officer charge in 1927. In 1976, just prior to his death, Mancini confessed to Violet Kaye's murder, knowing that he could not be tried again for the same crime due to the double jeopardy law. Mancini gave his confession to the *News of the World*, undoubtedly for payment.

After their initial *News of the World* article on Sunday 6 October 1935 from Moffat in Dumfriesshire, Jock Rae and Jim Milligan were looking for other leads to follow. There would soon be major developments in the Ravine Murder case.

Other bundles of human remains, eventually reaching approximately thirty in total over the coming weeks, contained various body parts to add to the initial arm packed into the first bundle spotted by Susan Haines Johnson: a torso with no arms, legs, a thighbone, lumps of flesh, and the upper part of two further arms. It was obvious that two bodies were present, and then two skulls were discovered, the faces having been skinned in an obvious attempt to prevent identification of the victims through facial feature ID, although teeth were still present in one skull and dental research would help confirm identification.

Fingertips had also been removed from two hands to avoid fingerprint detection. Fingerprint evidence had then been in use as evidence in murder trials for thirty years in Britain, since it was first used to hang the Stratton brothers in 1905 for the senseless murders of an elderly shopkeeper and his wife in the course of robbery in Deptford, south-east London. A burglar named Henry Jackson had previously been convicted using fingerprint evidence in 1902, just a year after Scotland Yard's Fingerprint Bureau was established. But back to Moffat in 1935 – this was murder, and double murder at that.

The body parts were soon being examined by prominent Scottish forensic scientists Professor John Glaister from Glasgow University and his colleague Dr Gavin Millar of Edinburgh University, who had to piece together the bodies like a jigsaw. The English Home Office pathologist Bernard Spilsbury was also called from London to carry out post-mortems. He had particular expertise in dismemberment, as he had proved in the piecing together of the victim's body in the Patrick Mahon case back in 1924.

The first *News of the World* piece that ran on 6 October 1935 had stated that poison may well have been used on the victims, specifically arsenic. This was obviously what Norman Rae had carefully gleaned from police contacts they had made on the scene, who had been advised after early forensic analysis. It was also reported that the pieced-together taller body was thought to be male, and the shorter one female. Rae described the unidentified 'couple' as follows: 'The man – probably elderly, 5ft 8 or 9in tall, muscular condition and nutrition good, scarcely any teeth. The woman – between 30 and 40 years of age, about 5ft 2in tall, dark brown hair, no wisdom teeth, three vaccination marks on the left upper arm. Feet and hands well cared for, no ring marks on hands.' Bernard Spilsbury's post-mortem reports in the police case file confirm this analysis, as he refers to one of the bodies as a 'he'.

The finding and identification of three breasts showed that both victims were certainly female. Spilsbury also wrote, 'From the clean method by which both limbs were severed through the knee joints it is a strong presumption that it was carried out by someone having anatomical knowledge.' Glaister and Millar had also thought this, especially when it was confirmed that a knife, not a saw, had been used to dismember the two bodies, a far more difficult implement to use for the grim task, and one that would have taken real understanding of human anatomy. Their opinions were supported by consultation with Professor Sydney Smith, a leading pathologist from the University of Edinburgh, and several other experts in pathology, dentistry and anatomy from that university and John Glaister's own University of Glasgow.

It too had been reported that the body parts had been wrapped variously in a blouse (in the case of one skull), sheets, children's clothing and newspapers. It was the latter wrapping which would break the case wide open as to the identity of the two women and their killer, in an ingenious twist. The newspapers used were not named in the press at that early stage, but in fact they were all national newspapers which came out of Fleet Street: the *Sunday Chronicle*, the *Daily Herald* of 6 and 31 August 1935, and the *Sunday Graphic* published on 15 September 1935.

It was the *Sunday Graphic*, published two weeks before Susan Haines Johnson made her discovery, which would lead the police, and the *News of the World*, in the direction of the victims and the culprit. The *Sunday Graphic* chosen by whoever wrapped two upper arms in its pages was a special regional printing or 'slip' edition, published only in a small geographical area: the Lancaster and Morecambe areas of Lancashire in north-west England, around 100 miles (160km) south of Moffat. It was advertising a local festival in Morecambe, and just 3,700 copies had been printed.

Jock Rae of the *News of the World* had got the jump on Murder Gang reporters on rival papers with their initial splash, but by now representatives of other Fleet Street papers had arrived in Moffat, like aliens invading a small sleepy town. It was now that Rae showed real journalistic initiative and quietly made his way south to the Morecambe and Lancaster areas. So as not to alert the other rival Murder Gang reporters on the scene as to his new lead, Rae let it be known amongst the hacks that he had to return to London for personal reasons. The *News of the World* strengthened this journalistic alibi by sending Rae's crime colleague James Howie Milligan to Moffat from London to take his place, as other reporters would have been suspicious if the paper had withdrawn representation at the scene of such a big crime case.

James Howie Milligan was almost eight years Norman Rae's elder and a fellow Scot, born in Glasgow in 1888. At the time that he travelled to Moffat to cover the Ravine Murder case, Milligan was almost 47 years old, and he'd led an eventful life. On leaving school he went to sea, becoming a Second Mate, and on the outbreak of the First World War served as a navigation officer on troop ships. As Duncan Campbell points out in his seminal history of British crime reporting *We'll All Be Murdered In Our Beds*, Milligan was also a gifted comic songwriter in his spare time. He wrote the popular song 'Roamin' in the Gloamin" for the Scottish music hall and vaudeville singer and comedian Sir Harry Lauder, who also later recorded Milligan's song 'Pin Your Faith on the Motherland'.

Milligan entered journalism in 1920, joining the London branch of the National Union of Journalists on 7 November 1925, four days before his 37th birthday. By 1928 he was a crime reporter on the *Sunday Express*, where he quickly made his mark, securing an exclusive interview with King Carol of Romania that year which misleadingly became known as 'the interview that cost a throne'. The scandal-ridden King Carol had actually renounced his right to the Romanian throne in 1925 and was living in Paris with his mistress Magda Lupescu by the time Milligan interviewed him. Still, it was quite a scoop, and the first of many for Milligan.

James Howie Milligan moved to the rival Sunday paper *News of the World* to work alongside 'Jock' Rae in 1935, so he was new to the paper when he and Rae travelled up to Moffat in their native Scotland at the very beginning of October. Earlier that year in March, Britain's first driving test had been taken, 'Lawrence of Arabia', T.E. Lawrence, had been killed in a motorcycle crash in May, and the publisher Penguin had introduced the first of its famous paperbacks in July.

The small town of Moffat must have been bewildered by these hardened yet courteous Murder Gang hacks arriving from Fleet Street to get the real story behind Susan Haines Johnson's gruesome discovery, already the talk of every Moffat living room, shop and pub. The two most prominent hotels in the town were the Moffat House Hotel in the High Street, designed by the famous architect John Adam, and the Star Hotel, much later entered into the *Guinness Book of Records* as 'the narrowest hotel in the world', being just 20ft (6m) in width. Rae, Milligan and the other crime correspondents are likely to have stayed in these establishments, or one nearby. In fact, Rae and Milligan would be engaged on the case for the next six months on and off, all the while covering other less sensational murders, too.

James Howie Milligan would soon follow his colleague south once Rae had something concrete to go on, whilst other Murder Gang members stayed in Moffat, where the bodies had been found. Rae was moving where the action was in reality, surmising that as one of the newspapers used to wrap the unfortunate women's bodies like 1930s butcher's meat was read in that small area of north-west England, the real story was south of the border.

It has long been widely assumed that Norman Rae came up with the crucial evidence that led the police away from Scotland, as he was so quick off the mark in going there. It's extremely unlikely, almost certain, that Rae got his information about the newspaper Morecambe and Lancaster slip edition from a police contact, and that in itself shows his, and perhaps James Howie Milligan's, ingenuity and thorough working of the story. But it can now be revealed that the tip-off about the slip edition came from another source, in fact from another journalist not on the case, down in London, hundreds of miles from Scotland.

Tucked away in the Metropolitan Police files of the case, there is a letter dated 3 October 1935, four days after Susan Haines Johnson saw the first macabre bundle, and three days before Rae and Milligan published their first coverage of the case in the *News of the World*.

The letter was sent from the Press Club, based in St Bride's House in Salisbury Square, close to Fleet Street, and read:

I notice that it is stated that some of the human remains found in Moffat were wrapped in 'National' newspapers. A small point comes to me, which may be of interest, and it is this. All national newspapers print certain editions for various areas. If these papers are by any chance the *Mail*, *Express* or *Herald*, the editorial staff in either case could tell you which area it was printed for by reference to their files. This might help to localise matters. Yours Truly…

The sender of this letter was Colin Cathcart, who had been a member of the central London branch of the National Union of Journalists since 1918, and had worked as a journalist since starting as a reporter on the *Daily Express* in 1919, when he lived in Catford, south-east London. Born in 1872, Cathcart was aged 63 and nearing retirement, now living in Streatham, South-west London. He died on 8 April 1947, eleven and a half years after he gave the Metropolitan Police the crucial tip off they needed in the Ravine Murder case.

The letter was sent straight to the CID the following day, 4 October 1935. By this time Dumfriesshire Police had called in the then more sophisticated assistance of Scotland Yard and Inspector Jeremiah Lynch of the Metropolitan Police, a tough Irishman already very distinguished for his fearless uncovering of German spies operating in Britain in the First World War, his pursuit of the infamous conman Horatio Bottomley and as a member of the early Flying Squad. In a more administrative role by now, Lynch was tasked with checking all subscribers to that Morecambe and Lancaster slip edition of the 15 September 1935 *Sunday Graphic*.

At the same time, Dumfriesshire Police were far from idle. Chief Constable Black, the head of that force, had read about the disappearance of a young woman called Mary Jane Rogerson, who worked as a nanny and maid, then called a 'nursemaid', in Lancaster, which of course fell within the geographical radius of the slip edition of the paper. By liaising with his opposite number, Chief Constable Vann of Lancaster, it was learnt that Rogerson was the nursemaid to a Dr Buck Ruxton and his wife Isabella, who lived in Lancaster, and, most importantly, that Isabella Ruxton was missing too. Both women had not been seen since 15 September 1935, the very day on which the slip edition of the *Sunday Graphic* used to wrap one of the bundles was on sale in that area and being sent out to subscribers.

Norman Rae, now down in the Morecambe and Lancaster area far ahead of the Murder Gang curve, got to Dr Buck Ruxton by sheer investigative work, known as 'legwork', and local gossip learnt through copious and patient interviews, conducted in a relaxed 'bedside' manner that would have made any doctor proud. Colin Cathcart may have provided the tip that led the investigation towards Morecambe and Lancaster, and Rae used a police contact to glean that information, but he still had to follow through and build his story. It took a formidable range of journalistic skills and indefatigability. The indomitable Scotsman was soon making his way straight to Ruxton's house.

≡

Dr Buck Ruxton lived in a large and imposing Georgian house, 2 Dalton Square, in central Lancaster, close to the town hall. It was actually rented for between £80 and £100 a year, but Ruxton owned the furniture, and he'd done extensive redecoration inside. Rae met and interviewed the 36-year-old Ruxton, who was warm and receptive. But little about Ruxton was as it seemed – including his name.

The doctor's real name was Buktyar Rustomji Ratanji Hakim, and he was born on 21 March 1899 in Bombay (now Mumbai), India. Hakim was Parsi, a religion that follows an Iranian prophet and which fled to India from Persia (now Iran) in the seventh and eighth centuries to escape Muslim persecution. Hakim had French ancestry too, and this explained why he spoke fluent French, actually much better than his English. He first came to London to study at London University, but he'd soon returned to Bombay where with no language barrier his medical studies resumed and he graduated from the University of Bombay.

Probably largely because of family pressure, Hakim married a fellow Parsi, an older woman, in India, almost definitely an arranged or at least family-approved marriage, before joining the Indian Army Medical

Corps. After a stint, he returned to London alone, now estranged from his wife. By the time that Norman Rae knocked on his door at 2 Dalton Square, at the end of the first week of October 1935, Hakim had only been in Britain since January 1927, less than nine years, and a great deal had happened since then. Hakim was now called Dr Buck Ruxton, having anglicised his name and changed it by deed poll on 10 April 1929.

Ruxton had flitted between London and Edinburgh between 1927 and moving to Lancaster. In Edinburgh, he twice failed the exams to gain his Surgeon's Fellowship. He was always short of money, despite receiving funds from his family in India, who unconditionally supported him, although they were unhappy that his Indian marriage had not worked out. In London he was helped by other Indian families, receiving much kindness from that immigrant community.

But it was in Edinburgh that the event happened which would change the course of his life, and the lives of many others. Frequenting a tearoom, he began chatting to the manageress, Isabella Kerr, a tall woman with angular features. They were soon in a relationship, a rare mixed-race partnership then, and obviously very much in love. Ruxton, at that time known as Captain Gabriel Hakim, a nod to his military service and with an added romanticised Christian name, was smooth-talking, interesting and good-looking, a qualified doctor, who was able to find work back in London as a locum.

Isabella had married a Dutch man some years before, but they were estranged and she was able to get a divorce from him. Hakim called Isabella 'Belle' and she called him 'Bommie'. They were soon living together in London, she as his common-law wife. Hakim was, of course, still legally married, and divorcing his Indian wife may well have been too much for his parents.

Hakim and Belle's first child was born, a daughter called Elizabeth, and he soon began to look for a medical practice which he could take over and settle down with his family. To help meet the costs involved in this, Belle moved back to Edinburgh and worked as a manageress again, this time in a café at the Woolworth's department store, saving any money she could, while Hakim continued working as a locum in London and did the same. Then a medical practice became available in Lancaster in the north-west of England, and they successfully made an offer and moved there. He became Dr Buck Ruxton legally just before they arrived in Lancaster.

Buck and Belle now had three children, Elizabeth, Diana Rose and William Gladstone, named after the famous former Prime Minister, called 'Billie Boy' in the family. However, they had lost a baby boy in April 1932. They had also built up the medical practice together, Ruxton presenting himself as an attentive and then exotic doctor, who, as Jean Ritchie details in *150 Years of True Crime*, was known by his patients as 'the Rajah'. When Norman Rae first met him in early October 1935, Ruxton's practice on Lancaster's Scale Hall Estate was turning over £3,000 a year, at a time when the average income of a British solicitor was £1,238 a year and of a teacher £480 a year. But Ruxton had expensive and extravagant tastes too, and his financial situation was far from stable, as the police would soon learn.

James Howie Milligan had by now joined Rae in Lancaster, and the two took turns in talking to Ruxton and other key sources. Perhaps smoking Craven 'A' cigarettes, 'made specially to prevent sore throats', and wearing the requisite long coats and trilbies, the two *News of the World* colleagues interviewed around forty of Ruxton's patients over the following days, and soon realised that Ruxton had given a few different versions of his wife's and their maid's disappearance. There was also gossip mounting in local shops and pubs.

Rae and Milligan were building up a picture of Ruxton, Isabella and their missing 20-year-old nursemaid Mary Jane Rogerson, who had actually lived in Morecambe and commuted to and from 2 Dalton Square, Lancaster, doing the cooking and cleaning and helping Isabella with the three children. The hacks learnt that Isabella was well-known in Lancaster. She 'hobnobbed' with the upper-class 'town hall set', and did charitable work for young children in the area. The police were also of course investigating these avenues, but Rae and Milligan had a deadline to meet for that Sunday, and it was a front page.

RIDDLE OF DOCTOR'S WIFE AND MAID
Husband on Their Disappearance – Are They Victims of Ravine Crime?
News of the World, Sunday 13 October 1935

Rae and Milligan corrected the previous Sunday's early investigation misinformation about the sex of the victims, confirming that both bodies were female. But the most interesting revelations were their interviews with Dr Buck Ruxton, access that no other Murder Gang journalist had. Ruxton seems to have been relaxed chatting to the two journalists, and no doubt Rae and Milligan put him at ease. His wife and maid were officially still just missing of course. Ruxton had told them that it wasn't the first time that Isabella had gone away suddenly: 'She is a highly romantic and ambitious woman, and when she heard of anyone doing something unusual, such as flying the Atlantic, she always took the view that she could go one better.'

Ruxton was reported as saying that he had been in the bath on Sunday 15 September when his wife called up to him that she and the maid Mary Rogerson were off on their holiday, although they had planned to leave on the following day. 'She was definitely scheduled to go North [to Edinburgh] on that day [Monday 16 September], and I was not surprised when she left with the nurse on the Sunday. I do not know if they went by train or not, for, as I have said, I was in my bath at the time.' Dr Ruxton was also quoted as saying that the human remains found in Moffat were not his wife and maid: 'In the case of the younger woman's remains there are no teeth missing, but Miss Rogerson had four extracted in Lancaster recently.'

Ruxton had also expanded on the effect of the focus on him:

I am afraid of the talk affecting my practice. I am anxious to make it known that there is no truth in rumours that I am selling my practice is leaving the town, or that another doctor is working in my place. I am not leaving Lancaster, and I am conducting my practice as usual.

Having been asked about links between the remains found in Moffat and the disappearance of Isabella Ruxton and Mary Jane Rogerson in Lancaster at a police press conference the previous day, Saturday 12 October, Chief Constable Vann of Lancaster Police was also quoted as saying, 'I have no evidence of any such connection.'

But this was plainly untrue, and obviously for a reason. As delivery vans were distributing millions of copies of the *News of the World* that early Sunday morning of 13 October 1935, something major happened that completely contradicted Chief Constable Vann's statement. As the paper had gone to press the previous night, Rae and Milligan were not able to include it in the piece.

Dr Buck Ruxton was arrested and charged with the murder of Mary Jane Rogerson at 7.20 a.m., at his house in Dalton Square. There wasn't sufficient evidence yet to prove that the other human remains were those of his wife Belle, and body parts were still being found and examined. James Howie Milligan later recounted that in an interview, Ruxton had said to him, 'I did not kill my Belle. I tell you she had gone away. Tell everybody I am not guilty. Tell them I loved my Belle too much to harm her.'

Other Murder Gang members on the dailies capitalised on Rae and Milligan having to wait another week for the *News of the World* to go to press again. The next day, Monday 14 October, the case held the front page of the *Daily Express* with 'Ravine Riddle: Doctor Arrested: Murder of Lost Nurse the Charge' and the *Daily Mirror* had a report on Dr Ruxton's first court appearance on the following day on page 8: 'Doctor's "No" To Charge Of Murder: Missing Girl's Father In Tears In Court'– referring to the father of Mary Jane Rogerson. Both papers and others in Fleet Street reported the case that week, focusing on the fact that the police were digging around in Ruxton's back garden at 2 Dalton Square and searching the house. Meanwhile, Rae and Milligan went with 'Ravine Crime Hunt Intensified: Hikers Help Police in Search for Missing Torso' on page 13 of the *News of the World* on Sunday 20 October 1935. It wasn't looking good for Dr Buck Ruxton.

Dr Ruxton was a gambler, and very superstitious. He was often in poor credit, despite his high salary from his medical practice. Extravagant and reckless spending was to blame, and his wife Isabella was undoubtedly used to a high standard of living too. Plus there were the three children's upkeep and Mary Jane Rogerson's wages to cover too. But Ruxton was the real impulsive spender, bathing daily at a time when not many people did, leaving lights in his house on all night as he disliked darkness, having his numerous clothes professionally laundered. The Metropolitan Police file on the case is very enlightening as to Ruxton's character, containing details not available to even Rae and Milligan back in 1935.

On 2 June 1934, fifteen months before 'the disappearance' of his wife and maid, Ruxton wrote to a bookmaker in Regent Street London, Hendley & Co., Turf Accountants, wanting to open a credit account of between £25 and £30 to bet on the upcoming Derby. His letter shows that he was secretive about his gambling, and concerned about any potential damage to his reputation as 'the Rajah' in Lancaster that might result from credit checks and gossip: 'I believe I hardly need say you will make all your inquiries in a discreet manner without divulging my intentions as this is a small town of people of anti-gambling religious views.' The account was duly opened three days later, despite a poor credit reference from his bank, Midland Bank in Lancaster, which said that Ruxton 'seemed to be short of liquid capital at times,' although he could cover the £25–30 outlay.

An internal Hendley & Co. report stated that 'He does not bear a good reputation for payment of accounts, and we have heard of him being sued.' Between June 1934 and October 1935 when he was arrested, Ruxton paid just over £205 into this turf account, and was paid out £216, so Ruxton came out £11 ahead. But it was noted that he had often fallen behind with his account payments.

On 27 September 1935, twelve days after Isabella and Mary were last seen, Ruxton wrote to an astrologer, Mr A.E. Webber, in Finchley Road, north-west London, in what was to be the start of a lengthy correspondence, about completing a personalised horoscope. Ruxton wrote 'I am married most unhappily. I am neither on good terms with mother nor with the wife ... I have never been happy in my married life. Even a love affair ended in disaster. I came across a worthless woman who has left me for another man.' The police now knew, in Ruxton's own admission, that he was unhappy with Belle and had committed adultery.

On 30 September, the day after Susan Haines Johnson spotted the first body part in Moffat, Ruxton wrote to Webber again, asking for astrological advice. While on remand in Strangeways Prison in Manchester and just five days after his arrest, on 18 October Ruxton was asking for his horoscope to be completed, obviously anxious to know what lay ahead for him. Webber did not provide the horoscope, and the police were now reading all correspondence between Ruxton and Webber. Just a few days later, Ruxton wrote asking Webber which month – November or December 1935 – looked better for him. Ruxton was obviously thinking about his murder trial, which actually wouldn't take place until the following year. But he was due in the Police Court for a preliminary hearing on 22 October 1935, and he wrote to Webber, 'I will prove my innocence.'

Ruxton's obsession with astrology was confirmed when the police searched his house, and found zodiac symbols painted all over the walls, along with bright colours. Ruxton was impulsive and egotistical, but perhaps astrology gave him some kind of structure. But the stars were not aligned in Ruxton's favour now.

DOCTOR ACCUSED OF SECOND MURDER
'A Lie – It Is Driving Me Crazy!' Outburst
News of the World, Sunday 10 November 1935

Ruxton had begun ranting in court. Rae and Milligan's piece says that his knuckles had turned white while clenched around the dock railings at Lancaster Crown Court. When he was charged with the murder of his wife Isabella, Ruxton erupted:

> It is a positive and damnable lie. It is all prejudice. I cannot bear the thing … My home is broken up – my happy home … Do I look like a murderer? It is not my nature, and my religion would not allow me. I don't smoke. I don't drink. I observe the fasts. I cannot bear it. My blood is boiling!

When told to calm down and compose himself in court, Ruxton, almost screaming, said, 'I cannot help it. I have my children and my business!'

On 14 November, the *Daily Mirror* reported that Ruxton was going to sell his house. This was in fact untrue, as the house was rented, but he *was* going to sell the furniture. The first photograph of the tragic Isabella Ruxton was also published that day. Despite the case still being only at the committal hearings stage, a great deal of detail was being reported in the dailies. On Wednesday 20 November, the *Daily Express* told how Ruxton had regained his composure in court, running with, 'Error Makes Dr Ruxton Smile:"Remanded on Bail"'. The Chairman of the Bench at the Crown Court had mistakenly announced that Ruxton was to be remanded on bail, which he quickly corrected to 'remanded in custody'. Ruxton was seen 'smiling broadly' at this slip.

It was soon established that Isabella Ruxton had been strangled and the alleged motive was stated. On 27 November the *Daily Express* went with, 'Mrs Ruxton Strangled: Court Told Accused Doctor Was Jealous of Her'. Witnesses to the Ruxton marriage were giving evidence against him. The same day, the *Daily Mirror* told readers just how much press and public attention the Ruxton murders were getting: 'So great is the interest in this case that Pressmen from all over the world thronged the court. Only a fraction of the hundreds of spectators who queued were admitted.'

The following day, the *Daily Express* came back with an eerie story, taking the whole of page 7, about the now empty murder house, 2 Dalton Square: 'Woman Cries "That Curtain Moved": Excited Women Staring Up At Ruxton's House Swear They Saw A Curtain Move'. On 29 November, the *Daily Express* had, on the front page, 'Rush For Tickets', referring to the fact that 2 Dalton Square was being opened to the public to go over the furniture being sold, and tickets cost two shillings. The bathroom was closed off, however, as, in the opinion of the police, the dismemberment of the bodies had taken place in the bath in there.

That bath, which would be taken to the court for Ruxton's main trial as evidence, would later end up serving as a horse trough for Lancaster Police. On Saturday 30 November, the murder house was open to the public all day, and it would be stripped of all furniture just a few days later, much of it sold as macabre souvenirs – the very mindset which was the stock-in-trade of the Murder Gang of course. The *Daily Express* trumpeted on Monday 2 December that, 'Crowds view Ruxton House: Break Barrier.'

Ruxton's character was being badly damaged by people in court and in the public's mind through the papers, and he was coming across as sounding cold and self-centred when speaking of his wife to others while she was alive, although he was prone to emotional outbursts himself when he was in trouble. That week, various Fleet Street papers reported snippets which made him seem very callous and uncaring. But the reality would be established in the end – Ruxton may have been unfaithful, as he had admitted in his letter to the astrologer in the police files, but he did love Isabella. It had been a love-hate relationship, and the whole-page spread in the *News of the World* of Sunday 1 December, 'Sensations In Case Against Dr Ruxton' and inside the paper on the following Sunday, 'Tense Court Drama Of The Ruxton Trial', made it clear that the police thought that jealousy had indeed been the motive. But why had he killed the nursemaid Mary Jane Rogerson?

Rae and Milligan were supplying real detail, some of it repeating what the dailies had revealed to the public that week, but the way that the *News of the World* covered the case was superlative, Sunday after Sunday painting Ruxton's portrait in words, details building up the background, dab after dab adding colour and sensation. Dr Ruxton and his terrible alleged crimes were made for the Murder Gang, and Rae and Milligan knew it was their story now, and due to their unprecedented access to Ruxton pre-arrest, they had the handle on him. Other Murder Gang members could only look on and report the snippets they heard and the early court remand and committal hearings.

'Dr Ruxton to Face a Judge and Jury', Rae and Milligan announced in a banner headline on Sunday 15 December 1935, reporting that the forensic experts were 'Building Up Bodies From Ravine Remains'. Ruxton's trial wouldn't take place for another three months, at Manchester Assizes in March 1936. The intricate and time-consuming work of piecing together the body parts of the two women was taking time, and the prosecution wanted to ensure that Ruxton's defence had no wriggle-room in court.

There was true historical importance in the painstaking forensic work in the case against Dr Buck Ruxton, in what was then still known to the British public, courtesy of Rae and Milligan, as 'the Ravine Case'. There were at least two forensic breakthroughs achieved. The use of photographs to confirm the identities of the pieced-together bodies, by photographing the two skulls, blowing them up to fit life photos of the two victims – in the case of Isabella Ruxton a posed studio portrait, sitting for which was popular at that time, and two amateur, lesser quality photographs of Mary Jane Rogerson. The life photos were then superimposed on the enlarged skull photos, and both were found to be an exact match.

The Ruxton case also made pioneering use of the field of entomology (the study of insects) in a murder case. This was undertaken by Dr Alexander Mearns of the Institute of Hygiene at the University of Glasgow. Maggots found in the decomposing remains of both women were microscopically examined, the age of the maggots after hatching from flies being calculated, so revealing when the women died – Mearns found that both women had been dead since about 15 September 1935, the last time Isabella Ruxton and Mary Jane Rogerson had been seen alive. In his history of forensic science *Silent Witnesses*, Nigel McCrery asserts, 'Never before had entomology been applied forensically like this.' It would be used in many more murder investigations internationally, and is still used today as a means to establishing time of death.

So the Ruxton case was scientifically important, as well as capturing the public's imagination. The work of Norman Rae and James Howie Milligan at the *News of the World* did more than anything to create the huge interest, but of course they had great journalistic raw material. Ruxton himself, the Indian doctor who dressed flamboyantly and drove an expensive custom white-enamelled and blue-wheeled car, was seen as exotic, and the fact that he was married to a white woman and had children with her was rare at the time. Then there was the sheer callousness of the disposal of the bodies, so far away from home, so disrespectful, gruesome parcels left in a trail presenting a grisly jigsaw puzzle for the authorities.

It is interesting to note that Ruxton wrote to James Howie Milligan from prison, and not to Norman Rae. Milligan had interviewed Ruxton in the latter's expensively decorated library at 2 Dalton Square, just before his arrest. 'The library is no more. Only the bare walls of that spacious room remain to bear mute testimony of my choice of treasures,' wrote Ruxton, alluding to the stripping of his former home. Added to the pretentiousness of Ruxton's prose, this shows how material things were so important to Ruxton, a man who had recently and allegedly brutally murdered both the mother of his three children and their nursemaid. Milligan had obviously gained Ruxton's trust, making him feel comfortable enough to share his feelings with a Murder Gang member, who ostensibly just wanted his story. Rae had opened the line and found Ruxton first, but Milligan kept that line open after Ruxton's arrest, an exemplary example of journalistic teamwork.

Rae and Milligan and the rest of the Murder Gang were engaged on other stories in that lull in the Ruxton case between December 1935 and March 1936 while everybody awaited the main trial – the ultimate penalty of hanging looming over Ruxton, as it did for anybody facing a murder trial in Britain until the mid-1960s, raising the stakes for defendants, and massively increasing public interest, on which the Murder Gang thrived. The *Daily Express* of Saturday 25 January 1936 did have the fact that Ruxton had had three writs from creditors served on him in prison, and almost a month later on Monday 24 February, the same paper reported that 'Two Murder Trials Affect 8 Children'. This was reference to Ruxton's own three children, and the infamous 'Nurse' Dorothea Waddington, aged 34, then also standing trial with Joseph Sullivan, aged 41, for the murder of 80-year-old Louisa Baguley and her 50-year-old daughter Ada Louisa Baguley. Waddington had five children to add to Ruxton's two daughters and a son. All eight children were now in state social care.

The Ruxton trial began on Tuesday 3 March 1936. The *Daily Express* that day described the defendant in court: 'Dr Ruxton took voluminous notes throughout. His lips moved constantly. Sometimes he drummed with his pencil on his striped trousers.' The *News of the World* returned to the case on the following Sunday, still leading Fleet Street in the level of coverage it offered, covering a full page. 'Drama of Ruxton Murder Trial – Doctor Accused of Planning Perfect Crime' ran on Sunday 8 March. The sub-headline 'Unfounded Jealousy Alleged As Motive', pointed to the fact that the prosecution thought that Ruxton had murdered Isabella, his beloved 'Belle', in a fit of jealousy, thinking that she was having an affair, which was never either proved nor disproved, although she had spent time with a male friend, and Ruxton certainly felt as if he had been losing control over his wife. Mary Jane Rogerson was considered as a tragic afterthought, as some sort of terrible collateral damage after Ruxton killed his wife.

It came out in the trial that week that the marital bedroom at 2 Dalton Square had been ominously locked for five days after Isabella and Mary were last seen, as the *Daily Mirror* reported on Friday 6 March. Added to this, Ruxton had given a bloody carpet to a woman who did cleaning for him, telling her to dispose of it, but which she had kept. This of course was brought forward as evidence of a violent act having taken place, and the amount of blood pointed to the probability that a knife or a bludgeoning weapon had been used in at least one of the murders, and that one killing had taken place on the stairs where the carpet had been pulled up. Perhaps the saddest fact was that all three of the Ruxton children had been present in the house, sleeping through the massacre.

Ruxton may have gone to great lengths in dismembering the bodies and travelling to Dumfriesshire to dispose of the parcels, but his clean-up at home in Lancaster had left a trail of clues, welcome breadcrumbs for the hungry police after the jigsaw puzzle posed by the body parts. Ruxton had also denied going to Scotland or anywhere else, but this was disproved when it was shown that Ruxton had been stopped by a policeman on the way back from Scotland on 17 September 1935 at 12.35 p.m., two days after Isabella and Mary were last seen in Lancaster.

In Kendal in the Lake District, Ruxton had accidentally knocked a cyclist off his bike and his registration plate was noted and driving licence checked at a police roadblock set up in nearby Milnthorpe, to stop the driver. The policeman had also noticed that Ruxton had a small child with him in the car, obviously one of his own three children. Ruxton was in a rush to flee south home to Lancaster, the police reasoning that he had just scattered the parcels containing the body parts of his wife and maid in the area around the Devil's Bridge, just north of Moffat, which would later become known locally as 'Ruxton's Dump'. In court, Ruxton would claim when confronted with this evidence that he had been travelling back from a business trip in Carlisle, but no corroboration was ever found to support this.

It was looking distinctly bleak for Dr Buck Ruxton. His defence, led by Norman Birkett KC, tried to claim that the remains found were of three bodies and not two, and indeed an extra eye had been found, which the *Daily Mirror* gleefully called the 'Cyclops Eye.' However, Professor Glaister gave evidence that the eye was not in fact human, but that of an animal.

Ruxton continued to deny killing both Isabella and Mary, and when the lead prosecution lawyer J.C. Jackson KC put it to him in the witness box that he had strangled Isabella, he denied that too. Ruxton's day of cross-examination came on Thursday 12 March, and as the *Daily Express* relayed the next day, Ruxton broke down in tears several times. The judge, Mr Justice Singleton, reprimanded Ruxton when he rambled in his answers, 'It would be better for you if you would listen and answer the questions.' To which Ruxton replied, 'I humbly beg your pardon, but don't you see how he *(J.C. Jackson KC)* is driving me into a corner?' It was the prosecution's theory that Isabella had been strangled by Ruxton in their bedroom in a fit of rage, and that Mary Jane Rogerson had been on the stairs, and that Ruxton had either stabbed or bludgeoned Rogerson as she was a very unlucky witness.

Ruxton was found guilty of murder on Friday 13 March 1936, and sentenced to death. The *Daily Express* the following day went with 'Ruxton "Salaams" Sentenced to Die', meaning that Ruxton had made a very low bow with his right hand on his forehead, an Islamic gesture signifying peace. He also said 'I am sorry' to the court, but made no admission of guilt. The *News of the World* that Sunday led with 'Ruxton's Diary Of Hell On Earth', Rae and Milligan having gained access to Ruxton's personal diaries and letters, which had been used by the prosecution. They showed a 'love–hate' relationship between Buck and Belle, an unhappy marriage, but one in which love still existed, especially on Buck's side, but that this had turned to acute jealousy in the excitable and unstable doctor and paranoia about Isabella's alleged infidelity.

With allusions to Ruxton's superstitious nature, attention was given to the prevalence of the 'unlucky number thirteen' linked to Ruxton, in something of a journalistic stretch obviously designed to spook the readership: 'The doctor was arrested on Sunday October 13, sent for trial Friday December 13, sentenced to death Friday March 13, his prison number – 8410 – totalled 13, and his address, 2 Dalton Square, has twelve letters and one figure – 13 again.'

The following Sunday, 22 March 1936, Rae and Milligan focused on 'Ruxton Engrossed In Case for Appeal', explaining that Ruxton was sending 'day-by-day instructions from his prison cell'. This was complete with 'facsimiles' of notes that Ruxton had written to his solicitor during the trial, showing that Rae and Milligan, unlike any other Murder Gang reporters following the case, had cultivated strong relationships with either Ruxton's legal team or the police and probably both, giving them access to primary materials from Ruxton's own hand with which to feed their famished and ghoulish readership.

On Sunday 3 May, Rae and Milligan had 'The "Inside" Story of the Ruxton Crime', explaining how 'Police Play Spider and Fly', describing how the police slowly caught Ruxton in their web. The level of detail shows just how good their access was to the police involved in the case, and no other paper had anything like that depth. They also reported on Ruxton's 'Loyal but Heartbroken Wife in Bombay', to whom he was still legally married, Isabella having been his common-law wife. The *Daily Mirror* had managed to contact Ruxton's mother through its India correspondent back in mid-March, showing how far Fleet Street was prepared to go in big murder case coverage in the mid-1930s, when gathering sources was true legwork.

The next day, the *Daily Express* headlined 'Women Plead for Ruxton's Life'. Almost 900 people, most of them women, had signed a petition for Ruxton's reprieve, incredibly as Ruxton had been sentenced to death for the brutal murder of two women. The petition, organised by his solicitor, had been signed on a table on the porch of the Ruxton family's former and now empty house at 2 Dalton Square. But this reprieve attempt, just like Ruxton's appeal hearing, which he had attended in London on 25 April, failed.

Dr Buck Ruxton was executed at Strangeways Prison in Manchester at 9 a.m. on Tuesday 12 May 1936. There were at least 5,000 people gathered outside the prison, showing just how the case had entered public consciousness in this era before television. The *Daily Mirror* reported how 'While Dr Buck Ruxton was being executed, women with their children took front seats on the barriers used to hold back the crowds ...' Indeed, contemporary photographs of the scene show policemen struggling to hold people back.

Executions were a freak show at the time, just as the Victorians, including Charles Dickens, had crowded to witness public executions. Now the condemned were executed out of public sight, but the putting up of the black flag and the hanging of the death sentence notice, confirming it as having been carried out, on the prison gates, made the crowds rush forward. This was made worse on that day by an anti-death penalty demonstration, leading to a woman, Mrs Van Der Elst, being arrested for obstructing the road with her car and refusing to move it when asked. Conversely, Ruxton had been quiet and composed as he made his final walk.

But five days later, Norman Rae and James Howie Milligan got the biggest British murder scoop of the 1930s.

Ruxton Confesses His Double Crime – Exclusively to the 'News of the World'
News of the World, Sunday 17 May 1936

Trumpeted as Ruxton's 'Frank Avowal of Guilt on Single Sheet' and 'one of the journalistic sensations of the present century', it was an incredible coup, covering most of the front page and page 3 inside, and how it had come about was incredible too.

The following account of what happened came from Rae's own pen, a series called 'My Front Page Murders' which ran in the *News of the World* towards the end of his career. 'Jock' Rae claimed that he was present outside Strangeways on the day of Ruxton's execution, gathering material for the final coverage of the extraordinary case. Suddenly, a man approached Rae and gave him an envelope, obviously with a letter or note inside it. The man was a friend of Ruxton, and he had been given it by the doctor and told to keep it in a safe, and only to hand it over after Ruxton's death. The front of the envelope marked it as for the attention of the editor of the *News of the World*.

Rae followed protocol and took the letter back to the newspaper's offices, where the editor opened it. It was as described in that Sunday's paper, just a single sheet, and it had been written by Ruxton on 14 October 1935, the day after his arrest, almost exactly five months earlier, when he was still being held in Lancaster. It read:

I killed Mrs Ruxton in a fit of temper. I thought she had been with a man. I was mad at the time. Mary Rogerson was present at the time. I had to kill her. [signed] B. Ruxton'

It was a full confession to both murders, and confirmed the prosecution theory. Rae and Milligan wrote that Sunday 'how his secret was kept through his fight for life'. It has been claimed that Ruxton's Parsi faith had made him want to purge his guilt in the letter. But the fact that it was only to be handed over *after* his death shows that the opportunistic Ruxton was still playing the odds, with his life, like the horses. When he wrote it just after his arrest he still had strong hopes of being acquitted, at the very least escaping the hangman. As his confession to double murder would only ever come to light after his death through a trusted friend, Ruxton's secret was safe and could not damage him while alive.

But it is also possible that Rae was never approached by Ruxton's friend that day, and that an arrangement had been made between the *News of the World* and Ruxton for his confession in the event of his execution. The timing would have been right, with Rae and especially Milligan having Ruxton's ear just after his arrest. A deal offering payment may have indeed been struck between Rae and Ruxton's friend just after the execution, or the envelope may have been kept in the newspaper's safe, either opened or unopened, during those months between it being written and the execution.

It was common practice for Fleet Street newspapers to offer murderers money for their inside stories during the Murder Gang years, and Ruxton may have wanted to secure some money for his children were he to be executed. Rae's version is more colourful, but newspapers certainly didn't want to publicise the payments they made to convicted killers, and both possibilities of how Ruxton's confession came into the hands of the *News of the World* should be considered.

Ruxton had lost his gamble, paid the price, and there was nothing left to lose. But the three Ruxton children now had neither mother nor father. Ruxton had left a fund for them, but due to his debts they would receive nothing – unless the *News of the World* had secretly paid for their father's confession of course. Ruxton's first wife in India was left three guineas. He even left a set of silver forks to his lawyer, Norman Birkett KC.

In a final twist the *Daily Mirror* reported on Wednesday 18 November 'Ruxton's Dentist Friend Gassed – Trial Witness.' A 58-year-old friend of Ruxton, Herbert Anderson, a former friend and patient of Ruxton who had given character witness in Ruxton's favour at his trial, had gassed himself in his kitchen. Anderson had been ill for a long time, but he had apparently become weaker after the Ruxton trial. More than six months after Ruxton's execution, anything connected with him was still making national news.

Norman 'Jock' Rae's work on the Ruxton case made his name in Fleet Street, and he would go on to land many more scoops. For almost thirty years from then on he would be a leading member of the Murder Gang. The year following the Ruxton exclusive, at the end of 1937, James Howie Milligan, who worked so well with Rae and cultivated Ruxton, became the north of England crime man for the *News of the World*, covering a very wide area.

Now based in the seaside town of Blackpool, Lancashire, where he lived at 122 Park Road, Milligan was a member of the Manchester Press Club. But Milligan was to die on 18 March 1940, aged just 51, four and a half years after he and Rae had arrived in Moffat, Dumfriesshire. James Howie Milligan would never achieve legendary Fleet Street status as Rae did, but among those who knew him, worked alongside and were scooped by him, there was quiet professional respect.

2

I DID THIS MURDER TO PROVE I COULD GET AWAY WITH IT

GREAT MARLBOROUGH STREET POLICE STATION, LONDON, TUESDAY 25 JULY 1933

Statement of Nelson Leaver, 50 Kings Hall Road, Beckenham, Kent
Witnessed by Detective Inspector C. Campion, 'C' Division
I am the News Editor of the *Daily Sketch* newspaper, 200, Grays Inn Road. In October 1931, I got into touch with a man named Frederick Field regarding the murder of Nora Upchurch. I arranged with him, in return for his story, should he be arrested for the murder, that I would finance his defence. As a matter of fact he made no admission in the matter and told me that police were trying to fix it on him. No police action was taken against him and I heard no more of Field until the morning of the 25 July, 1933 …

Nelson Leaver had contacted the police earlier that day when Frederick Field came to him and confessed to the murder of a young woman called Norah Upchurch in September 1931. A month before Field had originally come to Leaver saying that he was being framed by the police and that he would sell his story to the paper in return for the funding of his defence should he be charged. It was the beginning of an incredibly tragic and almost unbelievable story, and shows the workings of the early Murder Gang at first hand.

Nelson Leaver was 53 years old when he gave that statement to the police in July 1933, having been born in Maidstone, Kent in 1880. He had joined the then Institute of Journalists in 1903, when he lived in Alton, Hampshire, and was on the staff of the *Bristol Mercury* newspaper in the southwest of England in 1906. By 1910 Leaver had made it to London and Fleet Street, working as a reporter on the *News Chronicle*, and joined the Central London branch of the National Union of Journalists in September, 1919, and he would also later become a member of the Newspaper Press Fund. By 1930, he was the news editor of the *Daily Sketch*, when he first met Frederick Field a year later.

The *Daily Sketch* began publication in Manchester in 1909, founded by Sir Edward Hulton, but from 1928 it was owned by Berry's Allied Newspapers, which later, in 1937, became the famous Kemsley Newspapers. Leaver's editor in 1933 was A. Curthoys, who was from Bristol, and may have recruited Leaver after meeting him during his *Bristol Mercury* days. Curthoys had two sons who also worked as journalists on the *Bristol Evening Post*. The *Daily Sketch* was a tabloid with conservative views, and often took moral positions on stories it reported. But it obviously wasn't above paying money to fund the defence of suspected murderers to get murder scoops.

Anna Louisa Norah (sometimes misspelt Nora) Upchurch had been found dead in an empty shop, just inside the locked doorway, at 173–179 Shaftesbury Avenue in the West End of London on 2 October 1931, although she had been killed on the night of 29 September. She had been gagged with a piece of white cloth in her mouth and strangled, a piece of green cloth still around her neck. Upchurch, a pretty 20-year-old with fashionably bobbed dark hair, was originally from Dollis Hill in London, and her father worked as a railwayman. But Norah had fallen into prostitution around Soho and the West End – the newspapers discreetly, or perhaps euphemistically, referred to her as a 'Soho waitress'.

Norah's body had been discovered when a policeman on the beat, Sergeant A.A. Ferridge, was approached by a sullen young man called Frederick Field in High Street, Bloomsbury, just north of Shaftesbury Avenue. Field said to Ferridge, 'Will you come round the corner Sergeant? There's a woman in the shop, and I think she's dead.'

Field had previously been in that shop on 29 September to take down a sign – he was a sign-fixer by trade, and had held the keys. Field was interviewed by the police in early October 1931, and he told them that a man 'in plus-fours' had asked him for the key to the shop while he was in there taking down the sign. The man apparently said that he was thinking of renting the vacant premises, and that he would arrange it with the letting agent. Field was obviously inferring that this stranger who had the key had killed Norah Upchurch later that day after taking her back to the shop.

There were other suspects too. A famous cricketer, Frank Foster, who had been captain of the Warwickshire county side and had played for England, had met Norah in Piccadilly in the heart of the West End on the evening which she disappeared – it was never proved that he had hired her services, and he claimed that he had just chatted with her, bought her a meal as she was 'hungry and faint', and then escorted her home to her flat 'because of some unknown terror that disturbed her'. Foster recounted his story for the *News of the World*, almost certainly the work of Norman Rae, on 24 September 1933, which ran with 'Famous Cricketer and Dead Girl'. There was also Norah's fiancé, a sailor in the Royal Navy, who was thoroughly looked into by the police, but had a firm alibi for the night of the murder.

Field's ruse worked, and the press were soon reporting the mystery man created by Field. The *Evening News* went with 'Soho Murder Puzzle', informing readers that 'the search for the 6ft 1in man who was known to be one of her last associates is going on'. The *News of the World* had 'Yard Baffled – Shop Crime Remains a Mystery'. Leading the police investigation into Norah Upchurch's murder was Superintendent Cornish, who amongst many high-profile murder cases, had secured the confession and conviction of 18-year-old hotel porter Henry Jacoby in 1922 when he was an Inspector. Jacoby had bludgeoned to death, in the course of attempted robbery, the wealthy Lady White, a resident elderly guest at the expensive hotel where he worked in Marble Arch, central London. Jacoby was hanged, despite his age. By the mid-1930s, Supt Cornish was called 'one of the big four of Scotland Yard' by the Murder Gang, making him one of an elite group of detectives.

Field claimed to Cornish and his police colleagues that he knew nothing about the murder, although the Metropolitan Police files on the case confirm that Field was a strong suspect, but there had been insufficient evidence with which to charge him. However, Field didn't know this of course, and in case he was arrested, had gone to the *Daily Sketch* with his 'fears' of being framed, Leaver, sensing a juicy news story for the *Daily Sketch*, making an offer for his story, should he be charged for Upchurch's murder, which he was not, in 1931. But less than two years later, Field had returned to the newspaper's offices with a very different story about the murder of Norah Upchurch.

When Frederick Herbert Charles Field went back to the *Daily Sketch* offices at the end of July 1933, he was 29 years old, a wiry and tough-looking young man with beady eyes and dark hair. Contemporary photographs show him suited wearing a fedora with a prominent band, a cigarette dangling from his lips, in the best tough-guy nonchalant pose of the time.

Field was born in Acton, west London on 18 April 1904, and attended the Rutlish School in Merton, south-west London. After leaving school at 14, he worked as an office boy at an engineering firm in Clapham for two months, and then left to become assistant operator at the King's Cinematograph Palace in Wimbledon. On 10 August 1923, aged 19, Field joined the RAF as an Aircraftsman on a six-year enlistment. On 7 April 1928, Field got married to Bessie Matilda, originally from Cardiff, Wales. On 10 August 1929, after his six years Field left the RAF, being released to the Reserve. He worked as an electrician in the City of London until November 1929, when he was made redundant. The police learned that while he was working there he'd had an affair with a woman who did not know he was married, and who stopped the romance when she learnt the truth.

It was a time of deep recession, and Field was unemployed for eighteen months, but at Whitsun 1931 he and Bessie had a baby daughter. By now they were living in Sutton, south of London. Finally, on 31 July 1931, he found a job as a sign-fixer for Messrs Hilder &

Co. Sign Contractors, who had offices at 23 Great Pulteney Street, in central London. It was while working for that company that he was sent almost two months later to take down a sign in an empty shop in Shaftesbury Avenue on 29 September, where the strangled body of Norah Upchurch was discovered three days later.

≣

At around 12.30 p.m. on Tuesday 25 July 1933, Frederick Field walked into the offices of the *Daily Sketch* on Grays Inn Road near Kings Cross Station and filled in a form at reception, asking to see Nelson Leaver, the news editor he had met in October 1931, about 'a confidential matter'. Leaver didn't at first make the connection with the young man called Field he had met and made a financial offer to regarding the Norah Upchurch murder. Field was finally sent upstairs to see Leaver, and Leaver recognised him immediately. They talked in a room alone. Field confirmed that he wanted to talk about the Norah Upchurch murder again.

Field was agitated and Leaver recalled to the police that 'He appeared to have some difficulty in starting his story.' Field asked for some water, and leaver sent for it. After he had drunk it, the busy Leaver said, 'What have you got to tell me?' Field said, 'I know I shall get a straight deal from you and I want you first of all to promise that you will say nothing until Saturday.' Leaver refused to commit to this, and once again asked Field to tell him what he had to say. Field hesitated, and then said, 'Well, I did it.' 'You mean that you killed Norah Upchurch?' 'Yes.' 'That's a very grave thing for you to tell me,' said Leaver. 'Yes I know,' said Field, 'I've been thinking about it for a long time and I know what it means.' Leaver then asked why Field had confessed to him.

Field replied, 'I have decided to surrender myself, but I want to get my wife and child out of London before I do it. I will tell you the story if you promise to help her to go home.' Field meant back to where she was from in Cardiff. Leaver again would make no promises: 'Well, you must leave any question of money to me until I know exactly what your story is.' Field agreed to tell the whole story, but Leaver told the police that he didn't press Field for details at this stage as he had 'already decided to pass him over to a member of the staff with more time to go into the murder'.

At Leaver's prompting Field said that he had not known Norah Upchurch before he killed her. Field had first seen Upchurch walking in the West End of London, and had seen her again later in Leicester Street, near Leicester Square by the Hippodrome, originally built for circus performances, then a music hall, but by 1931 used mainly as a theatre and for concerts – the first official jazz concert being held there back in 1919 when the Original Dixieland Jass [*sic*] Band played. Field spoke to Norah, and she agreed to come with him 'for the purpose of sexual intercourse', but Field told Leaver that sex was 'never in his mind'. His intention was to kill.

Field led Norah towards the shop on Shaftesbury Avenue just off New Compton Street where he still had the key after taking down the sign earlier. On the way to the shop, they had passed two policemen on the beat, and Norah had said 'Good Night' to them – she may well have been well-known to police in the area as it was her 'patch' to pick up clients. Field then made a remark about these policemen not having come forward when Supt Cornish was investigating the murder in October 1931, 'I don't think the constables were very sharp not to have remembered me.' They entered the shop at around 10.20 p.m.

Field said that as soon as they got inside the shop, he put his hands around her throat and started strangling her, and that Norah hadn't struggled at all. 'It was all over very quickly and it's a fact that I was home again, as I told the police at the time, shortly after 12 o'clock.' At the time, Field lived with Bessie and their infant daughter Nancy at 16 Manor Street in Clapham, south-west London.

Leaver then asked Field why he had killed Norah Upchurch, and recounted to the police that Field said that 'There had been much argument among his workmates, arising out of the Rouse case, and he maintained that it was possible for a man to get away with murder while an innocent man might be run in for it. I asked him what that had to do with Norah Upchurch's death, and he replied that as a result of the arguments he was anxious to prove his own theory.'

The 'Rouse case' refers to Alfred Rouse, a good-looking ladies' man who worked as a travelling salesman, who in November 1930 had killed an unidentified man – probably a transient he had picked up in his car, and then set fire to the car and ran away. The object was to make everyone believe that he himself had been burnt to death in the car; the married Rouse was under extreme financial stress having to pay for several secret illegitimate children under child support court orders. But Rouse had been spotted leaving the scene, and was soon caught. The press had covered it assiduously, and it became known as the 'Blazing Car Murder'. Rouse was hanged on 10 March 1931, just over six months before Field took Norah Upchurch into the shop to kill her, and so it had very likely been a major talking point among his fellow sign-fixers as he said.

Field also told Leaver that he had thrown Norah's handbag, for which the police had made a desperate search back in 1931, into a ditch along the Sutton bypass, south of London. When Leaver asked what he had done with the shop keys, Field said that he had put them inside the bag before he threw it away. Nelson Leaver had then turned Field over to one of his reporters to go and try to recover the bag. There was no moral impulse to call the police yet, that July 1933 day, just as the police had not been informed at the time about Field's first visit to the *Daily Sketch* offices in October 1931.

Great Marlborough Street Police Station, Central London, Tuesday, 25 July, 1933
Statement of John Davey, 14 Calthorpe Street, London WC1
Witnessed by Detective Inspector C. Campion, 'C' Division
I am a reporter in the employ of the *Daily Sketch*. About 1.30 p.m. on the 25 July 1933, I was called into my Chief's office (Mr Leaver) who introduced me to a man named Field. I had never seen him before. Mr Leaver explained that Field had had a conversation with him in which he confessed to the murder of Norah Upchurch. I asked 'Is this a joke?', and Field said, 'No, No, I want to confess.' I asked 'What did you have to do with it?' He said, 'Obviously by confessing, it means I did it.' I asked 'How did you do it?' He said, 'Everybody knows how she died.'

In 1933 John Davey's main home was at 39a Morris Road, Lewes, Sussex, some distance from London, and the address he gave to the police that day, which was not far from the *Daily Sketch* offices, may have been a flat where he stayed during the week. Like Leaver, Davey was a member of the Newspaper Press Fund.

The milieu in which journalists operated in the 1930s, in and around Fleet Street, is atmospherically described in a 1954 *Spectator* magazine article by the journalist John Beavan, later Lord Ardwick. He was editor of the *Manchester Evening News* in the early–mid-1940s, before becoming London editor of the *Manchester Guardian* from 1946 to 1955, when *The Guardian* was still in Manchester, and later worked at the *Daily Herald* and the Mirror Group up to the mid-1970s, when he turned to European politics and later became chair of the Press Freedom Committee until his death in 1994. Beavan wrote:

> Until 1939 Fleet Street lived with a belated Edwardian gusto. The pubs seemed to be full of parsons' sons noisily hellbent; of confident young Cells with a gleam in their eye and a work of genius on the stocks; of hard-drinking executives with soft Dickensian hearts; of shambling dipsos telling how the crew of the Pall Mall Gazette had slain the albatross; of elderly club men peddling London Letter pars to the provincials. On the nine guinea minimum, a bachelor could live like a bookie and the father of five (at a council school in Dulwich) could still pay his corner. Fleet Street was a hearty masculine club with its drinking competitions, hotpot and pigeon pie suppers and boozy harmonic smokers.

Beavan also recalled that 'in the Thirties, Fleet Street was still on nodding terms with literature'. He described how the famous writers G.K. Chesterton and Hillaire Belloc could 'now and then be seen drinking burgundy at the Bodcga', and also how literary men of the time, such as the Irish writer Robert Lynd and the literary critic and journalist Desmond McCarthy, often went to the Fleet Street wine bar El Vino, which was a legendary journalists' haunt for decades. Beavan remembered how 'Young Fleet Street men gaped at the giants and dreamed. They too wanted to write and looked to Fleet Street

– to provide them with adventures to write about.' Writing in 1954, Beavan was wistful and romantic about the past in a Fleet Street already changed dramatically.

But the journalists of the Murder Gang were a different breed. Whether in the 1930s, 1940s, 1950s or 1960s, literary merit was hardly the priority, although that's not to say that they couldn't write – they could, some of them very well, all providing crisp and scene-setting copy under real time pressure, in which readers could invest their time and imaginations. But for the crime hacks, it was the scoop, the sources, the 'gen' or information they could get on a story, the juicier and more gruesome the better. This often meant dealing face-to-face with murderers. Fleet Street may have been more literary and Dickensian in the 1930s, but back on 25 July 1933, John Davey, not a member of the Murder Gang, was tasked with taking Frederick Field, a self-confessed killer, to lunch, to put him at his ease and then get more information out of him.

When Davey and Field returned to the *Daily Sketch* offices after lunch, there was a car waiting for them, driven by a 40-year-old photographer called Herbert Muggeridge, who had been a journalist since March 1919 and a press photographer for nine years, since June 1924, when he worked for Kemsley Newspapers. In March 1933, he joined Allied Newspapers, which, as already mentioned, would be bought out by Kemsley four years later. Muggeridge was at this time floating between different Allied titles, but later, from 1945 until 1948, would be exclusively a *Daily Sketch* 'clicker' or photographer.

Muggeridge drove Davey and Frederick Field to the Rose Hill estate, south of London, and close to the Sutton bypass. They didn't speak about Norah's murder on the way down, as Muggeridge didn't know exactly why they were going there – Leaver had told Muggeridge to drive there, as they hoped to recover Norah Upchurch's bag containing her gold ring and the shop keys, Field having claimed he dumped it there of course. Leaver was trying to corroborate Field's story, in case he was just a fantasist. About 20 yards (18.2m) north of the bypass railway bridge, Field said, 'Stop here.' Field led them towards a large elm tree, and then looked down into the ditch in front of the tree. 'That's where I put the bag,' he said. He explained that when he had put it there at the end of September 1931, almost twenty months earlier, the ditch had been full of water. It was now bone dry. Field walked up and down the ditch, kicking up the bottom with his boots, but uncovered nothing. During this time, Muggeridge took two photos of Frederick Field.

The sceptical Davey asked him what he thought about not finding the bag, and Field said, 'Well, of course it was a cheap bag and after six months in water, might easily have become detached from its fittings and washed away. I am sure that if we looked long enough we might find the ring and the keys.' They went on to search for about an hour, to no avail. Davey then informed Field that only the police would be able to carry out a proper search for the items. They drove back to the newspaper's offices, and Leaver asked Davey to 'find out what Field had to say'.

Davey told Field that his news editor had been placed in a difficult position, and that Leaver had to inform the police as 'a newspaper could not accept a confession'. Field said, 'Well, I have explained that I want everyone to know that I have confessed, and I will give you my real reason for confessing. I did this murder to prove that a man could do what is called a perfect murder and get away with it.' Davey made the point that he wasn't getting away with it by confessing, and asked him to explain himself more, to which Field replied at length, expanding on what he'd previously told Nelson Leaver:

> I had many arguments with my workfellows, particularly a know-all called Duff, over the Rouse case and someone said to me, 'If you think you can beat the police on a perfect murder, get on with it.' Now that was in my mind for quite a long time and it became an obsession. The impulse to commit the murder came to me on the night [29 September 1931] that I left the premises [the empty shop] after having been working there. I left the shop at about six o'clock and went home to Sutton. I had my tea and told my wife that I was going out again. I intended to come back to the West End, but I told her I was going to Balham [south-west London] to see about a new job. I got to Leicester Square about 9.15 p.m. and walked around. I spotted Norah Upchurch and then lost sight of her. I did not know

her then, but it was obvious she was a prostitute. I came face to face again with her again in Leicester Street and I stopped and spoke to her. She was willing to go to the shop and we went there. I did not interfere with her – that was not my object. We stood talking for a minute and I had my left elbow on the wall of the passage [by the shop doorway]. I gripped her by the throat with my right hand and she collapsed right away, but I strangled her again when she was on the floor. I picked up her handbag and left the shop. It was about 10.15 p.m.. I caught the tube [London underground train] to Morden [end of the tube line in south-west London] and then caught a bus part of the way home.

Field also told Davey that before he dumped Norah's bag with her ring and keys in the ditch by the Rose Hill Estate on the Sutton bypass, he took some money out of the bag, Norah's money, in the form of four notes. Field swore that robbery was not the motive, as 'at that time I was fairly well off'. Davey asked Field again why he had really done it. 'Well, I have no use for life, and life has no use for me,' said Field. 'I have never had a break. I've always done the work and others have got the money. In the RAF I did all the work and others got the stripes.'

Field had been a witness at the inquest into Norah's death in 1931, and Davey pressed him about the evidence he had given. 'At the inquest I was pitting my brain against the Coroner and the police; I won.' Davey asked if he would have let any of the other witnesses take the blame for the murder if they came under suspicion – the penalty then for being found guilty of murder being execution, of course. 'I want you to believe that if the Coroner had charged any of them, I would have allowed them to go for trial, but I would have confessed before anything happened to them.'

Field also said something to Davey which perhaps best gets to the core of his mindset: 'One thing that has annoyed me all the time is my realisation that although I committed this murder and got away with it, the people I wanted to prove it to do not know. But they will now.' Field appeared to be a cold-blooded sociopath with narcissistic tendencies, perhaps a psychopath. Poor Norah was the collateral damage in his selfish game – if Field's confession was indeed true.

Davey then told Field that the police would have to be told, and Field said that he understood. Nelson Leaver then spent some more time with Field alone.

≣

Great Marlborough Street Police Station, Central London, Tuesday, 25 July, 1933
Statement of William Ashenden, 31 The Avenue, West Wickham, Kent
Witnessed by Detective Inspector C. Campion, 'C' Division
I am employed by the *Daily Sketch*. During September 1931 I was engaged in my duties on the murder of a woman named Norah Upchurch. During these enquiries I did not meet a man named Field. This afternoon, 25 July 1933, I received a telephone message from my News Editor, Mr Leaver, and I went to the *Daily Sketch* office at Grays Inn Road. This was about 3 p.m. or 4 p.m..

William 'Bill' Ashenden was a crime reporter, and a member of the Murder Gang. Unlike Davey, who was a general reporter, Ashenden was a crime specialist, so the murder of Norah Upchurch in September 1931 would have been a routine story for him. Interestingly, if Ashenden is to be believed and he was making a police statement, Nelson Leaver hadn't introduced him to Frederick Field in October 1931 when the offer of a deal was made, and this is undoubtedly because Field wasn't arrested at that time, and the deal was never finalised.

Bill Ashenden came from a Kent family. He was the grandson of a boot maker and the son of a journalist, also called William, who was on the staff of *Hansard*, the British parliamentary publisher which records all political activity in the Houses of Parliament, from 1909 until 1923. He had previously been temporary editor of the *Maidstone Gazette* in Kent around 1890, then rejected for a job on *The Times* in 1895. At the time of his death in 1924, aged 68, he was one of the oldest political reporters in the House of Commons. His son, William 'Bill' Ashenden, followed him into journalism, and was working for the *Daily Sketch* by the late 1920s.

Nelson Leaver filled in Ashenden about Field when he arrived at the paper's offices on 25 July 1933. Field was still out with Davey and Muggeridge looking for Norah's bag, and Ashenden, with his police contacts, made the first contact with the police, and this sensitive situation required going straight to the top. After trying several times, Ashenden finally got through to Supt Cornish, the leader of the original investigation into Upchurch's murder, at around 6.10 p.m. By now Frederick Field was back in the *Sketch* offices, and Ashenden remembered that Field told him that he was 'fed up, out of work, and wanted to get his wife out of London before he gave himself up'.

Ashenden then drove Field alone to where he and his wife Bessie and daughter Nancy lived at 16 Manor Street, Clapham, in south-west London, much closer than where they had previously lived in Sutton. In the motorcar, Field ruminated about what he was going to tell his wife to explain why he was asking her to go back to her family in Cardiff – he obviously wasn't ready to confess to her too. He eventually decided to tell Bessie that he had found a job there. But Bessie hadn't believed Field's explanation, and asked him what was really going on, and she said that she wouldn't leave London.

Ashenden and Field then drove back to the newspaper offices, and on the way Ashenden asked him if his confession was 'a question of conscience'. Field said, 'No. I have read about a lot of murders in the papers and it struck me it was easy to do and to get away with it without being caught.' Ashenden then advised Field to give himself up to the police immediately, and said that he would take a letter back to Bessie explaining everything. Back at the *Sketch*, Nelson Leaver agreed that Field should hand himself over to the police that night. Ashenden then got in touch with Supt Cornish again.

Leaver and Ashenden then went to Marlborough Police Station together and gave their statements, while Field stayed at the paper's offices with John Davey. Leaver and Ashenden went back to the *Sketch* at 9.30 p.m., and he and Davey took Field back to the police station, where Davey also gave his statement and Field was taken into an interview room and recounted the story he had told Leaver, Davey and Ashenden, beginning his statement with 'I have come to give myself up for the murder of Norah Upchurch on 29 September 1931, at an empty shop at Shaftesbury Avenue.'

≣

On the day that Field had gone into the *Daily Sketch* offices, 25 July 1933, that paper had a front page about the aviator couple Jim and Amy Mollinson, then household names in Britain like flying pioneers all over the world before and especially since Charles Lindbergh. A Scot, Jim Mollinson set several flying records in the 1930s, but they had crashed at 3 a.m. in Bridgeport, Connecticut, having taken off from Wales on 22 July en route to New York City. They had run out of fuel and were taken to hospital, their plane pulled apart by souvenir hunters. For those with a sweet tooth in that day's edition, an advert for Cadbury's Dairy Milk chocolate carried the slogan 'I'll continue to say … I want Cadbury's', while those feeling peaky may have turned to Andrews Liver Salts, as 'Andrews keeps you fit'.

The next day, the first *Sketch* piece about Field ran on page 3. It wasn't a front-page scoop.

AMAZING SOHO MURDER SEQUEL
Frederick C.H. Field, Sign-Fixer, Who Was Witness at Inquest on Norah Upchurch, Surrenders to the Police – 2-Year Mystery
Daily Sketch, Wednesday 26 July 1933

Field was to be charged with Norah's murder at Marlborough Street Magistrates Court that day, and page 5 of the next day's *Sketch* followed up with 'Norah Upchurch Murder: Man In Court – Alleged to Have Given Himself Up – Soho Crime – Prisoner Said To Have Made A Statement'. This was of course disingenuous, as Field had confessed to the very journalists who put out that edition. The fact that the *Daily Sketch* did not capitalise on their exclusive is very telling. Leaver and the paper's management, including the editor Mr Curthoys and the owners Allied Newspapers, had obviously been warned off, and this was undoubtedly due to the earlier contact between Field and Leaver in October 1931, during the full heat of the Norah Upchurch murder investigation.

Leaver had had to come clean to the police about that earlier meeting in July 1933, as Field would probably have contradicted him in police interviews. Field had not confessed to Leaver back then of course, but Field's desire to make a deal with the paper and Leaver's offer of payment for his defence if he should go to trial would surely have been of keen interest to the shrewd Supt Cornish and his team at Scotland Yard. The fact that Leaver had not alerted the police after that first curious meeting shows a news editor's hunger for an inside story connected to a murder, something which was surpassed by any ethical responsibility he may have felt.

One has to wonder if Field would have been arrested in October 1931 after being looked at more deeply, and the subsequent twisting and turning of events would prove that Nelson Leaver had made a big mistake in not alerting the police. Journalists are supposed to protect sources, but Field was not a source, just a man aiming to get money for his legal defence and also the subsequent national newspaper publicity, conveniently telling his version of events. Any other member of the Murder Gang and their paper would have splashed all over the front page with the inside story of the killer confessing to them. The fact that the *Daily Sketch* did not take advantage of its access to Field shows that the paper was not in a position to trumpet its involvement, and the wording of Field being 'alleged to have given himself up' and 'said to have made a statement', when Bill Ashenden took Field to the police station under his news editor's aegis, indicates that the paper was covering its unethical – if not illegal due to the obstruction of justice – tracks, probably having been leant on by the police. The newspaper would certainly have been prosecuted today.

The *Daily Sketch* did report that Field was 'collarless' and said 'I want it cleared up' in court. That same day, the *Evening News* went with 'The Murder of Norah Upchurch – Man in Court Charged with Soho Crime after Two Years' and the next day the *Daily Express* ran 'Man Gives Himself Up for the Murder of Norah Upchurch – Arrest of Police Station Visitor'. On Sunday 30 July, the *News of the World* carried 'Strangled Girl in a Soho Shop – Dramatic New Turn to Mystery of Two Years Ago – Inquest Witness Charged'.

Whether the rest of Fleet Street knew of the *Daily Sketch's* involvement in Field giving himself up is unknown, but if other members of the Murder Gang did know, they would have kept quiet, as there was a code of professional journalistic respect and 'omerta' amongst the Murder Gang. They fought ruthlessly over scoops, but would never divulge the less than legitimate working practices of rivals, particularly as most them were prone to indulging in such practices too when in hot pursuit of a murder exclusive.

Field's trial was set for September 1933. But there was a last-minute minor postponement, when the judge, Lord Justice Goddard, was taken ill with toothache. This was Rayner Goddard's first trial at the famous Old Bailey after being appointed to the bench, and much later he would become Lord Chief Justice, gaining a reputation as a 'hanging judge' in the 1950s, presiding over trials such as those of Craig and Bentley and Ruth Ellis, also covered by the Murder Gang and later in this book. Back in September 1933, Mr Justice Swift was recalled from holiday to take Goddard's place at Field's trial, which began on 19 September, Field being defended by Mr Gansia and Mr Harrison.

It lasted just two days. Field took back his confession in court, saying that he'd never met Norah Upchurch. Field told the court on the stand: 'I wanted the whole thing cleared up properly – the whole thing was left in the air. People said, "This man has done it." I could not turn round and say, "I have been proved innocent." I could not do anything or say anything. I wanted to be arrested and put on my trial, because by doing that I could have my innocence proved properly.'

It also finally came out in court that Field had visited 'a newspaper's office' before going to the police, and that as he was broke he had tried to get money from them. The *Daily Sketch* wasn't named by Field in court, however. But he did admit that he had spent about nine hours with the 'newspaper's representatives' and that he had been with them for five or six hours before he told them that he was going to hand himself in to the police. This prompted the judge to ask, 'Did it occur to you or the newspaper representatives that you might be indicted together for interfering with the course of justice?' Field replied that he hadn't thought about that. The judge went on to say that Field had tried to exploit the newspaper, and that the newspaper representatives had tried to exploit him.

The judge decided that there was no other evidence proving Field's guilt apart from Field's own, now retracted, confession. The judge said of Field and his actions, 'That he is a thorough liar is obvious. But you cannot find a man guilty of murder because he is a liar and because he has been trying to exploit newspapers.' The judge ordered Field's acquittal, and formally pronounced him 'Not Guilty'.

Field did finally get some money from Fleet Street, through the Murder Gang. The following Sunday, the *News of the World* had Field's personal story: '"I Confessed Because I Was Not Guilty" – Frederick Field Tells the Truth of His Motive.' There would have been a sizeable payment offered for this story straight from Field's voluble mouth. Meanwhile, the murder of poor Norah Upchurch was still officially unsolved, almost exactly two years after she was killed.

There was no significant movement on Norah's case reported by the Murder Gang for sixteen months, but then on 26 March 1935, when Isabella Ruxton and Mary Rogerson were still alive in Lancaster and Dr Buck Ruxton was almost six months from becoming a double murderer, on that day, the *Evening News* had a brief piece headlined 'Norah Upchurch Mystery – Statement by Man in Australia: "Yard" May Reopen Inquiries'. There was little detail, but the Reuters news agency in Adelaide reported that an Englishman named Sydney Smith, who had moved to Australia, had made 'a statement' about Norah's murder. He had been doing temporary work in the grounds of a mental hospital in that city, but had apparently vanished since making the statement.

This intriguing development was followed up in more, yet anticlimactic detail on the following Sunday 31 March 1935 in the *News of the World*: 'Soho Crime Echo: Man in Australia and Norah Upchurch – Startling Developments Unlikely'. Sydney Smith had previously lived in Leighton Buzzard, Bedfordshire. The Metropolitan Police had dispatched 'a Flying Squad car' down to Leighton Buzzard and officers had interviewed Sydney Smith's mother. Norman Rae and his colleagues had obviously spoken to the police, and wrote, 'The *News of the World* learns that there is little likelihood of any startling development as a result of the statement.'

But interestingly, one paragraph of the article shows tantalising inside knowledge of the police's thinking at the time about Norah's murder:

The identity of the murderer of Norah Upchurch is known to the officers who carried out the investigations at the time, but they have never been able to secure sufficient evidence against him to justify an arrest, and so far as the general public is concerned, it will remain a mystery.

Later, Frederick Field is mentioned as having been acquitted after confessing. Of course, Field had been arrested, so the hot suspect was not him, and the Metropolitan Police files on the case infer one particular suspect after Field's acquittal, the original 1931 suspects having been exonerated in the eyes of Supt Cornish and his colleagues then. But subsequent events, just over a year later, would shock even the hardened and informed members of the Murder Gang.

LONE WOMAN DEAD
Locked Flat – Pillows on Her Face
Daily Sketch, Monday 6 April 1936

Blonde Found Dead In Flat – Mystery of the Seven Pillows
Daily Express, Monday 6 April 1936

All-Night Guard on Red-Haired Woman Found Dead in Flat
Daily Mirror, Monday 6 April 1936

The dead woman's hair colour may have been in dispute, but her identity was not. Beatrice Vilna Sutton, aged 48, had been found dead the previous day, in her locked flat at 8 Elmshurst Mansions, Edgeley Road, Clapham, south-west London. She had been working as a prostitute, having been separated from her husband for around fifteen years, and she had previously lived in the Brixton area. At first, it was thought that she may have died of natural causes – which is strange as those seven pillows were found on her face. The *Daily Mirror* reported on 8 April, the day of Beatrice Sutton's inquest, that a further examination the day before 'indicated that death was due to a heart attack'.

But that same day, the *Daily Sketch* had 'Surprise Move in Flat Mystery – Police Visit Gaol to Visit Friend of Dead Woman'. Bill Ashenden likely wrote the piece, explaining 'Just before midnight last night Scotland Yard officers paid a visit to a man who is on remand in a London prison. He is believed to have been a friend of the dead woman and to have seen her shortly before her death.' Who was he? Nine days later, the *Daily Sketch* was the first to confirm that Beatrice Sutton had been murdered with 'Flat Death Surprise – Woman Smothered under Pillows'. Readers were informed that at first it was thought that Beatrice may have 'died from a seizure or that it was a case of suicide'. It was also revealed that 'in former years Mrs Sutton posed for the "Perfect Mother" advertisement of a well-known baby food'. It was also confirmed that a charge was going to be made against 'a male'.

But who was he? The *Daily Sketch* revealed his identity the following day: 'A man named Frederick Field (31), an aircraftsman of the Air Force, was charged yesterday with the murder of Mrs Beatrice Sutton.' There was no mention yet of Field's acquittal almost three years earlier for the murder of Norah Upchurch, or indeed Field's visits to and dealings with Leaver, Ashenden and Davey in both 1931 and 1933. The paper was maintaining its silence over the matter, and expressed no surprise at his being arrested and charged for the murder of another unfortunate woman. In fact, the *Daily Sketch* went very quiet about Field and the Beatrice Sutton murder over the following weeks and months, while the rest of the newspapers and Murder Gang hacks went in hard on the story.

That same day, Saturday 18 April 1936, the *Daily Mirror* told how Field had been identified by his initials on a knife, and it published a photo of Field and the *Evening News* ran with how Field's diaries for the two weeks up to Beatrice Sutton's murder were being read at preliminary court hearings by the prosecution, and that he had written,

'I just murdered her because I wanted to murder someone.' Two days later, the *Daily Mail* went with '"I Wanted to Murder" – RAF Man's Alleged Confession'. Field had given exactly the same motive as he had for Norah Upchurch's murder to the *Daily Sketch* journalists and the police on 25 July 1933, which he of course later retracted in court.

≡

Since being acquitted of Norah Upchurch's murder in 1933, Frederick Field had re-joined the RAF on 17 June 1935, which was then running a recruitment drive. Still married to Bessie, Field had deserted her and his daughter Nancy, and was living in RAF quarters at Hendon Aerodrome in north London. Bessie and Nancy were by now living in Cardiff, Wales, where Bessie's parents also resided. Bessie took Field to court on the grounds of desertion during his second stint in the RAF, and she was awarded maintenance support. But on 24 March 1936, Field stole four cheques from an office and went AWOL from the RAF.

Field had been having a relationship for about a year with a woman called Mrs Florence Elizabeth McGregor, who was separated from her husband and lived in Tooting, south-west London, not far from where Field's own parents lived in Streatham. They had been 'teenage sweethearts' about fifteen years earlier, before either of them was married, but the relationship had become more intense since July 1935 when they met up again. He went to stay with Florence McGregor while he was AWOL, but they had a big quarrel on 28 March 1936, and she told him she didn't want to see him again. Field, despondent, left and bought a bottle of the disinfectant Lysol with the intention of committing suicide. Field would also later claim to that he had tried to kill himself using gas, but both times he failed to carry it through. On 4 April 1936, he murdered Beatrice Sutton at her Clapham flat. The night before, Field had slept rough in a garden allotment.

Field was held at Brixton Prison in south London after his arrest, and the Metropolitan Police files show that he was 'quiet and reserved' whilst awaiting trial. Incredibly, Field had no previous convictions before the murder charge, the stolen cheques now being of little relevance, but it was becoming increasingly apparent that his retracted confession to the murder of Norah Upchurch five and a half years earlier had indeed been true, at least in the eyes of the police and the Murder Gang, and increasingly newspaper readers also. But Field himself would never admit to killing Norah. On 21 April 1936, Field attended Beatrice Sutton's inquest, the second murder inquest he had appeared at, but declined to give evidence this time, and he was taken back to prison in a taxi by two warders. The coroner singled out the detective work of Det. Inspector Robert Halliday and his team for their work on the Sutton case.

Back in the South Western (London) Police Court in the next days, the pathologist, Dr Temple Grey, who carried out the post-mortem on Beatrice Sutton, gave evidence that she had been 'susceptible to strangulation' due to a medical condition, and that 'slight pressure would easily kill her'. Of course, it looked like Field had tried to kill her, but this might affect the prosecution's case in court if Field should testify that he hadn't meant to kill her and hadn't applied great pressure to her neck.

But in a chilling echo of his Norah Upchurch confession, the *Evening News* of 28 April reported that Field had said in a police statement after his arrest for Beatrice Sutton's murder: 'I had not seen the woman before in my life, and had not the least ill intention towards her. I just murdered her because I wanted to murder someone.' Would Field try to pull off the same trick again and take back this confession at trial?

The RAF had first captured Field for desertion before he was arrested for the murder and before any connection had been made between him and Beatrice Sutton. As the *Daily Express* informed readers on 2 May, at the Police Court an RAF corporal stated that Field had said to him as they were being driven back to Hendon Aerodrome, 'Look here, corporal. I haven't seen a paper since Saturday night, yet I know there has been some trouble at Edgeley Road, Clapham … I know something about it.' Field was again desperate to be the centre of attention in a murder. When the RAF corporal asked him how he was involved in the 'Clapham affair', Field replied, 'You may as well go over the boat one side as the other. I was just browned off. I don't even know who the woman was.'

Field's lover, Florence McGregor, had also told the court that before the RAF took him back to base, Field had turned up at her home in

West Gardens, Tooting, and said, 'I have done something. I will try and tell you what it is, but if I do not do so you will read it in the papers.' The *News of the World* on Sunday 3 May 1936 carried on McGregor's story and went with 'Midnight Visit from Accused Airman'. Field had turned up at her house at that late hour on 4 April, the very same day that he had murdered Beatrice Sutton, in fact less than an hour before. It came out in court on 8 May that Field had told a policeman, Det. Inspector Brown, who interviewed him, 'I did it. I went to her place about 11.30 p.m. Then I done her in and put myself on the spot.'

Det. Inspector Halliday, leading the police investigation, confirmed that Field's statement was 'surprisingly accurate' in relation to what had actually happened. Halliday said of Field at the time he was interviewed, 'There was something that struck me about his eyes and demeanour that made me think he was not normal at that time … he was a man who wanted to tell me the whole truth, and that he was a very intelligent man.' When asked if he wanted to give evidence, this time Field 'stood to attention' and said 'I plead not guilty and reserve my defence'. Once again it seemed that Field was going to try to get away with murder. As he left the Police Court that day, Field was 'smiling at someone'.

Field's trial for the murder of Beatrice Sutton took place in the second week of May 1936 at the Old Bailey, where he had been acquitted of Norah Upchurch's murder in 1933. Once again he was claiming to be not guilty. He was prosecuted by Mr Eustace Fulton. Field claimed from the witness box that he had slept secretly in 'cupboards' in Edgeley Road in Clapham, where Beatrice Sutton lived in Elmshurst Mansions – probably in an alcove or outhouse outside, around the time of her murder. Field's story when he gave evidence in court was as imaginative as ever:

On the night of the murder, I was going again to spend the night in one of these cupboards. I had got halfway into one when I heard somebody quarrelling in the flat. A man's voice was abusing another person. I could not see who it was. I thought then that the best thing I could do was to get away. I knew if the police were to come it would be discovered that I was a deserter. I began to get out of the cupboard. As I did so, the front door of the flat opened and a man came out. He was of average height, wearing a fawn-coloured raincoat and a trilby hat. I saw, as the man went out, that he had left the front door open … I thought I would go in and see what was wrong. I saw the woman on the bed as I have described in my statement. There was a big fire burning brightly and I could see everything in the room. The woman had a pillow over her face as I described. For a moment I did not know what to do… Then it occurred to me that if I were to take the blame for anything wrong in there I could accomplish what I had not the courage to do, that is, to commit suicide.

In the evidence he gave in his own defence, Field claimed that he had concocted his story about how he had murdered Beatrice Sutton by hypothesising to himself how the killing had taken place. The details he invented were well thought out – he even added that the he had seen the man in the fawn raincoat and trilby earlier in the evening 'talking to a woman at a gate' in the same road. The ever vain Field knew that his new version would make him sympathetic as a near suicide, and seem fiendishly intelligent, which undoubtedly he was, but would the jury also think him a fiend? Or would he get off a murder charge again?

Field's luck didn't hold out this time. Ironically, the depth of detail he had given about the murder of Beatrice Sutton 'did for him' in the end. Nobody believed his story about the man in the coat and trilby. He was found guilty and sentenced to death on Wednesday 13 May 1936. He was 32 years old, and showed no reaction in court, and during the whole proceedings, the *News of the World* would report that Field had worn 'a half-amused smile'. But Field had no history of mental illness and had been cleared to face trial.

The Murder Gang hadn't been able to report on Field's previous acquittal for the murder of Norah Upchurch, due to the law of contempt in that it could prejudice the trial. This was a cardinal rule that the crime hacks had to obey, and they rarely broke the law; they knew how far they could go. But now they were free to report freely on Field's extraordinary past. Unsurprisingly given what we now know about the *Daily Sketch*'s connection with Frederick Field in 1931 and 1933, that paper noticeably hardly reported on Field, during or after his trial. Of course, the 1936 British public had no idea that the *Daily Sketch* had been so linked to this murderer.

The *Daily Express* of 14 May had 'Doomed Man Twice Tried for Murder', and had an exclusive interview with Field's wife Bessie from her home in Cardiff. A reporter had been sent there the previous day. Bessie had not attended the trial, as she said that she could not go through what she had gone through at the 1933 trial again. 'I came here [to Cardiff] to forget the past, and the torment of those days and nights ... He was found not guilty then. Today it was impossible for me to attend my husband's second trial at the Old Bailey. This is the end.'

Then Bessie had started to cry in front of the *Express* man, and her 5-year-old daughter Nancy, described as 'a pretty, delicate child with fair hair and blue eyes, unaware of the tragedy in her mother's life', said, 'Don't cry Mummie.'

Bessie, long estranged from her husband, had received a letter from Field about a month earlier, and the paper printed the contents:

My dear Wife – You will have a shock when you know why I am here. I have been short of money and fed up. Whatever happens I shall plead guilty, so that the end will come quick. It is a pity we could never be really happy together. Don't trouble to visit me here – you are well out of it in Cardiff. It would mean too much fuss – Fred.

Field had, of course, pleaded Not Guilty and had done everything he could to escape justice.

Field's lover Florence McGregor had attended his trial and sat, as the *Daily Express* reported, 'with a pensive face'. The Metropolitan Police files show that Field continued to write to McGregor from prison after being sentenced to death, and that she replied too. The *Daily Mirror* of 14 May went with 'Five-Year-Old Writes to Death Cell' and recounted that little Nancy had heartbreakingly written the words 'Waiting for Daddy'.

On Sunday 17 May, the *News of the World* had 'Acquitted of One Murder – Found Guilty of Another'. The next day it was announced that Field would be executed on 2 June. He was writing to both his parents from prison – telling his mother that he had given them nothing but worry, that his wife Bessie whom he called 'Til' had always been good to him, and how he loved his daughter Nancy. His father visited him in Brixton Prison too. Field launched an appeal, and the Home Office sent psychiatric experts to examine him. On 15 June, his appeal was dismissed, W.F. Martin of the *Daily Mail*, reporting the next day, wrote, 'RAF Man Unmoved as Plea Fails'.

Frederick Field was executed at Wandsworth Prison in south London at 9 a.m. on 30 June 1936. The *Daily Sketch* didn't even announce that he had been executed. The next day, the *Daily Mail* ran an editorial titled 'Human Tigers', which was actually a reference to a speech once given by the great criminal judge Mr Justice Stephens. He had classed killers like Field and several other infamous murderers named in the piece as 'human tigers', and that 'there was nothing to be done with them but to eliminate them'.

It was Norman Rae of the *News of the World* who got the final scoop on Field. The murder of Norah Upchurch is still officially unsolved, even today, and Field could not have been tried again for that terrible crime due to the then Law of Double Jeopardy, which stated that a defendant could not be tried again for the same crime, and which stood in statute in Britain until the early twenty-first century. But almost everybody knew that Field had killed Norah in 1936. And the *News of the World* got closer than anybody to prove that Field had committed the murder, by getting the inside story from Field's father.

Herbert Field opened up and his story was published on Sunday 5 July 1936. Field's father supplied the headline 'My Son Was Guilty of Two Murders'. Herbert Field said: 'I will begin by saying frankly that my son murdered Norah Upchurch a few hours after he had talked to me about being fed up without money. My son was guilty of the murder of Mrs Sutton, and although officially he held out to the end that he was innocent, he let me know by means only a father and son could use that he was equally guilty of this second murder as he was of the first.' Herbert Field thought that his son, once 'a very likeable fellow', had become a 'self-willed, extraordinarily violent-tempered man', and been close to insanity. 'I am satisfied now that he was not sane. I have seen him when his eyes seemed about to fall from his head, when every nerve was twitching, and when little more than a thread's breadth divided him from sheer insanity.'

The paper also revealed that Field had tried to gas himself soon after he murdered Norah Upchurch in late 1931, his father saying that it only hadn't worked because the gas appliance had stopped working. A facsimile of a suicide note that Field had written to his father was printed that day: 'Dear Dad, I killed Upchurch and it has got me down at last. Goodbye. I am putting an end to it all by the gas. Fred.' Herbert Field admitted that he wished his son had been successful, as then Beatrice Sutton would have still been alive. Herbert let it be known too for the first time that his son had been investigated for 'Brighton Trunk Murder No.1', when a dismembered partial corpse was found in a trunk, which had also led to Dr Buck Ruxton being looked at for that still unsolved crime. Ruxton had gone to the gallows just seven weeks before Frederick Field.

Nelson Leaver, the *Daily Sketch* news editor who struck a deal with Frederick Field in October 1931 and received his confession in 1933, died aged 65 on New Year's Day, 1946, and the photographer Herbert Muggeridge died aged 55 while still working for the *Daily Sketch*, on 22 December 1948. John Davey, the *Daily Sketch* reporter who was assigned by Leaver to deal with Field on 25 July 1933, died in December 1936, less than six months after Field went to the gallows. William 'Bill' Ashenden, who also dealt with Field that day, would be a Murder Gang stalwart for years to come, later moving to the *Daily Graphic*.

3

BRUTALITY IN THE BLITZ

Britain had been at war with Germany for twenty-two months. Mr Benjamin Marshall, a demolition worker, was sifting through rubble and detritus in the damaged church, which hadn't actually been used for worship since the late nineteenth century. It was hard, tiring work, and as he lifted up stones from the floor, he needed frequent breaks. Dust was rising into the air, but his face mask protected him from the worst of it. Other workers were nearby, clearing and piling.

Then with a big effort, Marshall lifted up a heavy stone slab, and when he had pulled it off, was surprised to see human remains underneath where it had laid. He was surprised, but not shocked – workers had found other bodies around the site since it was bombed on 15 October 1940, in which a huge fire had added to the bomb carnage, with around 100 people losing their lives. More generally, bodies and burnt remains had been pulled from thousands of bomb-damaged buildings in London since the early autumn of 1940, and this unfortunate person was probably another victim of German bombs.

Under that slab lifted by Marshall was a skeleton, terribly scorched. It was not intact – the skull was separated from the body, the lower jaw was missing, and parts of the limbs, both legs and arms, were absent, having been cut off at the knees and elbows. Marshall told his foreman, and the police were alerted, with Det. Inspector Keeling and Det. Inspector Hatton soon arriving.

As always, the cause of death had to be officially ascertained, and the remains were taken to Southwark Mortuary for examination. It was the start of a hunt, and that would lead to gasps of horror from the British public, although many were by now hardened and desensitised to the horrors of war. It was to be another story for the Murder Gang.

The first London Blitz bombing had been almost two years earlier, on 7 September 1940, when 348 German bombers, protected by 617 Luftwaffe fighter planes, hit London at 4 p.m., and then carried out a second wave of destruction at around 6 p.m., which lasted until 4.30 a.m. the following morning, killing 430 Londoners and critically injuring 1,600 more. On 15 November that year, another huge bombing raid hit almost every part of London, including many key London buildings, the aim being to undermine British culture and civilisation, and therefore morale and wartime cohesion.

St Paul's Cathedral had famously survived the onslaught, although back on 31 December 1940, the *Daily Mail* had published Herbert Mason's famous photo of that symbolic London landmark engulfed in smoke from surrounding bombings, and captioned it 'War's Greatest Picture'. Two days earlier had been the most damaging night of the whole Blitz, when 1,400 separate fires were recorded, some covering very large areas, and many lives lost.

Much of London was now a bombsite, whole streets having been razed by German bombers. Rubble lay everywhere in sections of the city, particularly around the East End, the docks and central London. Hitler had focused on destroying London and sites in other key cities when he decided not to try to invade Britain, after his airborne defeat in the Battle of Britain. The Fuhrer's aim now was to wreak as much destruction as possible through the total destruction philosophy of Blitzkrieg. At 11 p.m. on 10 May 1941, the last huge Blitz raid had taken place, when 500 German bombers killed 1,486 people and made 11,000 families homeless. But at least many children and some women had been evacuated to the countryside.

German bombing raids on London would continue randomly until 1944, including by the dreaded V2 bomb, and whilst very damaging, would never have the sheer power of those eight months of Blitz raids and the enormous loss of life of individual raids. Hitler was now focusing on his invasion of Russia, which would be doomed. In London, the end of the Blitz had meant that clearing of bombsites was taking place, before plans were made for reconstruction after the war, the very reason why Ben Marshall had been tasked with clearing out the Vauxhall Baptist Chapel on Kennington Lane on 17 July 1942.

The remains were examined by the Home Office pathologist Dr Keith Simpson at Southwark Mortuary. Simpson would go on to distinguish himself by the evidence he gave in many big murder cases, including his seminal examination of the remains of Mrs Olive Durand Deacon after the war in the late 1940s, the last victim of the notorious Acid Bath Killer, John George Haigh. After his primary post-mortem, Dr Simpson asked permission to take the remains back to his lab at Guy's Hospital, which was granted.

As there was no lower jaw, there were no teeth too, but the upper jaw had four teeth still in it, and these contained fillings. It looked like the person, now identified as a woman, had worn a partial dental plate in her upper jaw, but this was missing. He also found that there was a tiny fracture of a bone in the voice box, and this would usually indicate that asphyxiation or strangulation had taken place. He did not have the internal organs to confirm this cause of death, but it raised enough doubts of murder in his mind to keep digging. He was also able to tell the police that the woman had been between 40 and 50 years of age, was around 5ft in height, and the few hairs left attached to the skull enabled him to say that she had dark brown or black hair that was going grey.

Returning to the Vauxhall Chapel, Dr Simpson tried to find the portions of lower legs and arms, but was unable to locate them. Something did catch his experienced and trained eye, though – there was a yellowy colour to some of the earth under where the slab had been, and samples were taken back to the lab and analysed. It was found to be slaked lime, which actually preserves bodies as it fends off maggots. Whoever had placed the woman down there in the chapel basement had used the wrong type of lime – quicklime would have decomposed the body. Dr Simpson estimated that the woman had been dead for between twelve and fifteen months, and whoever had put her there had tried to prevent identification by removing limbs and by placing her in lime. Neither bombs nor fires did that. Dr Simpson informed the police.

It was now a murder investigation, by a murderer who had tried to take advantage of the chaos of wartime – how many other murders had been committed during the London Blitz and passed off as bomb or fire victims, or just missing and presumed dead? There must have been some.

Scotland Yard now put all efforts into identifying the dead woman, the only way to find her killer.

It was a time of severe rationing, with many food and everyday products being restricted, and the Ministries of Agriculture and Food tried to placate the public and instil responsibility for food production in them with adverts, such as that in *Home and Country* magazine in 1942, 'Dried Eggs are my eggs, my whole eggs, and nothing but my eggs', and *Food* magazine had 'Do you remember when the headlines said – "No potatoes for this Sunday's Joint" – Dig for Victory Now!' Newspapers had also been affected, the paper shortage meaning thinner papers, and crime news, like every area of coverage, had been cut back.

But the Murder Gang kept reporting and giving readers what they wanted, sometimes murder being a macabre, more personalised distraction from the mindless terror of the war and blanket bombings. On the case of the woman's remains found in Vauxhall Baptist Chapel, Percy Hoskins of the *Daily Express* would very much lead the Murder Gang way, as he would on many cases over the years.

If the Murder Gang was ever said to have a leader – which it did not as it was highly competitive – perhaps more than anyone else Percy

Kellick Hoskins would have been the crime reporter-in-chief. Until the late 1950s, Stanley Bishop was a close competitor as to veteran status, as was Sid Brock of the *Daily Mail*, who had excellent police contacts; Norman Rae of the *News of the World* and Harry Procter of the *Daily Mail* and then the *Sunday Pictorial* were close competitors when it came to scoops, and Sam Jackett of the *Evening News* was a master of getting to a story first.

But especially in the late 1940s, '50s and '60s, Hoskins would undoubtedly have taken the title for whom the other Fleet Street crime hacks looked to for guidance and help. The sheer and increasing range of his police, judiciary and celebrity contacts was breath-taking. Nobody else in the Murder Gang would later have been able to be personal friends with the FBI Director J. Edgar Hoover and the film director Alfred Hitchcock. He was also the one they watched – if the large-framed Hoskins moved quickly, a murder scoop was afoot and it would lead tomorrow.

Percy Hoskins was born on 28 December 1904 – St Innocent's Day, as he would gleefully tell his colleagues, as he was so immersed in crime – in Bridport, Dorset, and he would never lose his thick West Country accent, despite years of living in London. Hoskins, who came from a family of sailors, would also enjoy recalling that Bridport was where they made the hangman's rope that was to be used on many of the murderers he reported on and met. He was in the choir at school, and by all accounts had a very good bass singing voice.

Hoskins was 19 years old when he first came to London in 1924 to join the *Evening Standard*. Thrust straight into crime, one of his first assignments was to cover the murder of Elsie Cameron by her boyfriend Norman Thorne. He had killed her as she was pregnant, and he wanted to be free of her. The police were searching all over his small piece of farming land, as Elsie had last been seen walking towards it. Norman Thorne told Hoskins, 'I don't mind what the police do so long as they don't disturb my chickens.' Hoskins told the police, 'She's in the chicken run,' where they then dug and found her body. Thorne was hanged.

In 1932, at the age of 28, Hoskins moved to the *Evening Standard*, where he would stay for the rest of his long career. He quickly made a name for himself, especially due to his incredible police contacts. In

1938, the IRA was carrying out a terror campaign in London, making balloon bombs and leaving them to explode in train station cloakrooms. Morley Richards, the news editor of the *Daily Express*, asked Hoskins to investigate where the bombs were being made. The next morning, when Hoskins arrived at the paper's offices, he told Richards that the bombs were being made in Richards's own cellar. 'Special Branch has just arrested your Irish butler,' said Hoskins. Later, Hoskins, who was a great raconteur, told the story that Richards had been sleeping above enough bombs to blow up the whole of Oxford Street.

Hoskins would not only cover all the major murder cases in Britain for decades in the Murder Gang, he would also write books and write crime scripts for radio and television. Hoskins was fast becoming the 'respectable' face of the Murder Gang, and he would increasingly become a member of the 'establishment' as the years passed. He was a responsible crime reporter, but he wasn't above cutting corners to get a story. He was a great believer in justice, however, and revered the work of the police.

The case of the woman's body found in the basement of Vauxhall Baptist Chapel would be included in Hoskins's 1951 book *No Hiding Place*, nine years after the grim discovery, and Hoskins used his police contacts at an early stage to start getting information, although due to the war and other cases that he had to cover with reduced page space, it would be a few months before the Murder Gang started reporting on the case, while the police investigation continued.

Hoskins, along with his *Express* colleague Montague Lacey, had recently reported on the murderer Gordon Cummins, known as 'the Blackout Ripper', the RAF Leading Aircraftsman who had murdered and mutilated three women, attempted to kill a fourth and who was suspected of a further murder, all in central London in the space of a week in February 1942. He was found guilty and hanged. Pre-war, this case and the furore caused would have warranted reams of crime coverage, but the war was treacherous and all-engulfing at this stage. In his book *An Underworld At War*, Donald Thomas wrote:

> With the entry of the United States into the war, it seemed impossible that it could be lost by the Allies. But El Alamein and

the first victories lay some months in the future. In the face of present reverses, even a Blackout Ripper rated little more than a few column inches.

≣

It was a difficult and tenuous task to identify the woman, and Scotland Yard had to look at all missing women fitting her age range, height, hair colour and who had worn an upper dental plate. Families of missing women were questioned, one after another, and by a process of elimination over a few weeks, it finally led to a woman named Rachel Dobkin, who had last been seen on 11 April 1941, fifteen months before the body was discovered, and just within Dr Simpson's limit of time of death.

But it still had to be confirmed that it was Rachel Dobkin, who was aged 47 when she vanished, had black hair with grey tinges, was 5ft 3in tall with a medium build, had an upper dental plate and, as the Metropolitan Police case file states, was wearing a fawn-coloured coat with a brown fur collar, a blue woollen jumper together with two woollen cardigans (dark and light blue), a navy blue skirt, black shoes, a brown hat and a wedding ring, when she was last seen in Dalston in east London at 4.30 p.m. on 11 April 1941. Mrs Dobkin, who was Jewish and of Russian parentage, was separated from her husband, and had been living at 44 Cookham Buildings, Old Nichol Street, Bethnal Green, in east London.

Rachel had been reported missing by her younger sister, Miss Polly Dubinski, a 38-year-old shorthand typist, the day after she was last seen. Polly lived with her mother, a Russian citizen, a 40-year-old sister and a 43-year-old brother, Nathan. The Rachel Dobkin missing person inquiry was led by Divisional Inspector Davis of the Metropolitan Police, but Sergeant Dawes of the Flying Squad would later take over from him. It was due to Polly Dubinski's perseverance and pestering that the inquiry was deepened, leading to the match-up with the remains found in the chapel basement. But this still had to be proven.

On the same day that Polly reported Rachel missing, a day after she was last seen, Rachel's handbag, containing her essentials of National

Registration Card and wartime ration book, were found on the counter of a sub-post office in leafy Guildford, Surrey, south of London and a long distance from Rachel's normal East End city environment. Rachel had no previous known connection with Guildford, although she had temporarily gone missing once before and had been found suffering from 'loss of memory' at St Clement's Hospital in Bow in the East End. This led the police to wonder if she had wandered off again.

Inspector Davis had circulated a search report for Rachel Dobkin on 23 April 1941, and a Metropolitan Police report dated 2 March 1942, almost a year later, shows that Polly Dubinski had viewed twenty unidentified bodies, none of them her sister. Rachel's photo and her particulars had also appeared in the *News of the World* three times by then, and there had been a wide search of the whole of her East End of London, all with negative results.

But long before Ben Marshall found the remains in the Vauxhall Baptist Chapel on 17 July 1942, Rachel's sister Polly had been telling the police that Rachel's estranged husband Harry had killed her. In a letter to the police on 16 January 1942, almost exactly six months before the chapel discovery, Polly's solicitors Shield & Son wrote, 'She [Polly] is quite determined, and so are her people, that [Harry] Dobkin has made away with his wife.'

Polly kept up the pressure on the police, and she was a very frequent visitor to Commercial Street Police Station in Whitechapel, as the somewhat harassed police noted. They also knew that Polly firmly believed in psychics and had visited several mediums, who had given her various explanations about what happened to Rachel. Mediums were very popular then, especially due to the life-and-death uncertainty of the war, and psychics regularly advertised their services in the national press. For instance, in 1941, Mrs Forncett Osborne, 'Clairvoyante' of Ravenscourt Park in London, was offering 'Inspirational Messages by Post – No Article Is Required – Questions Answered', presented along with a ghostly grainy photo of the profound, somewhat frightening face of an old woman.

It's understandable why the police, realists by both nature and need, thought that her psychic visits were having 'a depressing effect' on Polly Dubinski. The police had already turned their attention to Harry

Dobkin anyway, as a matter of routine. But until the woman's remains matching Rachel Dobkin were found in that basement, there was no proof of murder. But what was inexplicable wasn't so much her disappearance, as the bombings meant that some people never came home, but the discovery of her handbag. How could Rachel have survived without her ID card and ration book? Had her handbag been left in that Guildford post office as a ruse to make it look as if she had last been in Surrey?

Harry Dobkin was born in London in 1893, although he would later untruly claim to have arrived in London from his parents' native Russia when he was two months old. As a young man, he grew into a well-built man with dark hair and a solemn, knowing expression, and worked as a kitchen hand on several ocean liners and lived in the United States for a few years. Fond of wearing a wide-brimmed black bowler hat, black suit and tie, he was masculine and strong, very much 'a man's man', and from a tough working-class environment in the East End of London.

Harry married Rachel Dubinski at Bethnal Green Synagogue, Bethnal Green Road on 5 September 1920. It had been arranged by a Jewish 'marriage broker'. They moved into lodgings together on the fourth floor of Brady Street Buildings, just off of Whitechapel Road, then a thriving Jewish area. But just three days after moving in they had a huge row and Harry moved out. They tried to reconcile, briefly living together on two further occasions. The marriage was certainly consummated, as their son Stanley Emanuel was born in 1921, and so was presumably conceived on one of these temporary attempts at staying together.

For years, Harry sold aprons, handkerchiefs and other accessories in street markets, just like his father. But after the outbreak of the Second World War, 'bad trading conditions' meant Harry became a nightwatchman and 'fire-spotter' or 'firewatcher', a very necessary, common and sometimes dangerous occupation during the Blitz. Just one example of the hazards of fire-spotting is illustrated by another

East End Jewish firewatcher, Isaac Amiel, born on the Mile End Road, who was killed while on duty on 10 May 1941. He later had Amiel Street named after him, his name chosen by lot from among many victims of the bombings. So Harry Dobkin was a brave man, but his new, potentially lifesaving, job would be intrinsic to the police investigation into his wife's disappearance and the identification of those female remains, those of a murder victim.

By the time of Rachel's disappearance on 11 April 1941, she and Harry had been separated for around twenty years, and their son Stanley, by then aged 19, hadn't spoken to his father for a decade. There was good reason for this. Rachel had gone to court to force Harry to pay maintenance for Stanley's needs, and Harry was ordered to pay her 10s a week. He was supposed to leave these payments every Monday at Old Street Police Court. This order had been in force for years, but Harry had often reneged on his responsibilities, and on several occasions he had been committed to Brixton Prison for non-payment and maintenance arrears.

Strangely, Rachel had religiously gone to the court for her payment every week, the last time being the week before she vanished. Even more strangely, since she disappeared, Harry had made his payments every week without fail, but these had obviously not been collected. As the *Daily Express*'s Murder Gang man Percy Hoskins points out in his book *No Hiding Place*, a court official would joke with Harry Dobkin when he made those post-disappearance uncollected payments, 'Now Harry, you know you've killed your old woman, what have you done with the body?'

But the missing person inquiry remained open until the summer of 1942. The Metropolitan Police case files reveal the police's viewpoint before that point, having already made extensive enquiries, under the watchful and devoted eye of Rachel's sister Polly. 'The fact still remains that in view of this woman's mental history, she may have committed suicide, possibly by drowning, and her body has either not been found, or has been buried as unidentified.' It seemed that Rachel had been mentally unstable at times, although this cannot have been helped by her husband's behaviour and the stress of bringing up Stanley alone.

Polly, her other sister, her brother Nathan and mother all vehemently thought that Harry had murdered Rachel, of course. And when he was interviewed by the police on 24 January 1942, Stanley, now a young man, said that his mother 'had never threatened to commit suicide'. Stanley, who now lived in Slough, Berkshire, had been interviewed several times and hadn't seen or heard anything from his mother since early April 1941 either, and it transpired that not only had he seen his father just once in the past ten years – Harry had to be pointed out to Stanley by relatives – but they hadn't spoken.

Harry Dobkin had himself been interviewed by the police on average about once a month since mid-April 1941, so they had been looking into him, seeing if he contradicted himself. Dobkin was living with his parents at 21 Navarino Road in Dalston, east London. At the time of Rachel's disappearance, he was 48 years old.

Harry Dobkin told the police one story, and always stuck with it. He said that he had 'neither seen nor heard' from Rachel since he left her on Kingsland Road – the main street in Dalston – at 6.10 p.m. on 11 April 1941. He filled in the details of that afternoon, in those hours before he left her. Between 2 p.m. and 3 p.m., he had been walking along Navarino Road, where he was living with his parents, when he saw his wife Rachel at the corner where it intersects with Graham Road. He said he told her, 'Please don't come around here and cause trouble. My mother is very ill.' Rachel had said, 'Well, where can I see you?' Harry said, 'OK, meet me in a couple of hours outside the Metropolitan Hospital in Kingsland Road.' 'All right,' said Rachel. 'I'll bring the boy along. He's home for Passover.'

Harry was saying that his wife was harassing him, but the police must surely have thought it strange that she was going to bring their son Stanley to see him, when they knew from Stanley's own mouth that he hadn't heard or spoken to his father in almost ten years at that time and, when he had once seen him, his own father had had to be pointed out to him. Harry claimed that he had met Rachel at the arranged place at 5 p.m. that day, but Stanley wasn't there. They both then went to a teashop at 374 Kingsland Road and had a cup of tea.

As they were chatting, Rachel told him that her brother Nathan was getting engaged to be married two days later (13 April) and she would like Harry to come to Nathan's engagement party. But Harry said that Rachel told him that he could only come to the party if he 'made peace with her' and went back to live with her. Harry refused to return to Rachel, and she said, 'If you don't make peace with me, I'll make trouble for you.' Harry told the police that although Rachel was talking 'in low tones', she was 'becoming hysterical'. So he'd said, 'Now, calm yourself. I'll consider peace if you will calm yourself and go home.' They both then left the teashop, and Rachel told him that she didn't feel well, and that she was going home to listen to the wireless. He saw her walk away at 6.10 p.m.

Harry also told the police that he thought that Rachel 'had gone mad' and that a prostitute had told him that Rachel had been 'associating' with a man who lived at 6 Wheeler's Row. So Harry had painted a portrait of his missing wife as unstable, close to being unbalanced, desperate to reconcile with him, and a woman who associated with a mystery man who knew a prostitute.

But as of 2 March 1942, the police's thinking, recorded in a report, was still 'There is not the slightest indication that Harry Dobkin has murdered his wife.' But the finding of the remains and the painstaking matching of them to Rachel Dobkin would thrust Harry right back into the police investigation, now a murder inquiry, and he was by then the number one suspect.

Dental records from the upper jaw were intrinsic to confirming that the remains were those of Rachel Dobkin. Rachel's dentist, Mr Kopkin, of Stoke Newington, was able to pull out his records and he recognised his work immediately. Added to this, the forensic photography process first used five years earlier in 1936 to identify the skulls of Isabella Ruxton and Mary Rogerson, which had led to the conviction and execution of Dr Buck Ruxton, was used on Rachel Dobkin's skull. Dr Keith Simpson's colleague at Guy's Hospital, Mary Newman, who was in charge of medical and forensic photography, superimposed a photo of Rachel in life on to the skull. It was an exact match. There was no doubt that it was Rachel Dobkin who had been murdered and buried under that slab in the chapel basement.

The police also did a thorough survey of all bombings around the immediate vicinity of the Vauxhall Baptist Chapel. Within a radius of 150 yards (137 metres) of the chapel at 302 Upper Kennington Lane, there had been twenty-one enemy action bombing incidents between 10 September 1940 and 10 May 1941 – in the worst incident in that area on 15 October 1940, when the church was bombed, over 100 people had died in surrounding streets, due to the fierce fire. But there had been no bombing incident between 11 and 15 April 1941, the key window when Rachel disappeared. This research not only showed the ferocity of the Blitz, but meant that Rachel dying as the result of a bomb hit could be discounted – Dr Simpson and his colleagues and the police knew it was murder by now, but they had to be certain in the heat and confusion of war.

The most incredible discovery would lead directly to Harry Dobkin, and prove Polly Dubinski and the rest of Rachel's family correct regarding his culpability. Harry had been employed as a fire-spotter tasked with overseeing a firm of solicitors, located right next to Vauxhall Baptist Chapel. It was an incredible and damning connection, linking Harry Dobkin directly with his wife's remains.

As the police knew, there had not been an air raid nor a warning siren in the key time period, but they went to work, canvassing people living in the streets all around the chapel. It paid off, and it came out that there had been a 'small fire' on the night of 15 April 1941, four days after Harry Dobkin said he last saw Rachel in Kingsland Road, Dalston, and the last day that anyone else saw her alive too. Smoke had been seen coming through floorboards in a school adjacent to the chapel, but neither Harry Dobkin nor any other fire-spotter had reported it to the fire warden as was the normal procedure.

The police had finally called the fire brigade after being alerted by a member of the public, when the small blaze had been going for around two hours. A policeman who had been on the scene that night and early morning was found and he remembered that a man had been loitering around the chapel at the time of the fire. When the policeman asked why he was there, the man had said, 'I'm the fire-watcher over there.' The man had then jokingly added, 'I didn't do it.' This was very revealing, as Rachel's bones were scorched, so her body had been exposed to fire, and

Harry Dobkin was soon identified as the man the policeman had spoken to that night. Subsequently, it was also learned that the remains of a burnt straw mattress had been found in the chapel basement on the morning after the fire, obviously having been used to keep the fire burning.

Harry Dobkin was called in and reinterviewed, but he kept to the story that he had told the police all along. He was even taken to the chapel basement, where everything was explained to him. He remembered the fire, but denied having anything to do with it, saying that he hadn't reported it as it didn't seem serious. It was a very limp explanation. Then, on 28 August 1942, Harry Dobkin was formally arrested and charged with his wife Rachel's murder 'at 302 Upper Kennington Lane, on or about 11 April, 1941'.

It was obvious that Dobkin had tried to set fire to Rachel's body, to thwart identification and damage it as much as possible, making it appear that she had died in a fire after a bombing raid, when her remains were eventually found, which he must have known would happen at some point. He had tried to use the brutality of the Blitz to get rid of his wife. Ironically, Russia, where he and Rachel both had their roots, had indirectly led to her remains being discovered sooner rather than later – Hitler's focus on his invasion of Russia meaning the Blitz came to an end and the clean-up began.

There was little Murder Gang crime coverage of the murder of Rachel Dobkin immediately, and the papers went with war coverage, only reporting on murders in brief. When Harry Dobkin's trial began at the Old Bailey, on 17 November 1942, the Murder Gang was straight on it. There was a shocked fascination and revulsion for a man who had used the war, in which everyone was suffering, to commit wilful murder, and the crime hacks knew it – if it morbidly interested their hardened palates, it would translate to their desensitised and war-weary readers. Dobkin himself was hardly a sympathetic character too, continuing to deny his guilt. What he had done went against the so-called 'Blitz Spirit' and the unity and tough resilience of blitzed Londoners.

Harry Dobkin was defended by F.H. Lawton and prosecuted by L.A. Byrne. The evidence against Harry was overwhelming, and his brief could only query the identification of the remains, trying to breed reasonable doubt within the jury that it wasn't Rachel Dobkin. But the fact that her estranged husband, the last person to see her alive worked right next to where her body was found, was hard for Lawton to overcome. The prosecution's theory was that Harry, tired of Rachel and her financial demands, had lured her to the chapel on 11 April 1941, strangled her, hidden her body in the basement, and then set fire to it four nights later.

Who Was She? Jury Will Be Shown Life and Death Photographs
Daily Express, 18 November 1942

Woman Made Death Picture – 'Followed Ruxton Case Technique'
Daily Express, 19 November 1942

Percy Hoskins was on the case, reporting on how the prosecution was confirming identity in court, illustrating the process of Mary Newman's photography technique to the jury.

On 19 November 1942, the *Daily Mail* went with 'Bombed Chapel Death Riddle'. Hugh Brady had been the main Murder Gang reporter on the *Daily Mail*, but in fact long prefigured that group of reporters, having covered crime for that paper since 1923, as well as being a motoring reporter and writing war stories. A Dubliner, he had joined the *Daily Mail* in 1904, aged 24, after having been a linotype operator on the *Evening News*. Brady had died at the end of May 1942, aged 62. On his death, the *Newspaper World* led tributes, writing 'For more than twenty years Brady has had a reputation as a crime investigator which has probably never been equalled. No other single man in that time – whether on crime or general news – has obtained from his paper so many scoops.'

The next day, Friday 20 November 1942, Hoskins and the *Express* was back with 'Murder Accused Alleges The Police Left Him Alone For An Hour, Then Read "Wheels of Justice" Poem.' This was a reference to an ancient Greek poem, which gained popularity when translated into English in the seventeenth century, and which contains the line 'The Wheels of Justice grind slowly'.

Harry Dobkin was claiming that the police had taunted him by reading the poem while he was in custody. Dobkin had said in court the previous day:

> They [the police] left me alone in a room for an hour. The detectives told me that if I did not confess I killed my wife they would hang me. After that hour a man began reading that Wheels of Justice poem. I told him he would make a better hangman than a poet.

Hoskins also noted that 'Dobkin, in the witness box, covered his head with a handkerchief to take the oath in Jewish fashion.'

Science Proved It Was Murder: 20-Minute Jury End Mystery of 19 Months
Daily Express, 24 November 1942

The previous day, Monday 23 November, the jury had taken just twenty minutes to return a verdict of guilty, and Judge Wrottesley, later a Lord Justice of Appeal, sentenced Harry Dobkin to death. Hoskins reported that in reaction to his death sentence, Dobkin pulled a piece of paper from his pocket and read it to the court: 'The charge against me is very poorly invented. I do not like giving evidence against the police, but I claim this charge of murder, as I have mentioned, is simply invented.' The same day, the *Daily Mirror* had 'Sister at Séance "Saw" Murder Plot', a paranormal twist referring to one of Rachel's sister Polly's visits to a medium.

Harry Dobkin appealed against his sentence of death on 7 January 1943. It was dismissed, the *Daily Express* running 'No Reprieve For Cellar Murderer' on Tuesday 26 January. Harry Dobkin was hanged at Wandsworth Prison in south London at 8 a.m. the following morning. Just prior to his execution, Harry Dobkin finally confessed to his wife Rachel's murder. He wanted her out of the way, and he had been sick to death of her haranguing him for the money for their son's maintenance.

4

LIFE IS CHEAP ON THE BLACK MARKET

It was an Opel Saloon, registration DKR388. Parked opposite No.12 Chepstow Place, just a long stone's throw from where the serial killer John Christie was living at 10 Rillington Place, having already begun his depraved killings; from where the sexual sadist Neville Heath killed his first victim the following year in Pembridge Road; and from where John George Haigh was already dissolving his victims in acid, just a little further south in Gloucester Road.

But in Chepstow Place that morning, just a week short of the six-month anniversary of Victory in Europe (VE) Day, when the Second World War ended, there was a very different kind of darkness. The man slumped on his left side in the back seat of that Opel car had been shot through the back of the neck. The 'driving wheel' of the car was extensively blood-stained, the inside lamp was smashed, and a bullet had dented the metal roof.

The man would soon be identified as Reuben Martirosoff, known as 'Russian Robert', and as Percy Hoskins of the *Daily Express* would splash over the front page the next day, 'Murder Victim Had A Past'. In the language of the Murder Gang and its readers, this could only mean that Martirosoff had been involved in criminality, and it would soon come out that his shady dealings were international in nature, and that he had been 'making a killing' in the thriving black market of wartime London, before now being killed himself.

Notting Hill Gate was far from the fashionable and expensive area that it is today, being known by many then as 'Rotting Hill', as it was so faded, dilapidated and neglected, a state of affairs that the notorious slum landlord Peter Rachman, and his henchmen, including a brain-damaged bodybuilding dwarf of immense strength, would exploit in the 1950s and early 1960s. But unscrupulous landlords in this area of inner west London were already buying up properties, and often tenants, to rent them out at higher rents, in the mid–late 1940s. As Shirley Jackson tells us in her 1979 book *Rachman*, 'In 1946, the value of houses with vacant possession rose by 62%, in 1947 it rose by 93%, and in 1948 it rose by 127%.'

Osbert Lancaster, the art critic, author and cartoonist – a colleague of Percy Hoskins on the *Daily Express* from 1939, where he developed the 'pocket cartoon', a single panel cartoon reflecting the news which was published on the front page, which amused many during the hard war years – described 1940s Notting Hill in his 1963 memoir *All Done from Memory*. Lancaster was writing about the area around Kensington Park Road, which is just a ten-minute walk from where Russian Robert was found shot dead in Chepstow Place:

> The vast stucco palaces … had long ago been converted into self-contained flats where an ever increasing stream of refugees from every part of the then civilised world had found improvised homes … Long, long before the outbreak of war these classical facades had ceased to bear any relevance to the life that was lived behind them; the eminent KCs and the masters of City companies had already given place to Viennese professors and Indian students and bed-sitter business girls.

So where Reuben 'Russian Robert' Martirosoff was found murdered was hardly salubrious anymore, although the once grand houses still held a haunting, if seedy majesty of times past. The cartridge of a bullet was discovered inside the car, on the floor by the driver's seat. By 9.45 a.m. that morning, Fred Cherrill, Scotland Yard's ballistics 'whiz', was at the scene, and he was soon able to say that the bullet was of .32 calibre and nickel-plated, and that the murder weapon was a Walther .32 Automatic pistol.

The post-mortem report in the Metropolitan Police case file reveals that the bullet that killed Martirosoff had 'entered the nape of the neck at close range, went through the brain, and came out of the skull through the forehead over the right eye'. It also disturbingly details that Martirosoff would have lived for about twenty minutes after being shot, but would have been 'incapable of moving'.

Despite his underworld moniker 'Russian Robert', Reuben Martirosoff was in fact Armenian, but was a stateless subject at the time of his death, and had been since 1920, when he was living in Constantinople (now Istanbul). He arrived in England in 1928, and over the next seventeen years he'd accumulated five convictions for larceny, offences against alien (immigration) regulations and for frequenting gaming houses. Martirosoff had also been travelling in Europe, and had another five identical convictions there, plus for receiving stolen goods, all in France and Germany.

A contemporary Metropolitan Police report summed up Martirosoff. 'He undoubtedly has been living by receiving stolen property for years past and during the war has been engaged in black market deals in foreign currency, gold and suchlike transactions.'

The Second World War had seen the black market thrive, the chaos of bombing and the war effort allowing black marketers, then known as 'spivs' with their slicked back Brylcreemed hair, cheap sharp suits, pocket handkerchiefs and quick-fire sales patter. From restricted supply robberies when so many products were rationed, through to lorry hijackings and street spivs selling nylon stockings and other shortage goods to desperate customers, from a battered suitcase on the major streets of big cities, ready to pick up that suitcase and run at any sign of the law.

Russian Robert was very much part of this criminal scene, and he was a major player. It's no wonder that the day after his murder, the very well-connected Percy Hoskins of the *Daily Express* reported that 'Russian Robert' Martirosoff, who was aged 39 at the time of his death, 'had a past'. Although the war had been over for some months now in Europe, severe shortages and rationing would continue until 1947 as Britain regained some peacetime economic stability and the rebuilding began, so those operating on the black market, such as Russian Robert, were still prospering at the end of 1945.

Russian Robert had settled in London and ran a café and billiard hall in Bloomsbury, just behind Denmark Street, London's Tin Pan Alley, in the mid–late 1930s. On 2 May 1940, he married Yetta Slotsky, a prostitute with forty-three occupational convictions, at Caxton Hall in Westminster. Martirosoff gave his job on the marriage register as 'dealer', and he was dealing in watches and jewellery. But within hours of getting married, he was arrested for committing an offence against wartime curfew restrictions placed on aliens, for which he went to prison for nine months. When he came out, Russian Robert and Yetta lived in a flat at Langham Place, London W1, but she soon threw him out due to his heavy drinking and way of life.

On 18 June 1945, Yetta divorced Russian Robert at the Royal Courts of Justice on the grounds of adultery, although the last time that she saw him was in December 1944 at a divorce hearing. His new lover Auriol Rose Martisoroff (she had taken his name by deed poll) was co-respondent in the divorce. Auriol had first met Russian Robert in 1935, but they had bumped into each other in Marks & Spencer's in Oxford Street in January 1941, and that was when their affair began again. They lived together at 30 Hogarth Street in South Kensington. Russian Robert's daily routine was to leave the house at about 11 a.m. and return around twelve hours later.

Until the middle of 1945, Russian Robert ran a bookmaker's in Brewer Street, Soho, but he sold it as it wasn't making enough profit. He was now solely living off his deals and lucrative black market activities. He was a well-known 'face' around the West End, frequenting shady spiv-magnet clubs such as the Cromwell on Baker Street, the Quebec on Old Quebec Street, Jerry's Club on Archer Street and No. 12 on Frith

Street, Soho. He'd bought the Opel Saloon car in which he was murdered for cash four or five months earlier, and was known to carry a 'large roll' of money – around £400 at a time, an enormous sum then, not just for show, but also undoubtedly to facilitate last-minute cash deals.

On the last day of his life, 31 October 1945, Russian Robert had lunch in Gerrard Street, Soho, and then visited two female friends at 11 Bentinck Mews, just off of Bond Street, very close to where the Cambridge Spies – Guy Burgess, Donald Maclean and Anthony Blunt and Kim Philby visiting once or twice – would often congregate during the war at a house on Bentinck Street. Incidentally, Percy Hoskins would get the scoop on Burgess and Maclean's defection to Russia for the *Daily Express* in 1951. At 9.30p.m., Russian Robert was at Jerry's Club on Archer Street, and fifteen minutes later he was spotted at the Crown and Sceptre pub on Foley Street.

Russian Robert's new partner Auriol told the police that she had received a call at home in South Kensington that evening asking for 'Robert', not Reuben, as she called him. The man on the phone said that he was a Polish naval officer, and he obviously knew Martirosoff by his street name. Russian Robert came home at about 11 p.m., and the Polish man immediately called again. Russian Robert told Auriol that he had to go back out and meet the man at Edgware Road underground station. He left in his Opel Saloon at 11.05 p.m., and she never saw him alive again.

At 11.30 p.m. Russian Robert was seen entering the Quebec Club on Old Quebec Street with two men, and he left with them at 12.15 a.m. on 1 November. At around 1 a.m., three men were seen walking away from Russian Robert's Opel car in Covent Garden by a policeman on the beat. Thirty minutes later, the men returned, got back into the car and drove off towards west London, where Russian Robert was found shot to death in the back seat of the Opel in Chepstow Place, Notting Hill, later that morning.

Percy Hoskins of the *Daily Express* was by now emerging as a leading figure of the Murder Gang. One of the key reasons for this was his networking – by this time Hoskins had cemented very close contacts, and sometimes friendships, with the police, and these would only solidify over coming years. Many Murder Gang members had good police contacts, notably Arthur Tietjen of the *Daily Mail*, Norman 'Jock' Rae of the *News of the World*, Sam Jackett of the *Evening News* and Tom Tullett of the *Daily Mirror* particularly. But one very influential connection made at the end of the Second World War would move him into a different league, above his Murder Gang peers.

Towards the end of 1944, when it was obvious that the war was nearing its end at last, the British Home Secretary Herbert Morrison asked Harold Scott, then Permanent Secretary of the Ministry of Aircraft Production, to become Commissioner of the Metropolitan Police. Britain's largest and most influential force, covering London and a surrounding radius, and importantly encompassing Scotland Yard, and the elite Murder Squad and Flying Squad, which would help other forces on difficult murder and robbery cases all over the country. The choice of Harold Scott was a radical one – he'd been a civil servant his whole career, whereas all other commissioners had risen through the police ranks or come from a military background. Only the first Co-Commissioner of the Metropolitan Police, Richard Mayne, a lawyer, appointed way back in 1829, hadn't been of police or military pedigree before Scott.

When Harold Scott became Met Commissioner in November 1945, he soon made it clear that he wanted to improve the image of the police with the public, and launched a public relations drive, largely through television, radio and film, allowing Met Police resources and access in the making of a police-themed film and television series in the late 1940s and early 1950s. The actor Jack Warner was central to this too – starring as a heroic policeman in the film *The Blue Lamp* and the reliable yet tough Police Constable George Dixon in the long-running and very popular television serial *Dixon of Dock Green*, which would create a positive public image of the beat policeman or 'bobby' in British minds for several decades.

That was where Percy Hoskins was useful to Commissioner Scott, and of course a close working relationship with the highest-ranking policeman in the country was very beneficial to Hoskins too, with regards to access to information and trust, and Hoskins had always been very responsible when dealing with police information when reporting. Hoskins would go on to work with Scott in devising a BBC anti-crime crusading TV show called *It's Your Money They're After*, which apparently actually ended up doing little to reduce crime. Hoskins would continue to consult and sometimes write for crime television and radio programmes through the 1950s, as well as writing his books. But his friendship and collaboration with Scott lifted him into a rarefied police information Valhalla about which other Murder Gang hacks could only dream. Harold Scott remained Met Police Commissioner until 1953, and by then Hoskins was very firmly 'in' with the police, and his scoops would reflect that.

Included in Percy Hoskins's first coverage of the case the day after in the *Daily Express* of 2 November 1945 was the sub-headline 'Notting Hill Car Murder No.2'. This referred to the murder of Frank 'the Duke' Everitt, a London black cab driver who also had dealings in the black market, so much so that on his modest cabbie's wage he owned properties in Streatham and Battersea in south-west London, a large country house in Gloucestershire and a very healthy amount of money in the bank. Everitt had been found shot dead at close range on Thursday, 18 October 1945, just thirteen days before Russian Robert's murder. His body had been stuffed into the wall cavity of an air raid shelter on Lambeth Bridge. His taxi had been discovered abandoned in St Helen's Gardens, a mile away from Russian Robert's Opel in Chepstow Place, the reason for the Notting Hill car murder link made by Hoskins and of course the police.

Added to this, Frank 'the Duke' Everitt had been seen letting two elegantly dressed men into his taxi close to the Houses of Parliament in Westminster shortly before he was killed. Could they be the same two men seen with Russian Robert at the Quebec Club and getting in and out of his car on his final night?

Chief Inspector George Somerset led the Russian Robert murder investigation. Percy Hoskins obviously had excellent access to Somerset, as he reported a stream of details in the coming days and weeks, more than any other Murder Gang reporter. On Saturday 3 November, the *Daily Express* had 'Russian Robert Carried £900' –

this was an exaggeration, as we now know from the police file that it was £400, and there was speculation that Russian Robert's unnamed 'Beaten-Up Friend Vanishes', a lead which would go nowhere, but excited readers not acquainted with the shady black market at first hand, even if some were indirect customers, buying hooky goods from that spiv-with-a-suitcase in the street or in a pub.

Chief Inspector Somerset had soon traced the two men seen with Russian Robert on the night and early morning of 31 October – 1 November. They were both deserters from the Polish Army, absent without leave (AWOL), called Marian Grondkowski (alias Robert Granat) and Henryk Malinowski. Both were also heavily involved in London's black market. Chief Inspector Somerset gained the co-operation of the Polish military police to fill in the two men's backgrounds.

Grondkowski was 32 years old with blonde hair and blue eyes, 1.68m tall and weighed 76kg. He had served in the Polish Army as a driver and engineer, and also trained as a parachutist and sniper. He'd been AWOL since 1 April 1945. The police evaluated him as 'more shrewd than clever' and 'talkative'. Malinowki was 24, had blonde hair and light hazel eyes, 1.63m tall and weighed 64kg. He had no training or profession, and he'd been in the Polish Army since June 1943. After deserting, he was sentenced to fourteen months in prison on 29 November 1944 for theft and forgery, and had been released early not long before the murders of Frank 'the Duke' Everitt and Russian Robert. The police noted that he was 'capable' and 'drinks a lot'.

Both Grondkowski and Malinowski were arrested for Russian Robert's murder, and made their first appearance at West London Magistrates Court on Monday 5 November 1945, just four days after Russian Robert's murder. The next day, the *Daily Express* had 'Former Wife Tells Life Story of Russian Robert'. Percy Hoskins had made a deal with Russian Robert's ex-wife Yetta to tell her story of life with the murdered black marketer, prompting the smaller headline '£50,000 Jewel Swindler was Greengrocer at £5 a Week', describing Russian Robert's rags-to-riches legally downward trajectory, and the fact that he'd been arrested and 'Jailed on Wedding Day' was a detail to savour, as was the paper's headline on the front page of 8 November – '£2,000

Gems Locked Away By Russian Robert', referring to his secret stash.

The *Daily Mirror* of Monday 12 November got in on the Russian Robert story, the Murder Gang's Harold 'Jeep' Whittall making a connection between Russian Robert and a Polish airman who had been found dead near the Houses of Parliament, 'whose body was the second to be found in the shadow of Big Ben within three weeks', referring to the earlier discovery of Frank 'the Duke' Everitt's body on nearby Lambeth Bridge. Whittall focused on the possible connections between the murders, informing readers that 'the murdered Pole, a warrant officer, was well-known among the international gangs in Soho and had dealings with Russian Robert'.

Grondkowski and Malinowski appeared at West London Magistrates Court again on Tuesday 20 November, when their counsels let it be known that both Polish men blamed each other for Russian Robert's murder, and they were remanded to appear again on 4 December 1945. The coverage then died off until the trial started in February 1946.

Russian Robert Was Shot On Whiskey-Running Trip – 'Partners' Says Accused Man
Daily Express, Wednesday 13 February 1946

Henryk Malinowski had told the packed Central Criminal Court at the Old Bailey the day before that he and Marian Grondkowski had gone with Russian Robert to meet a lorry consignment of black market whiskey in Notting Hill when Russian Robert was shot. Malinowski pointed the proverbial finger at Grondkowski, saying that he 'saw a flash' and then saw 'Robert's cut'. That same day, the jury went out and sentence was quickly passed.

Russian Robert Man Jeers at Sentence – Dock Packed
Daily Express, Thursday 14 February 1946

Grondkowski and Malinowski were sentenced to death. They listened to the sentencing first in English and then in their native Polish. As Percy Hoskins witnessed along with the rest of the court, Grondkowski 'grinned and jeered' in reaction. 'Jeep' Whittall of the *Daily Mirror* was there too, the same day running, 'Killers Hear Fate in Two Tongues', and described the relationship between the two killers and Russian Robert: 'In handsome Russian Robert, who was known to lose £100 on a card, they found a friend. He was known to police all over the world. Women and money were his main "hobbies".'

The seedy glamour of international criminal Russian Robert's lifestyle and his brutal end was prime Murder Gang material in bombed-out, rationed Britain. In fact, Russian Robert would leave an estate of just £1,900, less than five times what he carried daily, perhaps symptomatic of his easy-come easy-go way of operating, but a character like him may well have secretly stashed away much more of course.

Both Grondkowski and Malinowski filed Appeals against their death sentences, and both were rejected. It was a cold-blooded murder, obviously committed for money – Russian Robert's pocket roll of money and probably for his share of the lorry-load of black market whiskey too, if the two Poles ever got their hands on it; that was never proven. Malinowski had already admitted being there when Russian Robert was shot, saying that Grondkowski pulled the trigger of the Walther Automatic. Grondkowski never admitted anything. They were hanged separately, one after another by Albert Pierrepoint at Wandsworth Prison on 2 April 1946, five months and a day after they killed their black market 'partner'.

Percy Hoskins was back the next day, using his inside track with the police to inform *Daily Express* readers about the 'Gallows Secret of the Duke'. This of course referred to the murdered taxi-driver Frank 'the Duke' Everitt, Hoskins saying that Scotland Yard detectives were 'almost certain' that Grondkowski and Malinowski had shot the Duke dead too. The *Daily Mirror*, in a front-page splash of the same day, 'by *Daily Mirror* Crime Reporter', aka Harold 'Jeep' Whittall, went with 'Yard Men Quiz Killers in Death Cells'. On the eve of the execution of the two Poles, detectives had gone to their cells at Wandsworth Prison and tried to get confessions to the Duke's murder, as the two men had nothing to lose. But no admissions came.

Frank 'the Duke' Everitt's murder remains unsolved, but it seemed highly likely that the same two killers had carried out that killing just under two weeks before the slaying of Russian Robert. But Percy Hoskins and his colleagues would have the last word on Russian Robert, eleven months and a week after his murder, and over six months after his killers were hanged. On Wednesday 8 October 1946, the *Daily Express* ran a front-page piece by Ralph Champion – 'Murder for Secrets – Taxi-Man's Wallet Taken: £38 Left in Pockets'.

A 6ft-tall taxi driver named Joseph Thomas Desmond had been shot to death, in fact shot five times. His body was found early the following morning in Ladbroke Grove, a fifteen-minute walk from where Russian Robert was discovered dead in Chepstow Place, Notting Hill. The police 'believed' that while Desmond knew underworld 'faces', he was not a criminal himself, as the Duke and of course Russian Robert had been. Grondkowski and Malinowki were now firmly entrenched in their unmarked graves in the unconsecrated grounds of Wandsworth Prison. Had the same killer or killers murdered the Duke and Desmond, or was being a taxi-driver a more dangerous than usual job in immediate post-war London?

The year 1945 would also be a landmark one for the Murder Gang, with the formation of the Crime Reporters' Association. As crime historian Steve Chibnall asserted in his excellent 1977 study *Law-and-Order News*, the Crime Reporters' Association was established to have 'the dual function of pressure group for better facilities for gathering information, and businesslike organisation whose members the police could distinguish from less responsible practitioners of Fleet Street journalism'. British crime reporting was becoming more organised and professional, and the skills more sophisticated, greater resources and sources, and undoubtedly the Murder Gang wanted ever closer relations with the police, through both official (the Scotland Yard Press Bureau) and unofficial (personal police contacts/informants).

Relations and contact between the police and the press would continue to become closer and closer entwined over the following decades, with up-and-down periods of more and less co-operation and sometimes personal friendships. But it wasn't until the end of the first decade of the twenty-first century, with the phone-hacking scandal – Fleet Street crime journalists hacking the voicemail functions of celebrities, families of crime victims and even a missing teenage murder victim, which closed the *News of the World* after 168 years, and led to the Leveson Inquiry and Report, which looked into media behaviour and the possible need for more regulation, that relations between the police and the press cooled dramatically. Elizabeth Filkin was employed by the Metropolitan Police as an independent advisor on police–media relations in the wake of the phone-hacking scandal, and she gave key evidence to the Leveson Inquiry.

As Dominic Ponsford of the *Press Gazette* reported on 14 November 2013, 'Crime reporters scrap annual drinks with police officers in the wake of mass boycott by Scotland Yard' – many police officers hadn't gone to the Crime Reporters' Association (CRA) Christmas party in 2012. As Ponsford wrote, 'Last year, Elizabeth Filkin published a report calling for strict controls on the way police officers interact with journalists. It was adopted by the Met Police which warned officers against drinking with journalists and told them to keep a note of any contacts.' John Twomey of the *Daily Express*, then President of the CRA said, 'It really is an indictment of the current state of police/press relations that so many people boycotted it last year. One can only hope that one day soon, someone will see sense at the Yard.' Almost eighty years after the Crime Reporters' Association came into being, links had broken down and show very few signs of regrowth, the Metropolitan Police now preferring to issue press releases to journalists than work with them closely as they had for so long.

Rewinding back into the mid-twentieth century, the late 1940s and 1950s would be the truly vintage years of the Murder Gang, with key members at the top of their game – Percy Hoskins, Norman 'Jock' Rae, Harry Procter, Sam Jackett, Tom Tullett and the veteran Stanley Bishop of the *News Chronicle*, who would retire at the end of the 1950s. That's not to say that this new era of professionalism meant that rogue methods were not employed – the period 1945 to 1960 would see some of the most extreme, unorthodox and sometimes distasteful if not immoral methods used to get scoops. It was the most competitive era for the Murder Gang too – newspaper circulations peaked in the

1950s, and crime scoops fed this arguably more than any other area of news – creating more front-page splashes and street newspaper placard headlines to attract readers. Crime simply sold in the media, as it still does of course.

The place of Murder Gang reporting in London urban culture at this time can be seen in the unfinished 1947 novel *The Dark Diceman* by Julian Maclaren-Ross, which was commissioned by none other than the novelist Graham Greene, when he was managing director of the London publisher Eyre and Spottiswoode, but which the hugely talented though unreliable Maclaren-Ross never delivered. The newspaper mentioned is a fictionalised amalgam of *The Star* and the *Evening Standard*, which Murder Gang members Cecil Catling and Victor Toddington reported for respectively:

In the Tottenham Court Road it's sticky hot...a paper-man is stationed, *Star News Standard*: a late final full of crime, CAR BANDITS ESCAPE, 200 CASES OF WHISKY STOLEN, SUSSEX BATH MURDER STILL UNSOLVED...

The Murder Gang and its work was now at the very centre of everyday British culture.

5

THE PERILS OF HAVING A GO

CHARLOTTE STREET, CENTRAL LONDON, TUESDAY 29 APRIL 1947

Men in overcoats, camel hair and Crombie, notepads out, in and out of shops, pubs and cafés, pressing for leads, scanning the street, getting a feel, a taste, led by instinct and experience. Its three o'clock in the afternoon and the Murder Gang are at the crime scene. Response time: less than thirty minutes. About fifteen of them are here: Len Hunter of the *Daily Express*; Percy Hoskins, otherwise professionally engaged, will arrive later; Reg Foster of the *News Chronicle*; Bill Jones of the *Daily Herald*; loner Syd Brock of the *Daily Mail*, who will soon phone his news editor Lindon Laing, who in turn will confer with Murder Gang reporters Arthur Tietjen and Harry Procter; then there's Harold 'Jeep' Whittall of the *Daily Mirror* and Norman 'Jock' Rae of the *News of the World*, among others, on site. It's a hot one.

Some are drinking at the bar at the Red Lion pub near New Scotland Yard, professional measures of halves of beer which often turn into pints after rounds started, when a colleague runs over from the Press Bureau at the Yard to 'tip the wink' about the shooting in Soho. All the hacks leave their drinks on that stained yet polished bar top. Others rush from their newspaper offices after police tip-offs fresh from the Murder Gang wire.

Charlotte Street is buzzing, members of the public watching the commotion, the heroic, still man under the blanket now taken away, policemen milling about where he'd lain so unceremoniously next to the kerb in that dirty gutter. A photographer, just passing, had got a photo of the have-a-go hero lying there. Mr Barnett, proprietor of the café next door to the jewellery shop the gunman and his accomplices ran out of at just after 2.30 p.m., and another passer-by were snapped for posterity trying to help him.

Len Hunter, Bill Jones and Reg 'Fireman' Foster – the latter would later do a short prison stretch for refusing to name a source, making him a hero of the Murder Gang – are questioning Mr Barnett, getting all the 'gen' they can to build the stories for their individual papers. Many other interviews are going on, and will for hours. Victor Toddington of the *Evening Standard* is under pressure to file for that day's final, as is a rookie reporter from the *Evening News*. Norman 'Jock' Rae of the *News of the World* and Fred Redman and Victor Sims of the *Sunday Pictorial* have days to finish their reportage, but they will be assigned to other stories too before their papers go to press on Saturday, so they want to 'wrap it up' as far as they can today.

The man lying kerbside in Charlotte Street was Alec de Antiquis, aged 31, a married father of six who ran a motorcycle repair shop south of the Thames. He had bravely tried to block the path of the three armed robbers as they emerged at speed from Jay's Second-hand Jewels & Silver. Mr Barnett's café was on one side of the jeweller's, and a vacant plot of freehold land on the other. Three robbers, wearing scarves as face masks, had entered the shop just before 2.30 p.m. and pistol-whipped the manager around the head with a revolver before making off.

Alec de Antiquis happened to be passing down Charlotte Street on his motorcycle and courageously tried to block the getaway of the three men, and one of them shot him through the head for his trouble. De Antiquis died at that kerbside, while the three robbers, one now a murderer, and the other two seen as killers in the eyes of the law because of the law of Joint Enterprise, escaping into the bustling West End on foot.

Scotland Yard sent one of its best murder detectives, Chief Inspector Robert Fabian, to handle the murder of Alec de Antiquis, and he would be ably assisted by Det. Inspector Bob Higgins and Det. Inspector Fred Hodge. The immaculately double-breasted suited Fabian, all slicked back hair and purposeful yet calm expression, was a boy's own detective hero who would become a celebrity in the 1950s.

It was a nasty and pointless murder. There had been no need to shoot de Antiquis; they could have pistol-whipped him too, or the three of them could have overpowered him and pushed him off of his motorcycle to escape. The gunman had obviously shot in panic, but he and his accomplices had walked into Jay's with a gun, and that meant with intent to use it in legal eyes. Alec de Antiquis, who had been a corporal in the Home Guard during the war, training men to defend their area in case of a German invasion, had done his best to thwart what the Murder Gang and their readers called 'bandits', but had paid the highest price.

Another 'ordinary' hero, naval officer Captain Ralph Binney, aged 56, had died doing the same – trying to stop smash-and-grab jewellery raiders – in Birchen Lane, to the east of Charlotte Street in the City of London, in December 1944, less than two and a half years earlier. The Binney Medal was instituted by the Metropolitan Police in his honour for public bravery and sacrifice, and Alec de Antiquis would be posthumously awarded it, a small but important consolation for his proud widow Gladys and their six children.

Percy Hoskins and his colleague Len Hunter went to work. Len Hunter was born in 1908, and became a journalist in 1926, first working for the *Evening News* in London, and during the Second World War he was posted to Tripoli in Libya, where he worked on the *Tripoli Times* as well as the *Union Jack* services newspaper. Journalists were in demand when posted abroad, as British forces news was very much in demand, between service men and women themselves in different outposts, but of course with a patriotic, morale-boosting flavour, to get past Churchill's censors. At the end of the war, Hunter joined the National Union of Journalists on 9 November 1945, and became a reporter on the *Daily Express*, working closely with Percy Hoskins on Murder Gang stories, such as the de Antiquis case. The day after de Antiquis's murder, it took the front page:

Murder, London W1 – Yard Identify Two Bandits
Daily Express, Wednesday 30 April 1947

Beneath the headline was the photograph taken by the passing photographer of Antiquis being tended to in the street, with arrows pointing to Tottenham Street one side of Charlotte Street, and on the other side the very busy Tottenham Court Road.

There were no details given yet as to how the police had identified two of the men. This could have been because Hoskins's police contact, Fabian, didn't want it to be known publicly yet – or it could have been a Fabian–Hoskins bluff to make the real culprits sweat. In fact, Fabian and his team had not yet actually identified any of the robbers, although they may well have had strong suspects in mind, which Hoskins had learnt and reported tentatively.

The headline on page 5 of the *Daily Express* the following day, Thursday 1 May, 'Calling All Informers "Get These Killers"' was preceded at the top of the page with the smaller headline 'Six Columns Cover Britain's Crime – Sheet Today', was a call for London's organised crime elements to come forward: 'Sir Harold Scott, Metropolitan Police Commissioner, last night authorised one of his senior officers to appeal to London's underworld to have the courage to show its disapproval of the shooting of Alec de Antiquis by helping the yard to arrest the gunmen.'

Underneath the sub-headline 'Wanted for Murder' were the descriptions of the three suspects, as gleaned from various witnesses interviewed by the police. Hoskins and Hunter had given the three 'bandits' the titles of The Leader, Pupil No.1 and Pupil No.2, one robber thought to have led the raid, the other two more subservient followers. The Leader was described as 'Aged 35 to 40, 5ft 8ins, medium build, clean-shaven. Wears cap and dirty green-coloured raincoat. Has a criminal record.' Pupil No.1 was 'Aged 25, 5ft 6ins, slim, pale complexion, broad forehead, thin jaw, clean-shaven, long dark hair, no record.' Finally, Pupil No.2 was 'Also aged 25, 5ft 10ins tall, slim build, pale complexion, clean-shaven. Was wearing a raincoat. No known criminal record.'

The fact that the suspects were not named was not unusual of course – under the contempt law it could prejudice any trial – and the descriptions, apart from the ages of 'The Leader' and 'Pupil No.2' were not so far off, once the real robbers were caught. The response from the underworld was one of disgust, as gang leaders such as Billy Hill, whom *The People*'s Duncan 'Tommy' Webb was close to, Jack 'Spot' Comer and their like recognised that de Antiquis's murder had been totally unnecessary. Harold 'Jeep' Whittall of the *Daily Mirror* reported on Saturday 3 May on the front page that 'Spivs and "Easy Money" Boys Are Questioned' and that 'The three gunmen are believed to be amateurs'. The 'professional' underworld would never have killed an innocent, ordinary man, so said the code, and there was real truth to that.

Chief Inspector Fabian and his colleagues made extensive enquiries and followed up several dead-end leads, but then learnt from a taxi driver that he had seen two of the three masked men run into a building called Brook House, on nearby Tottenham Street. An extensive search of the building was made, and a scarf, made into a rudimentary face mask, and a raincoat were found there. This would provide the vital lead, and in fact it was the raincoat that was traced to Charles Henry Jenkins, aged 23, known as 'Harry Boy', who already had a criminal record. Through detective work, the second and third robbers were found to be known associates of Jenkins – Christopher James Geraghty, aged 21, and Terence Peter Rolt, aged just 17.

'Harry Boy' Jenkins was found and arrested, put on an identity parade, but witnesses to the Charlotte Street murder didn't pick him out. When interviewed, both Geraghty and Rolt said that Jenkins had shot Alec de Antiquis, and they hadn't been armed with guns. The revolver used to pistol-whip the manager of Jay's and to murder de Antiquis was luckily found by a schoolboy on Wednesday 14 May, on the marshy embankment of the Thames, where it had been dumped, leading the *Daily Mirror* to splash on the front page next day, 'Children Find The Antiquis Death Gun'. It would soon be obvious to the police that 'Harry Boy' Jenkins had indeed been the shooter, Hoskins's 'The Leader', and Geraghty and Rolt 'Pupil 1' and 'Pupil 2'.

≣

Percy Hoskins actually got a named byline several times on the Alec de Antiquis case, a sure sign that he was releasing exclusive information. Only the top members of the Murder Gang, the ones which the crime journalist and writer Duncan Campbell has called 'the Sultans of the Newsroom' – the likes of Percy Hoskins, Norman Rae, Harry Procter, and Sam Jackett on occasion – could command named bylines, and only then when they had something special. Hoskins's police tip-offs were getting him regular small scoops, and sometimes really big ones.

But it was the *Daily Mail* which got the real splash on the de Antiquis case – not on the police investigation and court case, which was Hoskins's forte, but by working with Gladys, Alec's widow, to get the inside story. These emotive inside stories of the impact of murder on the loved ones of the victim were another stock-in-trade of the Murder Gang. Legendary newsman Lindon Laing, news editor of the *Daily Mail*, orchestrated the Gladys de Antiquis story, and she was interviewed gently at length by the *Daily Mail*'s John Hall, with her brother Mr Collins there to support her. She told of her bereavement, the sadness of her six children and the difficulty of explaining what had happened to the younger ones.

Lindon Laing was famously taciturn, and had the habit of calling everybody 'Mister', no matter how well he knew them; 'Yes, Mister' or 'No, Mister' was his usual refrain. He also had a deadpan, very dry wit and sometimes made ingeniously funny remarks. He worked with the likes of the Murder Gang's veteran Arthur Tietjen and the tenacious rising star Harry Procter, and when the *Daily Express* purchased a helicopter to get to stories faster, Laing quipped, 'The *Express* may have a helicopter, but we've got a Harry Procter.'

Laing was probably the best news editor in Fleet Street, and knew everybody of importance in the British newspaper world. He was strongly against the death penalty – ironic since he oversaw so many Murder Gang *Daily Mail* stories that ended on the scaffold – and he also campaigned for the release of the very large number of German prisoners held in detention centres during the Second World War. In his 1958 memoirs, Harry Procter wrote about how demanding Laing was, how he learnt a lot from him and how very much he respected him.

Laing was born on 1 June 1907, in Durham, the son of a coal miner. He joined the Brighton branch of the National Union of Journalists (NUJ) in September 1928, when he took a reporting job on the *Brighton Herald*, where he was assigned to the infamous Brighton Trunk Murders. In 1935, he entered Fleet Street from a distance, when he became the *Daily Mail's* Brighton correspondent. Laing transferred to the Central London NUJ branch in July 1936, when he became news editor of the *Daily Express*, the direct boss of Percy Hoskins. He remained in that role until 1941, when he became a reporter on the *Daily Mail*, often covering crime again, and the following year became that paper's news editor.

As well as working with the widow of Alec de Antiquis on her story, Laing helped arrange, with his editor Frank Owen, the 'Daily Mail De Antiquis Fund', which Chief Inspector Fabian noted in a police memo of 27 November 1947 had raised £5,926 by that date for the de Antiquis family, and a bungalow had been bought for his widow Gladys and their children. The Home Secretary Charles Chuter-Ede, in Clement Attlee's radical labour government, awarded a police grant to the de Antiquis family too, in recognition for Alec's and the family's sacrifice.

On 17 May 1947, the journalist and writer Hilde Marchant, a brilliant and trailblazing female journalist who had covered many important stories at home and abroad, largely as a freelance after working for the *Daily Express*, and published several books during the Second World War about the conflict's impact at home, published a long feature article in the famous and popular London weekly photo-reportage magazine *Picture Post*. Heralded on the cover under the unrelated photograph of a wistful young woman lying in some undergrowth, the article's title was 'Fleet Street's Murder Gang'.

In a very atmospheric and entertaining piece of incisive reportage, Marchant captured the essence of what it was like to be a Murder Gang journalist, and the focus was the de Antiquis case, complete with the photograph of de Antiquis on the pavement already run in several papers. Along with that incredible picture were the fantastic photographs of the legendary photographer and chronicler of British life Bert Hardy, and this journalistic subculture of Fleet Street crime hacks was brought to the attention of the British public as an entity for the first time in outstanding words and pictures, although the term 'Murder Gang' had been used around Fleet Street for a few years by then. But it's no exaggeration to say that Marchant's article vastly increased the Murder Gang's public profile and put characters, and with Hardy's photographs, some faces, behind the macabre stories that readers devoured daily.

Marchant made some juicy revelations about Murder Gang members, but she did not name the individuals themselves when the inference to their behaviour was less than legitimate, or it would divulge too much detail of Murder Gang trade secrets. For instance, she wrote tantalisingly for *Picture Post* readers in 1947 that 'There have been several cases where crime reporters have got information ahead of the police and on at least two occasions have been responsible for the conviction of a murderer.'

There were also mentions of how individual Murder Gang members got their information. 'There is one crime reporter who is successful because he looks so naïve and slightly slow, which makes people want to confide all their troubles to him: such a nice understanding gentleman.' Then there was one which undoubtedly referred to the Dorset-born and accented Murder Gang veteran Percy Hoskins. 'There is another who, in spite of twenty-five years in London as a crime reporter, has retained the accent of a West Country farmer, and although he is possibly one of the shrewdest of them all, he appears as a genial and gentle soul. One murderer went so far as to confide to him the place where the body was hidden.' The latter was a reference to the murderer Norman Thorne who had inadvertently alerted Hoskins to having buried his girlfriend Elsie Cameron under his chicken run way back in 1925, Hoskins's first big murder case.

Lindon Laing is mentioned, unnamed in the text, but captioned in a photo by Bert Hardy where he's conferring, in a double-breasted suit and cigarette dangling from mouth, with Arthur Tietjen. Marchant wrote how the news editor of the *Daily Mail* (Laing), 'himself a former crime reporter', handled the coverage of the de Antiquis case by asking his Murder Gang hacks three questions: was the shooting done by the same gang and the same type of bullet used as in a previous shooting in Eastcastle Street, off of London's Oxford Street (five years later in 1952 the scene of an audacious and highly successful robbery orchestrated by London godfather Billy Hill)? Did the police think it was a professional gang and had they got a fingerprint match? And did the police have any strong evidential lead as to the gang's identity, or were they relying on an informant? It illustrated just how much Murder Gang work and crime reporting supervision was detective work in itself.

Five days after the Murder Gang was immortalised in the *Picture Post*, the Murder Gang's coverage of the de Antiquis murder was being discussed in a higher sphere – in Parliament. On 22 May 1947, just over three weeks after the murder, a question was asked of the Home Secretary James Chuter-Ede in the House of Commons. The *Hansard* records of debates that day show the following exchange. Sidney Marshall was the Conservative Member of Parliament for Sutton and Cheam from 1945 to 1954:

The Speaker of the House: 'Mr S. Marshall asked the Secretary of State for the Home Department to what extent the details and pictures in the de Antiquis murder case appearing in the newspapers were supplied by the police and whether these methods of publicity in crime detection had his approval.'

Mr Chuter-Ede, Home Secretary: 'New Scotland Yard kept in close touch with representatives of the Press at all stages of the investigation in order to secure the co-operation of the public in their investigations, but only one photograph – that of a woman who was believed to have associated with a man whom the Police were anxious to trace

– was issued to the Press. I do not think that there is any ground for criticising the action taken by the Police.'

The photo of the woman supplied by the police to Fleet Street was of a young woman called Doris Hart, and the *Daily Express* had run it on the front page just six days earlier, under the understated headline 'Yard Want to Meet a Girl'. Hart's photo was captioned above 'The police issue this picture…' and underneath 'Nearly everybody in Britain will watch for her today'. Percy Hoskins had sole byline on that piece, showing that he had been trusted with helping the police and with the photo. Hart would be found and released without charge a few days after her picture ran.

The Metropolitan Police files on the de Antiquis case show that the police had been warned about these Parliamentary concerns regarding police–press co-operation and sharing of information – of course one of the Murder Gang's key sources of information. A hurriedly written internal report shows that the issue had been addressed at length at Scotland Yard:

> During the first week or so after de Antiquis was shot the police had very little upon which to work, and at the request of 'C' Department we appealed to the Press – and not unsuccessfully – to publish stories on certain lines in the hope that their publication might bring us some clue…The case aroused considerable public concern, and from the very beginning it was deemed necessary to have the wholehearted co-operation of the Press and of the public. To secure that co-operation the Press were taken into the confidence of the Police.

This was slightly disingenuous, as the police had been sharing information with journalists for years, and sometimes almost dictated Murder Gang material, the journalists having to take the police line in order to maintain that open channel. Conversely, crime journalists then as now wanted criminals, especially murderers caught, and it was only when the hunger for a scoop was greater than the steady police hand that fed them information intravenously that crime journalists broke the rules, and this was increasingly becoming common in the late 1940s and early 1950s.

The sometimes very close to illegal, then clandestine actions of Harry Procter and Norman 'Jock' Rae, in the pursuit of the murderers Neville Heath, John George Haigh and John Christie between 1946 and 1953, outlined at length in my previous book, *Frenzy! Hwath, Haigh and Christie: How the Tabloid Press Turned Three Evil Serial Killers into Celebrities*, are prime examples of this. The phone-hacking scandal that closed Norman Rae's paper *News of the World* in 2011 showed us that these duplicitous methods used by journalists to get an exclusive by any means certainly did not die with the Murder Gang, even if some members of that group of crime hacks helped set that immoral template decades ahead of that early twenty-first-century newspaper controversy.

But the Murder Gang did sometimes push too far when given inside police information, and that May 1947 internal police report shows this in relation to the de Antiquis case. 'With the exception of one newspaper, these confidences were respected throughout in a public spirited manner.' That rogue newspaper was not named, and no recorded official action was taken against it, so there is no way of knowing which one. But that paper would undoubtedly have had an informal reprimand, and may have had police co-operation taken away for a time.

The de Antiquis case was a watershed for open police–press co-operation, however. The report concludes by stating, 'Probably never before have the Metropolitan Police had such co-operation from the Press in a particular case. But for that co-operation then later developments would have been delayed, and the Commissioner is grateful to the Press…'

There is also a police statement dated 21 May 1947, written by Mr H.L. Jackson on behalf of Percy Hoskins's friend, the Metropolitan Police Commissioner Harold Scott, which is almost exactly the same, almost verbatim, of the statement read out in the House of Commons by the Home Secretary the next day, which Chuter-Ede had obviously been supplied.

Chief Inspector Fabian and his colleagues had meanwhile also learnt that Jenkins and Geraghty, along with two other accomplices named

Walsh and Gillam had in fact raided another jewellery shop at 91 Queensway in west London, close to Notting Hill, just four days before the attack on Jay's and the murder of Alec de Antiquis in Charlotte Street. That robbery, on 25 April 1947, had netted them the very large sum of £4,500 – a good haul for young amateurs. This had obviously emboldened them – at least Jenkins and Geraghty and their younger accomplice Rolt, to 'take down' Jay's in the West End, expecting easy pickings, and not to be confronted by a have-a-go hero.

The Metropolitan Police file on the case contains a witness statement to the Queensway robbery – a jewellery buyer who had been on his way to the nearby famous Whiteley's Department Store, which itself had been the scene of murder back in 1907, when its founder, 75-year-old William Whiteley, was shot dead there by a young man who claimed to be his illegitimate son.

That jewellery buyer on 25 April 1947 saw three men (identified by police as Jenkins, Walsh and Gillam), one with a knotted yellow handkerchief around his neck (probably Jenkins), looking into a jeweller's shop in Queensway, and the buyer had almost sardonically told the police that the three men were 'not the sort to be interested in jewellery'. That raid would come back to haunt 'Harry Boy' Jenkins though. Walsh and Gillam were arrested, and Walsh would give evidence for the prosecution against Jenkins, Geraghty and Rolt for that offence at the trial for the murder of Alec de Antiquis in July 1947.

The evidence against Jenkins, Geraghty and Rolt for the murder of Alec de Antiquis was overwhelming, and all three were found guilty of murder. Charles 'Harry Boy' Jenkins and Christopher Geraghty were sentenced to death, and Terence Rolt was ordered to be 'detained at His Majesty's pleasure', as he was under the age of eighteen. Jenkins and Geraghty were executed together in a rare double hanging by Albert Pierrepoint at Pentonville Prison on Friday 19 September 1947, Geraghty blaming 'Harry Boy' for his plight to the end. Rolt was released on license nine years later, in 1956.

The last Murder Gang word on the case came from Harold 'Jeep' Whittall on the front page of the *Daily Mirror* on Tuesday 7 October. 'Black cat across his path kept gangster from Soho murder' was the lower-case headline, a conversational style often favoured in that paper. The 'gangster' was 23-year-old Michael Joseph Gillam, who had been arrested for taking part in the raid with 'Harry Boy' Jenkins and William 'Bill' Walsh on the jeweller's in Queensway just before the attack on Jay's that led to the fatal shooting of Alec de Antiquis.

Gillam had been the getaway driver in the Queensway robbery, after he had been released from borstal two days previously. It turned out that Gillam, Jenkins and Geraghty had planned a series of jewellery raids whilst in borstal together. Gillam had been assigned as getaway driver for the tragic raid on Jay's too, but had seen a black cat run across his path and backed out. Gillam had told this story in court before he received four years in prison for the Queensway job, the day before the *Daily Mirror* article ran.

In the police file, there is a letter written by William 'Bill' Walsh to Chief Inspector Fabian, dated 13 October 1947 – Walsh had received five years for receiving stolen goods several months after giving evidence against Jenkins, Rolt and Geraghty. In the letter, Walsh claimed that he had received two threats against him in prison, one saying that he would 'have your face cut up so your own mother won't recognise you'. Walsh pleaded with Fabian in the letter, 'The squeak has gone all round the joint that I shoped *(sic)* Harry Boy, and got him toped *(sic)*. I think his brother is still here yet, and what he and his mates are going to do… I've got no chance…' There's no record of whether Fabian recommended Walsh's transfer or not.

The veteran Lindon Laing, veteran journalist and news editor of the *Daily Mail* left the scene prematurely in 1948, the year after working so hard on securing the inside story of Gladys de Antiquis. On the night of 26 August 1948, Laing was found dead with head injuries in a London Victoria to London train. An inquest verdict of death by misadventure was recorded, and as Laing's own paper the *Daily Mail* reported after the inquest, 'A railway ganger gave evidence that he found a fresh graze on a girder of Long Edge Bridge, Clapham Junction.' The coroner said that Laing 'must have put his head out of the window on feeling ill'. The workaholic Laing had been on his way home to Hassocks, West Sussex, leant out of the window of his train compartment to get some air, and his head struck the girder somehow. His body was found at his home station of Ditchling. He was aged just 41, but had looked much older. Laing left a widow and one child.

Laing's memorial service at St Dunstan-in-the-West church in Fleet Street illustrated his high-standing in newspapers. It was attended by many of the biggest names in Fleet Street, including G. Ward-Price, the Director of Associated Newspapers, who represented the firm's Chairman Viscount Rothermere; Arthur Christiansen, veteran editor of the *Daily Express*; Percy Cudlipp, editor of the *Daily Herald*; Charles Ede, editor of the *Sunday Dispatch*; R. Prew, former editor of the *Daily Mail*; E.M. Dougall, deputy editor of the *Daily Mail*; Cyril Morton representing the *Daily Mirror* and *Sunday Pictorial*; G. Morton-Smith representing the *News Chronicle*; and Morley Richards, news editor of the *Daily Express*.

The priest, Rev. R.M. La Porte Payne, who was also the Chaplain to the Tower of London, read a tribute written by a friend of Lindon Laing at the service. 'Circumstances made a fighter of him. He had resolution. He had a quickness of brain that flashed like lightning ahead of the rumble of others' slower thoughts. In brief, he had genius.'

Laing's wasn't the only premature Murder Gang-connected death that year. In 1947, Len Hunter of the *Daily Express* had been promoted to assistant night news editor after his work on the de Antiquis case. But he didn't have long to enjoy his promotion as he died of a heart attack, only just having celebrated his 40th birthday, in November 1948. Percy Hoskins had lost a valued colleague.

The de Antiquis case cropped up just one more time, almost six years after the murder, but not in Murder Gang coverage. The *Daily Mirror* of Tuesday 27 January 1953 had a column 'Star Turn' by Donald Zec. Zec had previously been a crime reporter on the *Daily Mirror*, which he joined in 1938, and his biggest crime scoop was an incredible interview with the 'Acid Bath' serial killer John George Haigh at the hotel where he lived and met and cultivated his final unfortunate victim, the elderly Mrs Olive Durand-Deacon, in 1949, just before Haigh's arrest.

Since then, Zec had written more and more about film and conducted interviews with film stars. His column that day in January 1953 was headlined 'Don't Let Us Have This Film Here', and referred to plans to make a television film in America based on the de Antiquis murder, called *Murder In Soho*, starring Eric Corrie, which would also be released in British cinemas. Incredibly, apparently Corrie, who was slated to play 'Harry Boy' Jenkins, had known the real Jenkins well 'when he was a youth'. Zec wrote that, 'No-one in Britain wants to be reminded of that black day in London – Certainly not the Antiquis family, or Jays the jeweller's, nor the people of Charlotte Street. I advise the producers to mark this film "EXPORT ONLY". Not here please!'

The script followed every moment of the raid on Jay's and the shooting dead of the real-life hero Alec de Antiquis, and then every twist and turn of the murder investigation. The senior investigating officer in the de Antiquis case, who had brought it to a successful conclusion, the now famous Robert Fabian, now a Superintendent, whose 1950 bestselling memoir *Fabian of the Yard* was adapted into a BBC crime drama series, with him co-writing it and appearing in the epilogue of each fictionalised episode, with Fabian supplying his commentary on the real-life case upon which that episode was based. The thirty-six-episode series ran from 1954 to 1956, starting just as Metropolitan Police Commissioner Sir Harold Scott retired, Fabian being part of the police public relations drive that Scott had started helped by Percy Hoskins, who was a friend of Fabian too. The series was also broadcast in the United States as *Fabian of Scotland Yard*.

In November 1952, Fabian had published a long feature article in a magazine based on the Alec de Antiquis murder titled *Death in Soho*. The television film which Donald Zec referred to in January 1953, '*Murder in Soho*', was eventually transmitted as the eighth episode of *Fabian of the Yard*, on 15 January 1955. Eric Corrie was indeed one of the stars, but his character's name had been changed from 'Jenkins' to 'Turner'. There's no record of how much Robert Fabian was paid for his television work, but it shows that it wasn't just the Murder Gang and their newspapers that were making money out of crime.

6

DEATH OF A CAR SALESMAN

A sea of hats, macs, brylcreemed hair and razor-sharp suits, handkerchiefs proudly displayed in breast pockets, while some of the gleaming motorcars half-mount the kerb, others parked entirely on the pavement, with used car showrooms behind. It's a street of cars for sale and their salesmen, making quick deals, the pavement a showroom for these dealers, some of the cars stolen, some 'clocked' and displaying extra-low mileage. It really could be the living definition of the term 'wheeler-dealers', although that phrase came from the American gaming houses of the late eighteenth and nineteenth centuries, referring to the men who operated the roulette wheels.

Now an informal description of somebody with numerous business activities going on, the men of Warren Street literally deal in wheels – 'Looking for a new motor?', 'It's a great set of wheels,', 'I'll do a good deal for you, 'cos I like your honest face', 'I can do a quick deal for cash', 'You seem a nice fellow, let me see what I can do for you'. This street at the northern end of Tottenham Court Road in the West End has been full of second-hand car salesmen for decades, and in the 1950s, the future Formula One supremo Bernie Ecclestone will make his first fortune here. But by the end of the 1950s, just ten years from now, the dealers will have moved on, the street no longer spiv heaven.

But in late 1949, it's a nest of legitimate or near-legitimate businessmen, and of vipers, ranging from 'a little' to 'very' dodgy. Stanley Setty – real name Sulman Seti – certainly fits into the latter category. As well as being a 'motor trader', Setty, born in Baghdad to Iraqi-Jewish parents, who migrated to London's East End when he was four years old, is now also heavily involved in London's black market, a seriously connected and tough man, burly at thirteen stone (82.7 kg).

Dark suited and hatted, gregariously tied, with his trilby's brim slightly pulled down at the front, covering a receding hairline, his remaining hair slicked back and meticulously barbered, gravel-voiced and straight-talking Setty looks successful and is formidable. In fact, he's had setbacks in recent years, serving prison time for debt and bankruptcy charges, the police now watching his every business move.

Setty is re-establishing himself, and Warren Street's 'easy-come easy-go' commercial atmosphere, where usually untraceable cash is king, suits him very well indeed. Setty can also often be seen doing deals at the Fitzroy Café, on the corner of Fitzroy Street and Warren Street. Setty has been a major player, and is suspected by the authorities of 'supplying' airplanes to Jewish groups in Palestine just before the Arab-Israeli War of 1948.

It's another day and he's just made a good deal, selling a Wolseley 12 Saloon motorcar for £1,005. It's typical of Setty to have haggled for the extra fiver; he's a hard negotiator. The purchaser gave him a cheque for cash, which Setty will soon cash and leave the bank with the full amount in five pound notes, getting back into the Citroen car he's currently driving, and going north, to the Finchley Road, Golders Green, in north-west London. He's going to meet an associate to talk business, and as the other man is just as unscrupulous as Setty, it's hardly legal and above-board.

Stanley Setty had gone to visit Brian Donald Hume, aged 29, at his flat in the Finchley Road. Like Setty, Hume was a shady character involved in many illegal activities. He was born out of wedlock on 20 December 1919 in Swanage, Dorset in the West Country, not far from where the *Daily Express*'s Percy Hoskins was born. After having spent a lonely time in an orphanage and living with his grandmother – a common experience for illegitimate children, who were seen as socially embarrassing at that time – Hume was finally brought up by his mother, a teacher, as she had now married his father. But, confusingly for the young Hume, his mother posed as his aunt. He went to Heriard School, in a village near Basingstoke, Hampshire, where his mother taught, and then to Queen Mary's School in Basingstoke itself. But he left school in 1933, aged 14, as his 'conduct and progress' were thought 'unsatisfactory'.

Hume was then taken on as an apprentice electrician by F.G. Fox Estates Ltd in Paddington, west London, and after finishing his training he continued working for the owner Mr Fox, who became a kind of mentor to Hume, and also paid for the young man's food and lodgings. However, on 11 November 1937, Fox fired Hume, as Hume hadn't been attending night school to gain his formal electrician qualifications as had been the agreed arrangement. Just five days later, Hume became a polisher with the British Metal Engraving Co. Ltd, remaining there until the outbreak of the Second World War in 1939; Hume enlisted in the RAF on 7 September.

Hume trained as a pilot and then an air-gunner, but failed all of his exams, and didn't qualify as either. This would always rankle with Hume, who would later tell tales about his exploits as a pilot in the war, all of them untrue. Officially discharged from the RAF on 7 September 1941 after two years, Hume was described in his discharge papers as 'physically unfit for Air Force service, although fit for employment in civil life'. Hume suffered from cerebro-spinal meningitis. A specialist who assessed him at the Clifton Hospital in York said of him, 'having suffered from meningitis he has developed a degree of organically determined psychopathy'. Basically, Hume had psychopathic tendencies, brought on or worsened by the meningitis, in the opinion of the doctor. His RAF report did evaluate Hume's character as 'very good', but those with psychopathic tendencies can be very efficient at masking their mental deviancies, of course.

Until 6 October 1941, Hume worked as a roof-spotter in Acton, west London. His job was to spot and raise the alert for approaching German bombers, but he was fired from that post for missing three consecutive night shifts, and for having 'a quarrelsome nature'. Hume also stole some knives and forks while working on those premises. He next worked as an aero-fitter, but left there on 22 January 1942, presenting a medical certificate to his boss claiming that he was unfit to work.

On 3 April 1942, Hume was arrested for posing as an RAF pilot, using a false identity card to gain access to prohibited places (military) and getting loans from people under false pretences. Similar offences were also committed by the double-murderer Neville Heath, whom Harry Procter of the Murder Gang befriended when he was on the *Daily Mail* and who was executed in 1946. Hume stood trial at the Central Criminal Court of the Old Bailey on 24 June 1942, but as it was his first adult offence he was given a fine and probation. Hume was now 22 years old.

Hume went on to start his own business, Hume Electrical Ltd, operating from 620 Finchley Road where he also lived, and this company was registered in August 1943. But it was liquidated by court order in 1947, with liabilities of £4,647 and assets of £1,413. Hume soon formed another company, Little Atom Electrical Products Ltd, registered in Hay-On-Wye, near Hereford, in September 1947. But this was just a front for his illegal activities: supplying gin to West End bars, which were suffering an alcohol shortage in the immediate post-war period. But the main ingredient of his product was surgical spirits with just a little real gin added.

Donald Hume was now working for Stanley Setty, running errands for him in his illegal deals, and mainly smuggling goods for him. They first met in the Hollywood Club, located close to Marble Arch, and Hume had soon bought a small van from Setty, and they began to talk business. Although he'd never qualified as a pilot in the RAF, Hume could fly light aircraft, and he was soon transporting illegal goods to and back from the Continent for Setty, being paid a cut for his services. This was obviously a good set-up for Setty too, and Hume was so well known for these activities by 1949 that he was known around London black market circles as 'the Flying Smuggler', a soubriquet that the narcissistic and insecure Hume would boast about later.

Hume was now married to Cynthia Mary, and they had a 3½-month-old daughter, and they all lived at Flat 620B Finchley Road, Golders Green. Hume's boss Stanley Setty was a frequent visitor to set up new assignments for Hume. When Setty arrived there in his Citroen that early evening of 4 October 1949, with the vast majority of that £1,005 in fivers in his pocket, there was nobody in, but Setty let himself in with the spare key outside as he often did. After he walked through into that flat on a busy road in suburban north-west London, nobody outside would ever see Stanley Setty alive again.

Stanley Setty lived at 53 Maitland Court in Bayswater, west London, with his sister and brother-in-law. It was the latter, Mr Ali Armin Ouri, who reported Setty missing the following day, 5 October 1949, at 12.50 p.m., when Setty had not returned home, as he always did. There was no suspicion of murder yet of course, and the Metropolitan Police file shows that a potential sighting was made of Setty on Monday 10 October, five days later.

Harry Lauder was an attendant at the Prince Henry Room, where lectures were held, at 17 Fleet Street – also, of course, the street where many members of the Murder Gang operated from in their newspaper offices. At 5.30 p.m., Lauder thought he saw a man fitting Setty's description in the Black & White Milk Bar facing Fetter Lane. In fact, Setty had been dead for almost six days by then. Setty's sister, Mrs Ouri, now offered a £1,000 reward for anybody who could find her brother dead or alive, a very sizeable sum – and ironically almost exactly the same amount as Setty had cashed at the bank on 4 October.

It was soon learnt from his associates that Setty had had that large amount of money in £5 notes on him on the day he was last seen, and on 8 October the police issued serial numbers of these notes, which were luckily recorded by the bank. There was little movement on Setty's whereabouts until 21 October, when a farm assistant called Stanley Tiffin was knee-deep in the Essex marshes north of London trying to find some ducks to cook for dinner. Instead he found a large parcel, and when he opened it, to his horror, it contained a man's torso – the legs and head had been removed.

Dr Francis Camps, one of the top Home Office pathologists examined the torso and ascertained that the torso had been dropped from a great height, since there was impact damage. This of course meant an airplane – there are no mountains in that area – and the police were soon questioning ground staff at all airfields in the area. Due to early reporting by the Murder Gang, as directed by the police, it was soon discovered through a tip-off that a member of the United Services Flying Club in Elstree named Donald Hume had hired a small blue Austin light aircraft on 5 October and that he'd been seen loading a large package into it. The plane was located, and there was some damage to one of the windows. Had Hume caused the damage when he threw the package with Setty's torso out of the plane?

It was also learnt that Hume had taken a taxi home from Southend Airport after his flight that day, and had paid the fare for the long journey back to north-west London from a wad of £5 notes – a seeming link to the fivers that Setty had been carrying the day before. This was confirmed when a £5 note given to the taxi driver was found to have one of Setty's serial numbers. The police also soon discovered that Hume was a known associate of Setty, of course, and began focusing all their efforts on Hume.

On Saturday 29 October, Harold 'Jeep' Whittall and his colleagues on the *Daily Mirror* ran a front-page headline of 'Setty: A Man is Charged With Murder'. Hume had been arrested on Thursday 27 October at 7.30 a.m., at home in the Finchley Road flat he shared with his wife and baby. Police officers had been posted front and back in case the slippery Hume attempted to get away. Superintendent Colin MacDougall of Scotland Yard arrested Hume, and he was questioned at length by MacDougall and Chief Inspector Jamieson at Albany Street Police Station. Hume told them the incredible story that he would stick to at his trial.

Two days later, Percy Hoskins at the *Daily Express* had '8 Hour Shift at Hume's Flat', with a picture of Hume with swept-back hair and wearing a cravat, also on the front page. The police were searching the flat from top to bottom and, while some cleaning up had obviously been done, bloodstains were found under the floorboards. It was obvious that Setty had been murdered at Flat 620B Finchley Road. The police file also reveals that at the time of Setty's murder, Hume had just £1.19 in the bank. He banked at the Golders Green branch of the Midland Bank.

At the inquest in Chelmsford, Dr Camps gave evidence that Setty had died from stab wounds to the chest, and the *Daily Mirror* had 'Setty Was Killed by 5 Stab Wounds' on page 3 on Tuesday 1 November. It was also revealed that identification had been made from fingerprints – the hands hadn't been removed – and ingeniously by a laundry mark '498', found on the collar of the shirt that Setty's torso was still wearing, which matched the label put there by the laundry service he had used.

The police file shows just what detectives thought of Hume. 'There is no doubt that Hume is very imaginative and likes to create an impression on people. His flat is decorated with several alleged RAF war trophies and photos and caricatures of him as a flying officer and racing motorist, and he has even deceived his own wife in the belief that he was a pilot with an adventurous career during the last war.'

The environment in which Donald Hume and Stanley Setty operated, professional smuggling and the black market, was becoming the forte of *The People*'s Duncan 'Tommy' Webb, a crime reporter with very close underworld contacts, who in 1950 would make his name when he exposed the Messina brothers, the Maltese gangster-pimps who ran a vile prostitution racket around Soho. Webb's editor at *The People* was Sam Campbell, and as the journalist Robert Edwards wrote in *Goodbye Fleet Street*, 'Police contacts, bribed lavishly by Sam's standards, told Webb about the Messina brothers.'

Webb would go on to ghost the memoirs of 'King of the Underworld' Billy Hill, a native of nearby Seven Dials, just off of Shaftesbury Avenue. But while Webb, who would die young after catching an infection on a trip abroad, knew this professional criminal subculture better than any other member of the Murder Gang, he was otherwise engaged with the Messina investigation at this time, leaving other crime hacks to lead on the murder of Stanley Setty.

On Wednesday 16 November 1949 an article in the *Daily Mail* headlined 'Hume: 2 Trips in Hired Plane – Setty dismembered in flat, say Crown' was bylined 'by Arthur Tietjen and Harry Procter', two members of the Murder Gang who had worked closely under the late news editor Lindon Laing. Both Tietjen and Procter were prominent members of the Murder Gang, and in the 1950s Procter would rise to the very elite, especially after he moved to the *Sunday Pictorial*.

Joint bylines were rare then in national crime reporting, and it showed that Tietjen and Procter were following the preliminary court hearings very closely, and reporting it very descriptively. Donald Hume and his victim Stanley Setty were now becoming big news, giving readers an insight into the seedy and sometimes murderous nature of London's black market and smuggling worlds. Hume was described entering the dock at Bow Street Magistrates Court 'carrying a shorthand notebook an inch thick and had two newly sharpened pencils in his coat pocket'.

That same day, Percy Hoskins at the *Daily Express* ran, without a byline this time, 'Setty Witness with Parcel – "Valuable Property" too heavy to carry downstairs'. It seemed that, on the morning after Setty's murder, Hume had called a painter and decorator around to his flat and had asked the man to help him carry the package, containing Setty's torso, downstairs to his car. That man was now one of twenty-three witnesses called to give evidence against Hume.

There were rumours that Setty's Citroen had been found in St Pancras near Kings Cross station, but in actual fact the resourceful Hume had driven the car to Setty's lock-up garage in Cambridge Mews, in Wanstead, east London. The fact that Hume knew Setty well through working for him helped Hume in this respect. Hume's fingerprints were found in Setty's Citroen too, but that didn't prove that he had murdered Setty of course, just been in or moved his car. However, the hiring of the plane, having some of Setty's £5 notes, moving the heavy parcel downstairs with a witness and the bloodstains on the floorboards at his flat would be far more difficult evidence to navigate for Hume.

Harold 'Jeep' Whittall at the *Daily Mirror* had 'Setty Reward is Paid' on Saturday 24 December 1949. Setty's sister Mrs Ali Ouri had paid the £1,000 reward to Sidney Tiffin, who was described as 'a duck-hunter', who had of course found the wrapped torso on Essex Marshes. The trial of Donald Hume for the murder of Stanley Setty was now set for January 1950, and on 1 January, the *Sunday Pictorial*, most probably Fred Redman or Victor Sims, veterans of that paper, had 'Dr Teare to Speak for Hume'. This was referring to Donald Teare, who was described as 'the brilliant young pathologist'.

The legendary pathologist Sir Bernard Spilsbury, veteran of many murder cases since Dr Crippen, had committed suicide in his laboratory in December 1947, having suffered from ill health and depression after his son Peter was killed in London's Blitz in 1940, and another son, Alan, died of tuberculosis in 1945. In the next three decades, four men would be the leading Home Office pathologists in Britain – Donald Teare, Sydney Smith, Keith Simpson and Francis Camps, the latter the pathologist who had examined Setty's torso, and would now give evidence for the prosecution at Hume's trial, particularly over the high probability that the torso had been dropped from Hume's hired plane. The trial of Donald Hume began at the Central Criminal Court of the Old Bailey on Wednesday 18 January 1950. He was defended by Mr R.F. Levy KC (King's Counsel), and prosecuted by Mr Christmas Humphreys KC, who would be involved in some of the most controversial murder trials in British criminal history in the 1950s.

On the day after the trial opened, Harold 'Jeep' Whittall had a front-page story, continued on page 5, about the Hume trial with a spooky angle that the *Daily Mirror* often specialised in – 'The Flat Where the No.13 Bus Stops'. There was a photo of the outside of 620B Finchley Road, the flat where Hume lived with his wife and baby, and where Setty was thought to have been murdered. There was a bus stop right outside the flat, and the No.13 bus stopped there, the obvious inference being that it had been very unlucky for Stanley Setty.

The first day of the trial was also extensively reported in the piece, and Hume's version of what had happened in his flat was finally revealed to the public – the same story that Hume had told to the police after his arrest when interviewed. Hume claimed that he hadn't murdered Setty, but had been paid £150 by three smugglers to dispose of Setty's body by throwing it from a plane, and that was why the package with the torso had been in his flat. The three men, rough customers in Hume's version, were called 'Mac or Max', 'Green or Greeny', and 'The Boy'. Christmas Humphreys for the prosecution made the Crown's view clear – that this story was 'pure invention'. The names did sound made up – the film *Brighton Rock* was released that year, based on the Graham Greene novel of the same name about a teenage razor gang in a seaside town, both of which had the protagonist Pinkie, played menacingly by Richard Attenborough, also known in the book as 'the Boy'.

Mr Justice Lewis, who was presiding over Hume's trial, had suddenly become ill, so on 19 January Hume had to sit through the same twenty witnesses giving evidence against him again, with Mr Justice Sellers now in charge of proceedings. A statement given by Hume to the police was read by the defence, leading Percy Hoskins to run with 'The Boy Warned: Remember Your Wife and Baby' on page 5 of the *Daily Express*. According to Hume, 'the Boy' had threatened him by alluding to the safety of Hume's wife Cynthia and their baby daughter, by telephone. Police protection had been given to mother and baby, the police had confirmed, almost definitely personally to Hoskins.

When he took the stand, Hume was verbose, telling his story, and emphasising how frightened he had been of the three men who had paid him to dump Setty's dismembered body from a plane. On Tuesday 24 January, the *Daily Express* reported 'Hume – I Was Scared Stiff of the Gang Who Paid Me – Mac, Green and the Boy called at flat – They could have been killers'. The same day, Harold 'Jeep' Whittall on the *Daily Mirror* had a direct quote headline from Hume inside the paper, 'I Am Semi-Honest – But I Am Not A Killer, Says Hume'. Hume had also regaled the court the previous day with 'They called me the Flying Smuggler.'

Two days later on Thursday 26 January, Hoskins at the *Daily Express* somewhat disingenuously had on the front page 'Women Queue for Hume Verdict'. In fact, as the article went to inform readers, there were only four women in that queue, very different from some other murder trials of the period, such as Neville Heath in 1946 and John George Haigh in 1949, when women flocked to get a glimpse of these

The Murder Gang listening to Scotland Yard's Chief Information Officer Mr P.H. Fearnly. (Getty Images)

Fleet Street reporters Bill Ashenden and Tich Leach wait for news to break in the press room at Scotland Yard in May 1947. (Getty Images)

The busy newsroom of the *News of the World* newspaper on Fleet Street, 18 April 1953. (Getty Images)

Fleet Street crime reporters interview Mr Barnett in his Soho café, situated next to
the scene of an armed raid in 1947. From left to right, Mr Barnett, Len Hunter (*Daily
Express*), Reg Foster (*News Chronicle*) and W.A.E. 'Billy' Jones (*Daily Herald*). (Getty Images)

Crime reporter Norman Rae of the
News of the World phones the news desk
with the latest scoop. (Getty Images)

Crime reporters meet at 'the dive', St Stephen's Tavern, across the road from the Houses of Parliament, in May 1947. (Getty Images)

Dr Buck Ruxton, who was hanged at Strangeways prison, Manchester, for the murder of his wife, Isabella Ruxton, and the family housemaid, Mary Jane Rogerson. (Alamy)

Donald Hume seen here just after being freed from eight years in prison for flinging the dismembered body of car dealer Stanley Setty from an aeroplane into the sea. He later admitted to killing Setty. (Alamy)

Ruth Ellis, a model and nightclub hostess, was the last woman to be hanged in the United Kingdom after being convicted of murdering her lover, David Blakely. (Author's collection)

James Hanratty, also known as the A6 Murderer, was hanged at Bedford Prison after being found guilty of the murder of scientist Michael Gregsten in 1961. (Author's collection)

John Bodkin Adams was a British doctor and suspected serial killer. Between 1946 and 1956, over 160 of his patients died in suspicious circumstances, many of whom had left him money in their wills. (Author's collection)

Serial killer John Christie killed and buried eight people at his home at 10 Rillington Place in London. (Author's collection)

John George Haigh, better known as the Acid Bath Murderer, was found guilty of the murders of six people, whose corpses he dissolved in acid at his workshop. (Author's collection)

Murderer Neville Heath being taken into custody by police. (Author's collection)

extremely dangerous men. Hume's small female fan base was however made slightly more impressive by the fact that one of the four women had waited all night and was carrying a hot water bottle to keep her warm in that cold winter.

On the afternoon of 26 January at 3.03 p.m., the ten men and two women on Hume's jury came back into the court, and a minute later Mr Justice Sellers entered and all rose. The next day, the *Daily Express* had a description of Hume as he waited, written by an 'Express Staff Reporter', so not Percy Hoskins, who also had a large bylined piece on the same front page. The unnamed reporter wrote: 'All eyes turned to Hume. Tight-lipped, but outwardly calm, he hurried to the front of the dock and stood erect, his hands clasped behind him. Three warders stood round him, a prison doctor was behind. Hume looked at every juryman in turn.'

Mr Justice Sellers said to the jury, 'Have you any communication to make?' The foreman of the jury said, 'We are not agreed.' Most of those in court and even some members of the Murder Gang covering the case were shocked, including Percy Hoskins. It was a hung jury, and Hume would have to face a second trial. 'You have deliberated for a long time. Is that your final conclusion? You are not agreed?' said the judge. 'I feel doubtful that we shall reach a unanimous verdict,' said the foreman. Mr Justice Sellers immediately discharged the jury, and they slowly filed out.

According to the *Daily Express* reporter, Hume's defence counsel, Mr Levy KC was called over to the judge, at which point Hume 'shook his head vigorously'. Hume was also conferring with his solicitor and junior defence counsel. At 3.30 p.m., the prosecuting barrister, Mr Christmas Humphreys KC stood up and said in a low voice,

The possibility of a disagreement had naturally occurred to the prosecution, and instruction had been taken from the Director of Public Prosecutions … After full consideration, my view is that it is not necessary in the interests of justice that there should be a retrial on this indictment. Therefore, I respectfully ask that a jury should be sworn and then no evidence should be offered on this indictment.

Mr Justice Sellers concurred, and a new standby jury was swiftly sworn in, and directed by the judge to find Hume Not Guilty of the murder of Stanley Setty. This freed the judge to immediately inform Hume that he now faced the lesser charge of accessory to murder, as he had admitted dumping Setty's body. Hume, knowing how lucky he had been, pleaded Guilty to the new charge. Mr Justice Sellers sentenced Donald Hume to twelve years of imprisonment.

Percy Hoskins, bylined for his front-page splash in the *Daily Express* the day after Hume's conviction for accessory to murder, led with the huge banner headline 'Who DID Kill Setty? – Yard men will reopen case today'. There was a photo-stat copy of a note that Hume had written in court, almost definitely in one of those shorthand notebooks that Arthur Tietjen and Harry Procter had earlier described in the *Daily Mail*, which Hume carried into court hearings. The note read 'Carpet was nailed down, would take time to take up.' This had obviously been handed to one of Hume's defence team, and Hoskins had got hold of it. Hume was making notes to assist his legal team, and the difficulty of the carpet being pulled up in his flat was obviously a reference to the alleged clean-up he had done there.

Hoskins focused on the police view of the case, and the approach they would be taking in finding the real killer. Later, Hoskins would say that he was sure that Hume was guilty of Setty's murder, but for now he just outlined the way forward. Hoskins wrote that the new police enquiries would 'start back at the kerbside car market in Warren Street, off Tottenham Court Road'. One interesting detail was that Hume's wife Cynthia hadn't been in court to hear his verdict, and that she'd waited with the baby and her father at the Finchley Road flat. She had heard about her husband receiving twelve years by phone, and had cried while the baby slept in her cot. The police later somewhat insensitively, if going 'by the book', returned the four blood-stained floorboards and carpet they had taken from the flat before the trial.

Most of the front page that day was given to Hume, and there was also a plan of the inside of Hume's second-floor flat at 620B Finchley Road. A small piece by Arthur Cook looked at Hume's psychology too – 'The Little Man Who Tried To Be Big' – while a now familiar small headshot photo, reprinted in many papers over the previous weeks,

of a smug and debonair Hume, lay in the middle of the page. On that
same day, the writer and journalist Rebecca West, who had attended
Hume's trial every day, did a similar, but longer piece for the *Evening
Standard*, 'Hume – The Man Who Contracted Out of Humanity'. It
was an insightful piece about nefarious motivations, and used skills she
would later employ when profiling Soviet spies in the late 1950s and
early 1960s and their reasons for committing treason.

But it was Percy Hoskins at the *Daily Express* who had the last
'glimpse' of a scoop on Hume in 1950. On Saturday 11 February
he took a section of the front page in a bylined piece, which always
meant that Hoskins had been solely or majorly involved in an
exclusive. The headline was 'Hume Makes A Statement – New Line
on Setty Riddle?' It read: 'Brian Donald Hume, sentenced to twelve
years' imprisonment as an accessory to the Setty murder, has made a
new statement which may eventually give a fresh line on the mystery.
A copy of the statement has been sent to the Home Office and
Scotland Yard … The new statement was made by Hume this week,
shortly before he was transferred from Wormwood Scrubs to a long-
term penal prison.'

It wasn't explosive in content, but the potential was tantalising to
readers. What did Hume have to say? Hoskins knew exactly how to
ramp up excitement, and knew that readers would be waiting. In fact,
there would be no follow-up to this piece, and Hume had either been
playing games, or the police warned Hoskins, ever police-friendly and
for good reason, not to pursue the story. It's obvious that Hoskins had
visited Hume in London's Wormwood Scrubs though, trying to get
more out of him, and the fact that 'the statement has been sent to the
Home Office and Scotland Yard' obviously did Hoskins no damage
in his close relations with the Scotland Yard hierarchy. But both the
Murder Gang and the public would hear much more from Donald
Hume. They would just have to wait for a long time.

Hume had been moved to Dartmoor Prison in Devon, where he
would serve his sentence, although not the full twelve-year term.

Impeccably behaved, showing that he could be so when it suited him, Hume was released early on 1 February 1958, after serving just a few days over eight years. He was now 38 years old.

While he was in prison, several Murder Gang members had visited him on behalf of their newspapers. But after Percy Hoskins of the *Daily Express* very early on, it was the *Sunday Pictorial*'s now assistant editor and Murder Gang reporter Fred Redman and Murder Gang member Victor Sims who made the most effort to continually cultivate Hume in Dartmoor. Subtitled with the slogan 'The Newspaper for the Young in Heart', the *Sunday Pictorial* or 'the *Pic*' cost 4*d* every Sunday and had a circulation of 5,677,000 by mid-1958.

While Fred Redman, known as 'Red', had made most of the visits to Hume in prison, it still wasn't a done deal for the *Pic*. There is evidence that when he left Dartmoor, Hume visited several newspapers in Fleet Street and nearby, offering the true story of what happened to Stanley Setty back in October 1949 for a substantial payment. Percy Hoskins would later tell other journalists that he had been approached by Hume, but whether that was when he was still in prison or after his release is unclear. Hoskins may not have pursued the story, as it could have affected his relationships with senior police and judicial contacts, by 1958 very close and based on hard-earned trust. Or perhaps Hoskins just didn't offer enough money.

Fred Redman's groundwork paid off anyway – it was the *Sunday Pictorial* that won the sensational exclusive. In an article entitled 'Procter-Land Paradise' about the *Sunday Pictorial*'s Murder Gang member Harry Procter for the Gentleman Ranters website, the journalist Tom Mangold, who joined the *Sunday Pic* in 1959, a year after Hume's confession scoop ran, described Fred Redman at that time. 'Red, who always looked as if he had just fallen out of a tumble dryer, lit a cheap cigar, leaned back in his chair …'

Hume had nothing to lose. Just like Frederick Field back in the early 1930s, Hume couldn't be tried again after his January 1950 murder acquittal, due to the then law of Double Jeopardy, and so could sell his story. His only fear would be that of the law of perjury, but just like Field, he could claim that the 'true story' that he gave to the newspaper was in fact a lie, told purely for financial gain. That was

Hume's motivation of course, as well as the notoriety it would give him, feeding his deluded self-image.

The deal was made between Fred Redman of the *Pic* and Hume – £3,600, a very sizeable sum in 1958, enough to buy several modest houses or flats in London then. In return, the newspaper would give Hume ten days to leave the country before publication – Hume was rightly nervous of being recognised, but probably also enjoyed the excitement. In the weeks leading up to his true story appearing, Hume is known to have worn a disguise in London, illustrating his paradoxically attention-seeking and paranoid nature. But at that price, the scoop had to be big.

Sunday Pictorial reporter Victor Sims was tasked with getting Hume's inside story on the Setty murder. Sims would later tell a *Time* magazine journalist that 'It was the most terrifyingly bloody day of my life.' To get Hume in the mood, Sims took him to a country hotel near the Thames Estuary, where the parcelled torso of Setty was dropped by Hume from the plane. Sims was going to hear Hume's full and detailed confession to the murder and dismemberment of Stanley Setty. Hume lay on a bed in the hotel room, staring up at the ceiling, Sims sitting close by, pencil and reporter's notepad in hand.

Hume was well prepared before his story hit the front pages. He went to Somerset House, where all official British birth, marriage and death certificates were then kept, and found a man's birth certificate of his own age who had died – John Stephen Bird. He applied a got a passport in Bird's name, and once he got his £3,600 from the *Pic* in late May 1958, left the country, going to Zurich in Switzerland by plane, as a passenger this time. When the first instalment of the Hume confession appeared, it took the whole front page.

I KILLED SETTY...AND GOT AWAY WITH MURDER
Donald Hume's Startling Confession to the Pictorial
I, Donald Hume, do hereby confess to the Sunday Pictorial that on the night of October 4, 1949, I murdered Stanley Setty in my flat in Finchley-road, London. I stabbed him to death with a dagger while we were fighting. (Signed Donald Hume)
Sunday Pictorial, 1 June 1958

Inside, it continued over three more pages. There was even a photo reconstruction of Hume next to a plane like the Austin he had hired, a parcel floating in the water of the Thames Estuary. The details he gave over the next two weeks were sordid and so matter-of-fact, Hume's sociopathic/psychopathic mind is apparent. Hume shared his troubled childhood with readers, and said 'I was born with a chip on my shoulder the size of an elephant' and that he soon adopted the personal motto 'If you have an enemy, get rid of him.' Hume said of Setty, 'He had a voice like broken bottles and pockets stuffed with cash.'

That week's instalment inferred that Hume was getting jealous because Setty was trying to get close to his wife Cynthia, and that he then grabbed 'a dagger'. That was the cliffhanger for the actual murder revelations coming the following Sunday. In that part, the petty viciousness of Hume came across when he made a great deal about the fact that Setty had once kicked Hume's beloved pet dog when the dog ruined a fresh paint respray of one of Setty's cars. That does sound like something the hardened Setty might do, but the fight in Hume's flat was a very violent one to the death between the two men brutally and sensationally described:

> I was wielding the dagger just like our savage ancestors wielded their weapons 20,000 years ago ... We rolled over and over and my sweating hand plunged the weapon frenziedly and repeatedly into his chest and legs ... I plunged the blade into his ribs. I know – I heard them crack.

Hume had got the better of the bigger but older Setty by pulling out the dagger. After the murder, Hume hid the body somewhere in the flat and began to clean up the bloodstains before his wife returned home that evening – he did a good job, as she apparently suspected nothing. Many of the almost £1,000 in £5 notes in Setty's jacket pocket were heavily blood-stained from his injuries, but Hume managed to rescue about £100 in unstained fivers for himself.

Hume dismembered Setty's body with a hacksaw and a carpet knife, doing so when his wife Cynthia took their baby for a 10 a.m. hospital appointment in central London on 5 October 1949, the morning after Hume had murdered Setty. Hume said that he felt no qualms about cutting up the body: 'I felt no squeamishness or horror at what I was about to do.' It was only Setty's 'staring eyes' that at all unsettled Hume. He then drove away Setty's car, got the painter and decorator to help him move Setty's parcelled body downstairs, hired the plane and dropped the parcel, with some difficulty, from the small plane. Mac, Green and the Boy didn't exist of course.

There were four instalments in all that month, 1st, 8th, 15th and the last one on Sunday 22 June. It was a real coup for the *Sunday Pictorial*, and especially for Fred Redman and Victor Sims. It also attracted international interest, and an article in *Time* magazine on 16 June 1958, the day after the third Hume confession ran, summed up the situation nicely in its title: 'Murder for Profit'. The end of the article, whose author was unnamed, had an interesting insight into the reaction of the rest of Fleet Street to the *Pic*'s exclusive:

The prospect of a murderer – and a story – getting away has set Fleet Street to trampling out a foaming vintage of sour grapes. Cried the *Daily Sketch*: 'Arrest this man.' Huffed the *Star*: 'It is bad for a nation when a man can get away with murder and show a profit.'

But on 1 August 1958, just ten days after his confession stopped running, Hume was back in London, where he robbed a branch of the Midland Bank at gunpoint, shooting cashier Frank Lewis in the stomach in the process, and escaping with around £2,000. Luckily, Frank Lewis survived. The next day, Hume was back in Zurich, holed up with his unsuspecting new lover Trudi – Hume was long estranged from Cynthia and their daughter. Hume lied to Trudi, just as he'd lied to Cynthia about his wartime RAF piloting exploits, saying that he was spying for the Americans, and then the Russians.

In January 1959, Hume raided the Gewerbe Bank in Zurich, shooting a cashier called Walter Schenkel, who also survived. Schenkel was able to press the bank alarm, and when Hume ran out into the street, he was chased by members of the Swiss public down to the river. In a panic, Hume starting firing at the approaching crowd, and shot dead a have-a-go hero taxi-driver named Arthur Maag, aged 56.

But Hume was soon overpowered and arrested by the police this time. After a trial lasting months, Hume was sentenced to life in prison with hard labour.

Hume might have felt lucky that Switzerland had no death penalty, but the conditions of his hard labour sentence were very tough, and took a real toll on Hume, physically and mentally – so much so that over eleven years later, on Sunday 4 October 1970, the Sunday newspaper *The People* carried a report by Jack Gee, its Paris reporter, entitled 'The Agony of Donald Hume' and a sub-headline of 'Should we allow even an arrogant double-killer to suffer like this?' along with a photo of a broken Hume.

Hume was eventually judged to be mentally unstable by Swiss prison psychiatrists, and he was returned to Britain on humanitarian grounds in 1976, immediately being sent to the Broadmoor Hospital for the Criminally Insane. Hume remained there for almost twenty-two years, and he was finally released in 1998, aged seventy-eight. Several months later, a body was found in a wooded area next to a hotel in Gloucestershire. Just like his first victim Stanley Setty almost fifty years earlier, Donald Hume was identified by his fingerprints.

7

MAYHEM ON A ROOFTOP

There was a huge surge in violent crime in the decade after the Second World War, largely a result of the desensitisation brought about by the war and the higher prevalence of guns in society. This meant that more criminals were armed or 'tooled up' with firearms. Criminals had also enjoyed more latitude during the war, when the focus of the authorities was on defeating Hitler and dealing with brutally incessant bombing raids. This fertile criminal environment died hard. Successive governments in the 1950s would take a hard line in fighting this crime epidemic, including a very disturbing rise in juvenile and youth violent crime. Pressure would be kicked down from the Home Secretary to the Commissioner of the Metropolitan Police, to the senior CID ranks down to the policeman on the beat, and this upsurge in crime and the crackdown by the authorities was reported closely by the Murder Gang.

When 'The Velvet Kid' and Cyril Burney went down for twelve years for the armed robbery with a gun of a respectable couple in outer north-east London in 1952, the heavy sentences were a sign that the authorities meant business. Nobody had been killed, but the couple had been terrorised and threatened. The gang had made off with just £4, a lighter and some cheap pens, after believing their victim's plea that the keys to his safe were at his place of work. The Buick getaway car used by the gang, an American car still a rarity on British streets, was found abandoned and upside down – it later transpired that the getaway driver's sight was failing and that he was dying of heart disease. The driver had also left his fingerprints all over an object inside of the car and was arrested in the vicinity. Links to the Velvet Kid and Cyril Burney were soon established.

The robbery had taken place on 14 March, and exactly six months later, on 14 September 1952, Scotland Yard's Flying Squad moved in on the two ringleaders of the gang. The Velvet Kid and Cyril Burney were taking refuge in a small hotel behind Whiteley's department store in Queensway, west London. They took no chances – they arrived armed, mob-handed and surrounded the hotel. Burney jumped out of the window of Room 5, but was met by a Flying Squad Sergeant on the ground, and after a ferocious struggle, Burney was taken into custody.

Back in the hotel, The Velvet Kid was found in Room 4, in bed with his then girlfriend, his dark hair dyed vivid blonde to change his appearance. The Velvet Kid moved for the automatic gun under his pillow, a Luger, the same one used in the robbery. Another Flying Squad Sergeant rushed and pulled the loaded gun from the criminal's hand before he could fire it. According to Donald Thomas in *Villain's Paradise*, the Velvet Kid's girlfriend would later say that the Sergeant said, 'Now what would a nice boy like you want with a thing like this?'

In that acute crime wave after the Second World War, many offenders were not professional criminals like the London godfathers Billy Hill and Jack Spot, but teenagers and young men in their 20s. But most would probably develop into major players as time went on. The Velvet Kid's German Luger was a prime example of a gun which would have been very rare in Britain before the war, but was now easily obtainable. This added more menace to a society used to knives and razors, which could kill, slash and scar, but were not as immediately deadly and potentially fatal as the reckless use of firearms.

The early 1950s saw tough sentencing, including the death sentence, being employed as a deterrent. The authorities were truly cracking down. In the five years between 1950 and 1955, three of the biggest miscarriages of justice in British history took place, when three people were hanged. Firstly, Timothy Evans, for the murder of his baby at the infamous 10 Rillington Place in Notting Hill, which was almost definitely committed by the serial killer John Christie. Within a few years, there would be the controversial case of Ruth Ellis.

But in late 1952, a murder was committed which sent Fleet Street and the Murder Gang into overdrive, and lead to an execution which many believed then, and most do now, was a terrible miscarriage, and one for which the British government was eventually, decades later, forced to recognise and apologise. The person who committed that murder was shockingly young, and was none other than the younger brother of The Velvet Kid, whose real name was Niven Craig.

≡

ON THE ROOFTOP OF THE BARLOW & PARKER WAREHOUSE, CROYDON, SUNDAY 2 NOVEMBER 1952

'Hand over the gun, lad,' yelled a policeman at 16-year-old Christopher Craig on the windy roof, who was waving his revolver, a Colt New Service .455 Webley with the barrel shortened, around, and had already hit Detective Sergeant Fred (aka 'Fairy') Fairfax in the shoulder, who had nevertheless been able to keep Craig's accomplice, in the attempted warehouse robbery, 19-year-old Derek Bentley, in custody, but then Bentley was hardly giving much resistance, despite having a spiked knuckleduster and a knife in his pockets, and being physically very strong.

'Let him have it, Chris!' Bentley possibly – or probably not – hollered to Craig.

'Come on you coppers' shouted Craig, 'you just gave my brother twelve years!'

He was taunting the policemen who had just arrived as reinforcements, and Craig shot the first up on the roof to confront him, Police Constable Sidney Miles, aged 42, who immediately fell dead with a bullet through the head. Teenager Chris Craig was now what the Americans call 'a cop-killer', and Derek Bentley would be held just as responsible, although he'd pulled no trigger, landed no punch nor tried to escape once captured. But he had joined Craig in climbing up on to that warehouse roof at 9.15 p.m., the intent being to lower themselves down inside and steal what they could find, in legal terms a Joint Enterprise.

Then Christopher Craig, out of bullets, threw himself off of the warehouse roof, plummeting about 30ft (10m) into a greenhouse below, shattering the glass and fracturing his spine. Bentley was taken down to ground level by the uninjured police officers still on the roof.

One Faces a Murder Charge, Other is in Hospital – Derek Bentley, 19 – Christopher Craig, 16
Daily Express, Tuesday 4 November 1952

Percy Hoskins and his news editor ran photos of both Craig and Bentley on the front page, the day after Bentley first appeared in court, Craig still being in hospital, unable to walk due to his spinal injury, and his left wrist also badly damaged in the fall. On page 5, details of the court hearing told how a 16-year-old boy had come forward to give evidence that Craig had previously given him a gun. The injured Det. Sergeant Fred 'Fairy' Fairfax had been discharged from hospital, but of course PC Sidney Miles was in the mortuary. The next day, the paper reported that Craig was kissed by his mother while on a stretcher, and the day after, a photo ran of Christopher Craig looking surly, lying on that stretcher.

Chris Craig obviously had a profound hatred for the police after they gave his older brother Niven 'The Velvet Kid' Craig, whom he idolised, twelve years for armed robbery. At this stage, Craig got far more attention than Bentley in the newspapers, and rightly so as he was the shooter and murderer, and the murder of a policeman always shocked the public, as it was, and is, a rare occurrence in Britain, although another Police Constable, Nat Edgar, had been murdered by 22-year-old Donald Thomas, an army deserter, as recently as February 1948. Thomas also had the distinction of being the first criminal to be caught when the police asked the public, through the newspapers, for 'help with their inquiries'.

There was also a move towards abolishing corporal punishment, such as birching, at this time, and there was also a building liberal consensus to fight for the abolition of the death penalty. The Criminal Justice Bill of 1948 was a move towards the capital punishment debate. Thomas was tried and sentenced to death, but soon reprieved and given life imprisonment, as the Criminal Justice Bill just passed stipulated a trial five-year suspension of the death penalty for five years. But abolition was, as always then, not a popular move for society amongst the police top brass and the rank-and-file, and murders such as that of PC Edgar and that of PC Miles in November 1952, both low-ranking, front-line officers, just reinforced police opposition to ending the death penalty, and keeping control of a youth felt to be 'out of control' and an increase in post-war crime, with hanging being the ultimate deterrent, was the reasoning behind that.

This had been mirrored by Percy Hoskins of the *Daily Express* when Donald Thomas was reprieved in early 1948, when the immediately reactive headline was '4.50 p.m. At Old Bailey. The New Deal For Killers Had Begun'. It's hardly surprising that the ultra-police-friendly Hoskins and his paper the *Daily Express* owned by the press baron Lord Beaverbrook would take this stance, which was totally in line with the police, the establishment and the structure of society of pre-war times, now under threat from liberal 'enlightened' moral forces. But when the established order was under attack, it came out fighting, and this to a great extent chimed with the mood and fears of the British public regarding crime and punishment, which in turn was partially shaped by the Murder Gang coverage it read, written by journalists such as Percy Hoskins.

Christopher Craig's age, just 16, also fed into the fear of delinquency sweeping the nation in the early 1950s, which was making the authorities take a hard line, and indeed had ensured that Niven Craig got such a long sentence despite no murder having been committed, while his 16-year-old brother Chris had now taken the life of a policeman seen as a hero by the British public in the fight against this new phenomenon of juveniles toting guns and now using them. But over the coming weeks, Chris Craig would attract less and less press attention, with Derek Bentley taking the limelight in Murder Gang reporting.

Another sensational murder case was breaking in the newspapers that week too – a youth named Miles Giffard was charged with the murder of both of his parents on their farm in Cornwall, a macabre detail being that he had loaded their bodies into a wheelbarrow one after another, and tipped them over a cliff. But this gained far less Murder Gang coverage than the murder of PC Miles.

That Sunday, a whole-page scoop was delivered by Harry Procter in the special 'Magazine Section' of the *Sunday Pictorial*, which in fact was a section within the paper itself.

The Craigs of Norbury, S.W. – Memories in a family portrait
Sunday Pictorial, 9 November 1952

In that week between the murder of PC Miles on the Croydon rooftop and that Sunday's edition of the *Pic*, Procter had inveigled his way into the lives of Christopher Craig's family at their home in Norbury, south-west London, with the help of Madeline, a junior female colleague, to give him the additional advantage of female empathy and intelligence in the professional wooing of Craig's mother and sister. Procter would later write that he 'tactfully and gently' gained the acceptance and trust of the Craig family – who of course had their elder son Niven serving twelve years in prison for armed robbery and now their 16-year-old son Chris facing a murder trial as a cop-killer. Only their daughter Lucy was not involved in criminal activity.

Procter's way in, with the help of Madeline, was to use the angle of concern about the rise in serious crime amongst British youth. As the crime historian Steve Chibnall highlighted in his 1977 book *Law-and-Order News*, Procter wrote in his 1958 memoirs *The Street of Disillusion* about the reaction to the murder of PC Miles, 'When news of this terrible shooting burst upon a shocked world, newspapers, Churches and the Government were gravely concerned about a wave of violence sweeping the land…the terror-problem of the times made the Craig murder focus a grave social problem of the day.'

It was what his readers wanted, and Procter instinctively knew this. Also in his memoirs, Procter was very open about how he opened up the Craig family. 'Eventually the Craig family regarded Madeline and me as their truest friends. They gave us all their confidences, they sought our help over every problem.' Procter would use this access to the Craig family to keep them on board throughout their son's murder trial.

The article that Sunday, including a photo of Chris and Niven's ex-soldier father Captain Niven Matthews Craig, who now worked in a bank, their mother and sister Lucy holding the family's Corgi dog called Skippy in their living room, were portrayed as a normal family who had experienced great misfortune. Six other children – five older sisters/daughters and a brother/son had already left the family home and were living their own lives. Now with 26-year-old Niven in prison and appealing his sentence and Chris, described as 'the baby' of the family in custody, just those three were living in Norbury Court Road, and it would be 'the first Christmas without a tree for thirty years'.

Mrs Craig had great concerns about the problems of youth delinquency, which had now so affected her own family, and Procter reported that she had given a talk on a radio show called *War and the Young Offender and What is the Remedy?* Their son Niven, now aged 26, had been involved in crime for some time, and Chris had been going in that direction too, with tragic consequences. Mrs Craig emphasised that the family was not a deprived one often synonymous with a descent into crime – 'We have never been poor' and that four of their children, three of the elder daughters and the incarcerated Niven, had gone to good Grammar Schools, where academic standards were higher. The tone was very sympathetic towards the Craig parents and their parenting, but it was of course in Procter's interest to keep the Craig family onside and not waste all the efforts he and Madeline had made, at least until after the trial.

Harry Procter was born in Leeds, Yorkshire in 1917, and as a teenager worked in the vermin-ridden basement of a shoe shop. When he was sixteen, Procter entered journalism, becoming a reporter on his local rag, the *Wortley and Armley News*, at eighteen moving to another provincial paper, the *Cleveland Standard* in Redcar, North Yorkshire, where he was Chief Reporter, and then on to the *Northern Echo* in Middlesbrough, but was made redundant. Procter's next stop was the *Yorkshire Evening News* back in his native Leeds, but he had for some time hankered after getting to a national newspaper and Fleet Street, and during a holiday from the *Evening News* he did a week's temporary work on the *Daily Mirror*, who then offered him a permanent job, which he accepted, arriving in Fleet Street aged 22.

After a short stint in the RAF after the outbreak of the Second World War, Procter was made war correspondent of the *Daily Mail*, where working under his news editor, the late Lindon Laing, Procter began to report increasingly about crime, and his exclusives about the double-murderer Neville Heath, whom Procter had known as a drinking companion in Fleet Street pubs prior to his murders and kept contact with him before and after his arrest and up to Heath's execution, marked Procter out as a resourceful, driven and natural journalist. Procter stayed on the *Daily Mail*, often working closely with fellow Murder Gang member Arthur Tietjen, as on the Hume case, until 1952, when Hugh Cudlipp, the very influential editorial director of the circulation-hungry and increasing *Sunday Pictorial*, offered him a job there as a 'Special Investigator'. Procter hadn't been on the *Pic* very long when he delivered his first big scoop with his Craig family portraits.

The *Sunday Pictorial* cost 2½d in 1952 and 1953, and was broadly conservative in tone, with photographs being a prominent feature of the paper, as its name suggested. Procter's editor on the *Pic* was Colin Valdar, and his news editor was Reg Payne. Procter would increasingly have a difficult relationship with Reg Payne. But in his six years on the *Sunday Pictorial*, Procter would become one of the very elite Murder Gang reporters, achieving numerous exclusives, for instance, in December 1952, Procter was also reporting on the Soviet spy Allan Nunn-May.

Although as the title of his 1958 memoir *The Street of Disillusion*, a reference to how he felt about Fleet Street, revealed, this success, often using morally dubious methods when chasing scoops, took a burdensome personal toll, and Procter would fall out of love with Fleet Street and the Murder Gang, and the highly competitive atmosphere and sometimes hostile jealousies aimed at those like himself who got the best exclusives.

But in late 1952, Harry Procter was 35 and very much on the rise, a handsome man with swept-back dark hair, a heavy smoker and drinker, but then those vices were almost a rule in the Murder Gang, rather than exceptions. And his methods on the Craig scoop reveal a great deal about how he and the *Sunday Pictorial* worked, in the face of strong rivalry from other Murder Gang members, hungry for access to the Craig family. In his memoirs, Procter wrote, 'And for weeks Madeline and I, as paid and skilled journalists, had the tough task of keeping away the opposition reporters and photographers. The opposition never allowed us a day or night free from anxiety.'

The trial of Craig and Bentley for the murder of PC Sidney Miles was approaching, and although the Craig family was firmly in the pockets of Harry Procter and the *Sunday Pictorial*, Christopher Craig was making headlines everywhere. On Friday 21 November, Harold 'Jeep' Whittall and his colleagues at the *Daily Mirror* had 'Boy, 16, Sent for Trial' – this wasn't Chris Craig, but one of Craig's friends. Craig and this boy had allegedly previously done an armed robbery in their native Croydon together, walking into a house with 'pistols' out and robbing the householder of £5.

Both Craig and Bentley were charged with murder, and their trial ran from 9–11 December 1952. The Lord Chief Justice Rayner Goddard presided, Christmas Humphreys, who had prosecuted Donald Hume in 1950 and who was now Senior Treasury Counsel, prosecuted.

Harry Procter later wrote about how he had to protect his scoop and look after the Craig family at the trial. 'When the trial opened at the Old Bailey I had to organise my forces like a military operation.' Procter had to stop Captain and Mrs Craig and their daughter Lucy from giving any titbits to hungry rival Murder Gang members outside the court. Procter also recalled how a 'pirate reporter' had pretended to have interviewed Lucy, and Lucy had to officially deny that she'd ever spoken to that reporter through her solicitor. For the three days of the trial, the Craig family were ferried between their Norbury home and the Old Bailey in a gleaming Rolls-Royce driven by a liveried chauffeur, laid on by the *Sunday Pictorial*, and immediately after the verdicts, that same luxury car took them to an expensive hotel in the countryside outside London to escape the media pressures.

Procter himself had also been busy before the start of the trial, visiting Christopher Craig in Brixton Prison, gaining access to him by passing himself off as a relative, no doubt with the help of the rest of the Craig family. The results and Procter's take on that interview would be revealed the following Sunday after the trial ended.

The case against Craig was fairly straightforward, the only legal argument was whether he had meant to shoot PC Miles in the head or to kill him, or had been shooting aimlessly. It was proved by a firearms expert that the Webley revolver, on which Craig had shortened the barrel, was far from accurate. But the fact was that Craig had already injured Det. Sergeant Fred 'Fairy' Fairfax, who would later get the George Cross, and PC Sidney Miles the Police Medal for bravery, which his widow Catherine would be given by the new Queen Elizabeth II.

Craig gave evidence in court on 10 December, and 'Jeep' Whittall of the *Daily Mirror* was there to report on Thursday 11 December on the front page: 'Rooftop Taunts "Just Bluff" – Craig Tells Court his story of the gun battle'. Craig had also said, 'I liked guns as a small boy', that his older brother Niven had had a gun, he enjoyed watching gangster films at the cinema, that he fired into the air, and that he wanted to kill himself when he jumped from the roof. Somewhat damagingly for his co-accused Derek Bentley, Craig told the court that Bentley had previously 'dared' him to break into a butcher's shop.

As for Derek Bentley, the evidence at the trial was far less clear-cut. Much was made of the shout 'Let him have it Chris!' that Bentley was alleged by the police to have called to Craig. Bentley denied ever saying it, and Craig backed him up on this and even if he had, the fact it could have been a plea for Craig to pass the policeman the gun rather than a provocation to open fire, which was raised by the defence at the trial, but dismissed. In his 1990 book *Let Him Have It, Chris*, M.J. Trow raised very serious doubts, convincingly through investigative interviews, that Bentley had ever said those words. Derek Bentley, 19, was also challenged; he scored 66 in an IQ test at the end of 1948 and 77 in 1952, had a mental age of 12 and a reading age of 4½ – almost illiterate – and was epileptic.

The jury was out for only an hour and fifteen minutes, and when the verdicts were read out, both Craig and Bentley were found guilty, so Christmas Humphreys had automatically secured the death penalty on Bentley under the law of joint enterprise, with Lord Chief Justice Rayner Goddard donning the black cap, although the jury had given a recommendation for mercy for Bentley. Christopher Craig was too young to hang of course, and he was sentenced to be detained at Her Majesty's Pleasure, and would serve ten years, being released in 1963, still aged just 26, disappearing into obscurity and by all reports becoming a plumber. The question was now whether Derek Bentley would really hang, or if the recommendation for mercy would lead to a reprieve, and whether Lord Chief Justice Goddard would use his influence with the Home Secretary to help secure it.

Rayner Goddard was known for his strict, authoritarian sentencing – he once rejected six appeals in an hour. In fact, it has been claimed that Goddard had a particular personal reaction to sentencing people to death. The late writer and barrister Sir John Mortimer, creator of *Rumpole of the Bailey*, was informed by Goddard's former valet that Goddard would sometimes ejaculate during sentencing and his trousers had to be sent off to be cleaned as a result. Another version suggests Goddard reacted in this way when sentencing young men to corporal punishment.

Percy Hoskins ran a piece on page 2 of the *Daily Express* on Friday 12 December, the day after the convictions, entitled 'Five Phases in the Life of a Boy Gunman' showing five photographs of Christopher Craig between the ages of nine and sixteen, and that Craig's older brother Niven was also 'gun crazy'. Hoskins must have got the photos of Craig from friends or his school, as Harry Procter and the *Sunday Pictorial* certainly wouldn't have allowed Hoskins access to Craig family photographs.

Meanwhile, Harry Procter now used his access to the Craig family and to Craig himself in prison, running the front-page headline of 'My Failure by Craig's Father' and an explosive two-page piece in the magazine section of the *Pic*:

Killer Craig – A candid pen-picture by Harry Procter
Sunday Pictorial, Sunday 16 December 1952

No doubt under pressure from his newspaper and to give his readers what they wanted in the atmosphere of fear about delinquent violent crime that Craig represented, Procter's piece was very different to the one that he and his assistant Madeline had assembled about the Craig family back in early November, about five weeks earlier. This time the tone was noticeably unsympathetic towards Craig and the way that his parents had raised him. Procter opened with his first impression of Craig:

> Christopher Craig was lying in bed in a small, gloomy cell at Brixton Prison. The pale yellow walls around him gave a sinister pallor to his white face. He tossed back his coal-black hair, turned his strikingly handsome head. 'What a handsome youth!' I thought. And then he grinned. The grin broke the spell. As I saw the left lip curl and the impudent flicker creep into his eyes I knew I was watching just another of those brass-faced little hooligans of which this post-war world is so bitterly ashamed – a lazy, cowardly, selfish young lout.

Below this portrait of Craig was a photo-stat of his final class report from school, showing very low marks in exams and the fact that he had come eighteenth out of eighteen in his class. Perhaps the most contrastingly since the picture of a normal family he had given in his November article, it was soon clear that Procter had convinced Craig's father, Captain Niven Craig to denounce his son's actions and to admit guilt at having brought him up in the wrong way.

Also entitled 'My Failure' inside, Captain Craig admitted his mistakes, saying, 'I should have supervised his leisure. Fathers must realise that theirs is the responsibility of seeing to it that their children do something useful with their time.' In a reference to how the family had reacted to Chris's older brother Niven being given twelve years for armed robbery, Captain Craig said, 'It was wrong of us to talk so bitterly about that heavy sentence passed upon his older brother Niven.' The inference was that this had poisoned Chris's mind against the police even more, of course.

The *Sunday Pictorial* would run a piece in the following month, on 11 January 1953 by Barrie Harding, which would show the social pressures that Captain Craig faced, which reported how Captain Craig, a First World War veteran who had been Company Commander of his local regiment of the Home Guard, which had been formed to defend Britain from invasion in the Second World War, had been asked to leave by the overall Commander, Lieutenant-Colonel Marten-Smith. While Harry Procter had to persuade the Craig family to change its' position on their convicted-murderer son, social stigma may have been as much a factor in their decision to do so.

Craig's mother also spoke about how Chris had been an intelligent boy, and how they had been so shocked about what happened on that warehouse rooftop. She said of her youngest son, 'Above all his love for his elder brother Niven was one of the biggest things in his life,' alluding to the fact that Niven's long sentence had led Chris to 'go off the rails'. But finally, Mrs Craig said, 'The adolescent mind is very complex, and what changed that quiet boy in a few weeks into that on the rooftop is something which I may never know.' This was a very different account to the one 16-year-old Chris Craig had given of himself in court at his trial.

Procter wrote six years later about how he had gone to Captain Craig and said:

> I am going to condemn your son … Not because I bear him any grudge – I don't … But it is my solemn duty to condemn him so he is not glorified in the eyes of millions of other young boys … My duty is to assure these boys that Christopher Craig was a coward.

Procter went on to write that he'd told Captain Craig that it was 'wickedly wrong' for any newspaper to glamorise crime or compliment criminals.

Procter never enjoyed good relations with the Craig family after that piece went out, but then that didn't bother him professionally at all. Christopher Craig, now convicted, was now old news, and so was by extension his family. Derek Bentley, on the other hand, was the new focus of the Murder Gang, as Bentley potentially faced an appointment with the hangman, Albert Pierrepoint, his execution originally set for 30 December 1952. Harry Procter now shifted his attention to the Bentley angle.

The *Sunday Dispatch* was a Sunday competitor of Murder Gang coverage in the *Sunday Pictorial* (Harry Procter) and the *News of the World* (the veteran Norman 'Jock' Rae), although it's circulation was much smaller, but still an boasted an estimable circulation of around 2,300,000 in 1953. In 1950, the paper had been responsible for fuelling the huge interest in flying saucers in Britain, and later in 1953 would publish 'The Rommel Papers', edited by the historian Basil Liddell Hart, an insight to the leading Nazi who fought Montgomery in the desert war in North Africa with his 'desert rats' in the Second World War. The *Sunday Dispatch* had a strong military connection at this time – its editor Charles Eade had been Lord Mountbatten's press liaison officer during the Second World War.

On 4 January 1953, the *Sunday Dispatch* published a piece about Derek Bentley, then awaiting execution, headlined 'Youth Laughs in Death Cell' and included the sub-headlines 'No Parties Yet' referring to the fact that he hadn't earned a reprieve, and 'Room with Bath', as his cell had a bath. Attributed as being written 'by *Sunday Dispatch* Reporter', that journalist had had access to Derek Bentley's family. The article reported:

> His *(Bentley's)* parents told me how he laughs and jokes with his warders, bathes every night, sleeps soundly, and even asks about the latest film shows … On one occasion before Christmas when his parents visited him, he said, 'Don't forget, no parties til I get home, Mum.' His mother and father made this promise… 'They tell me he is no trouble,' Mrs Bentley told me. 'He is so jolly on our visits and there are often outbursts of laughter.' … His sister Iris bought Bentley a ticket for an annual dance after he was sentenced. 'I'll ask the manager to change it for another next year when he comes home,' she told me.'

This piece was most probably the work of James 'Jamie' Reid, the key Murder Gang reporter on the *Sunday Dispatch*. Known as being fiercely competitive, in the summer of 1953, Reid would take on Harry Procter and Norman 'Jock' Rae, trying everything to get the attention of the depraved Notting Hill serial killer John Christie in court, but fail, with Procter winning 'Christie's own Story' for the *Sunday Pictorial*.

In the police files on the Craig and Bentley case, there is a letter written by an outraged reader of that *Sunday Dispatch* piece, addressed to the Metropolitan Police Commissioner, Harold Scott:

Dear Sir, I enclose a cutting of today's *Sunday Dispatch*, which in my view is the most disgraceful piece of journalism I have ever had the misfortune to read – it makes light of the Death Sentence – also, makes out that the warders are laughing and joking, while one of their colleagues he murdered, and a widow weeps. I hope Derek Bentley pays the full penalty – and you will deal with the libel on your warders by the *Sunday Dispatch* to make them repute it publicly. –Yours etc., Kathleen Corry, Ladbroke Grove, London.

Of course Bentley had not killed PC Sidney Miles, Christopher Craig had pulled the trigger, while Derek Bentley was in police custody on the roof. But in the eyes of many of the public, he was equally guilty, as he had accompanied Craig, even if it hadn't been definitively proved in court that Bentley had known that Craig was carrying the loaded Webley revolver. In the eyes of the law of course, Bentley was jointly culpable of the murder with Craig – he was armed with a knife and a spiked knuckleduster, the latter of which the trial judge, Lord Chief Justice Goddard, had singled out in court as 'a shocking weapon'. When Bentley decided to shin up that drainpipe after Craig to get to the warehouse roof that cold November night, the law saw him as going armed and equipped to commit robbery, and whatever happened in the course of the crime, whether Bentley knew that Craig had the gun and would use it or not, he was equally guilty under British justice.

The *Sunday Dispatch* piece illustrates how Murder Gang reporting could inflame opinion, and in the then climate of post-war fear of youth violent crime, it was an irresponsible piece of reporting, when Bentley was appealing for his life, and the comments by Bentley's family and Bentley himself in prison were obviously trying to 'put a brave face on it'. They almost couldn't believe that he could hang, especially as Craig the shooter couldn't because of his age.

Bentley's execution had been postponed, and there was a huge public call for clemency on his behalf. The *Daily Mirror* had on the front page on Wednesday 14 January 1953, 'And the question still is … Will Bentley Hang?' A new execution date had been fixed for 28 January. On Tuesday 27 January, the *Daily Express* splashed the front page with 'Bentley: 50 MPs Plead – Execution Eve Row', which was penned by an *Express* Political Correspondent, showing that Bentley's fate was now temporarily out of Murder Gang jurisdiction, the fight for his life now being fought in and around Parliament.

On the day set for the execution, also by a political correspondent, the *Daily Express* led with '2am – Bentley Crowds March – 'Must Hang' – Official – Bevan led appeal by 200 MPs'. A petition was signed on Bentley's behalf by over 200 Members of Parliament, and the last minute fight for a reprieve was being led by the Labour MP Aneurin 'Nye' Bevan, who had been one of the architects of the British National Health Service (NHS) in the immediate post-war Government of Clement Attlee.

But the Home Secretary Sir David Maxwell Fyfe refused to commute the death sentence, and it was duly delivered, Derek Bentley being hanged at 9 a.m. on 28 January 1953 at Wandsworth Prison, by Albert Pierrepoint. The *Daily Mirror* reported that day, in a big front page written by several reporters, certainly led by Harold 'Jeep' Whittall, with a photo of the Derek's mother and sister captioned 'Their grief became nation's problem', that Derek Bentley's last words had been 'Cheerio.'

It was Harry Procter and the *Sunday Pictorial* that ran the final posthumous scoop on Derek Bentley. In another feat of journalistic ingratiation, Procter had managed to gain the trust of the Bentley family, just as he had with the Craig family, so Procter had managed to get the two big scoops that bookended the tragic murder of PC Sidney Miles, and the cases of Craig and Bentley.

Bentley: His Last Dramatic Letter from Death Cell
Sunday Pictorial, 1 February 1953

On page 3, Procter printed a photo-stat of a portion of the last letter that Bentley had 'written' to his parents, actually by dictation to a warder as Bentley was near-illiterate, and so that photocopy of the letter was in the warder's handwriting, even if the words most definitely came from Derek Bentley. It came with a warning to other newspapers: 'World copyright – reproduction in whole or in part is strictly forbidden'. It was a long letter, with many private family details, but the part about Bentley's execution just hours later, and how he felt about his fate was highlighted by Procter in his text:

> I tell you what Mum the truth of this story has got to come out one day, and as I said in the visiting box that one day a lot of people are going to get into trouble and I think you know who these people are. What do you think Mum? This letter may sound solemn but I am still keeping my chin up as I want you and all the family to do … That will be all for now. I will sign this myself. Lots of love, Derek.

The former Lord Chief Justice Goddard told the writer David Yallop seventeen years later that he had expected Bentley to be reprieved, and blamed the Home Secretary for the execution, although Goddard, as Lord Chief Justice of England and Wales, hadn't applied any pressure on Maxwell-Fyfe to save Bentley from the gallows in 1953. Bentley's parents and sister campaigned relentlessly for his pardon, achieving his exhumation from the grounds of Wandsworth Prison and reburial in a family plot in March 1966, but sadly all had passed away when, forty-five years later in 1998, Derek Bentley was finally pardoned.

Harry Procter would remain on the *Sunday Pictorial* until 1956, when he was 39 years old. His health was deteriorating, and he wrote in his 1958 memoir *The Street of Disillusion* of his years in top-flight journalism, 'But though I was big-time in Fleet Street, I was unhappy. I did not like some of the stories I was writing.' However, the lawyer John Parris, who represented Procter in three drink-driving court cases, and incidentally represented Christopher Craig in the Craig and Bentley murder trial, later alleged that Procter was fired from the *Pic* for stealing from colleagues. Procter went on to work back at the *Daily Mail*, in the paper's Manchester office for a short time, before leaving journalism. A leading light of the Murder Gang was gone. Harry Procter died of lung cancer in 1965, aged 48.

8

THE GREEN-EYED MONSTER

It was a disappointing summer in London that year, the average temperature that July being just 15.4°C, the highest 23°C. But for many people it was a good year, as rationing finally ended after fourteen years, having started in 1940.

It was about 11.45 p.m. and in the back garden of No.11 smoke was rising and the smell of burning wafting over next-door fences. A neighbour, John Young, letting out his dog, saw the smoke and the orange-yellow flames. They caused this usually private man to look over the fence to No.11, next door but one, where he saw the middle-aged Greek-Cypriot woman he'd sometimes seen before, standing over the fire, and what looked like a burning tailor's dummy or 'a wax figure'. It seemed an odd time to be having a bonfire, but he thought no more of it – neighbours kept a respectful distance in this calm, leafy and gentrified suburb. Young remembered that it was definitely before midnight, because the popular *Light Programme* was still on the radio, which broadcast from 8 a.m. until midnight.

About an hour later, around 1 a.m. the following morning, Mr and Mrs Burstoff were driving down South Hill Park Road on their way home, having just closed their restaurant for the night, and suddenly Mr Burstoff had to brake hard when a small woman with dark hair and a dark complexion ran out in front of their car. She screamed at the Burstoff's in very basic, heavily accented English, 'Please come! Fire Burning! Children sleeping!' Mr Burstoff hurried after the woman, then saw that it wasn't a house that was on fire. The smoke and flames were coming from the back garden. The fire was spreading, and towards the house, where the woman had told him that children were sleeping. He ran into a nearby house and called the fire brigade.

The blaze was extinguished before it could do any damage to the house, and the three children taken to safety. But what the firemen found still smouldering in the back garden, after the fire hose had been turned off, made them immediately call the police. It hadn't been a dummy that Mr Young had seen being burnt, but a real-life woman, a human being.

That year, the weekly left-wing political and literary magazine *Time & Tide*, which had a very different readership from the right-of-centre *Daily Mail*, was advertising Mrs Davey of Crediton, Devon, saying 'I wouldn't change it for anything…ELECTRIC COOKING is the most wonderful thing I ever had', for South Western Electric, which proffered 'the four foundations of modern living': cooker, water heater, refrigerator and washing machine.

In the *Daily Herald*, an article ran about 26-year-old Paul Raymond, whose 'theatrical ventures are packing in audiences throughout the country'. His credits were listed as 'Paris After Dark – The Web of Desire', 'Follies Parisienne', featuring the 'Only Moving Nudes' – Mr Raymond saying to the *Herald* hack, 'They're static really, but I present them on revolving stages', obviously to bypass the law – and his hit in seaside Margate, Kent, 'Piccadilly Peepshow.' Raymond would go on to establish a multi-million pound adult entertainment, pornography and property empire in Soho and surrounds.

But there was no frivolity that year at 11 South Hill Park, Hampstead, which was a house with four floors. Until that night of 29/30 July, the first and second floors had been occupied by the Christofi family, while the third floor was empty, having been vacated in October 1953 by Robert and Maria Cooper. An elderly couple lived on the fourth floor.

The Christofi family consisted of Stavros Christofis (Stavros had added an 's' to his name), his wife Hella, aged 37, and their three children, aged twelve, ten and nine, plus Stavros's mother, Styllou, aged 53. Stavros had come to Britain in October 1937 from his native rural Cyprus, and had worked in a series of catering jobs. He'd met Hella, who was born in Wuppertal, Germany on 3 May 1941. Hella had come to London in 1939, en route to the United States, but with the outbreak of the Second World War, as a German she was stranded, and after she met Stavros, settled in Britain when they got married in 1945 and started renting the flat at 11 South Hill Park. In 1954, Hella was working in a clothes shop.

Stavros's mother Styllou was from a small village called Rizokarpasso in north-eastern Cyprus, was almost illiterate and had very limited English, and had only been in London since July 1953, the first time she and Stavros had seen each other for twelve years. Styllou had persuaded her reluctant son to let her stay with them, so that she could find a job and send money back to his father in Cyprus – her husband had bought a small farm and the money she could earn in London would pay off the mortgage. In fact, Styllou hadn't been able to find a job, and had spent most of her time housekeeping and taking care of her grandchildren.

Life had gone less than smoothly since Styllou joined them a year earlier. The police file on the case reveals that Robert Cooper, who had lived with his wife Maria in the flat above the Christofi family until the previous year, with the couple still visiting the Christofi family sometimes, told police that Hella 'strongly resented' her mother-in-law Styllou's presence in their home. Styllou had been interfering and domineering, trying to manipulate her son to do things her way, not Hella's. It would also be learned that Styllou had moved out and back into 11 South Hill Park during that year, due to the tensions.

The police file also gives the police's opinion of Hella and Styllou, a stark contrast. Hella was described as 'a bright, wholesome type, who dressed smartly, though not expensively'. Styllou was meanwhile bluntly, condescendingly and with a whiff of xenophobia, summed up as 'a typical Cypriot peasant type, low intellect, somewhat miserable demeanour, and looking a dowdy old woman, years older than her age, except for her jet black hair'.

In the opinion of the police in August 1954, Styllou 'probably resented' her daughter-in-law Hella because she was German, because she spent money on clothes, and because Styllou had to stay at home doing the housework and look after the three young children while Hella went out to work. Stavros worked as a waiter at the famous Café de Paris, and often had to work very late and into the early morning, and this meant that Styllou and Hella were left alone together most evenings and nights, especially after the children had gone to bed. The police also concluded that Hella was probably 'also resentful of her mother-in-law and probably detested her peasant habits and mode of life, and was afraid she would transmit these to the children'.

Both of the women had visited doctors recently, and both confided in their doctors that they were 'unhappy in the home'. Styllou went to see a Cypriot physician, and she was diagnosed as suffering from 'anxiety, neurosis and a duodenal ulcer'. Hella, meanwhile, had been to her doctor on 3 July, twenty-six days before the fire, and was said to be in 'a highly nervous condition, pains in the chest, and hair falling out'. Hella's doctor had concluded that Hella was so anxious because of 'her mother-in-law's presence in the house'.

Hella's last visit to her doctor, just three days before the fire on 26 July, saw an improvement and Hella seemed to be 'much better, but she had lost weight, now weighing 9 stone 4lbs (59 kg)', which was still nevertheless slightly more than the smaller and slighter-framed Styllou, who weighed 9 stone 1lb (57.6 kg).

There is an explanation as to why Hella appeared to be getting better: she had given Stavros an ultimatum – either his mother left their home, or she and the children would. Hella planned to take the three children on a holiday to see her family in Germany in August, and on her return, she expected to see that Styllou had gone. To save his marriage, Styllou told his mother that she'd have to leave, which can't have been well-received. There was mutually deep resentment between Hella and Styllou, but in one of the women, that jealousy would prove to be murderous.

In a November 1954 article, 'Fleet Street 1954', he wrote for the *Spectator* magazine, the veteran journalist John Beavan, who had been working on nationals since the early 1930s, gave a perhaps nostalgic view of his journalistic past, but of course he had been witness to many changes. 'Fleet Street was a hearty masculine club with its drinking competitions, hotpot and pigeon pie suppers and boozy harmonic smokers. All this has gone. Nobody today has the means, the leisure or the taste for conviviality. The ulcer and not cirrhosis is the occupational disease; phenobarbitone, not scotch, the professional sedative.'

Fleet Street had undoubtedly become more fast-paced and demanding, more professional and specialist in terms of the skills required by journalists, and this had led to the use of drugs, uppers and downers, to add to the alcohol consumed. The reason was simple: there had been a massive increase in the circulations of both daily and Sunday newspapers, especially the latter. Beavan acknowledged this, but lamented that there had been a decline in standards of coverage.

> Fleet Street's success has weakened the quality of journalism. Since 1939 the *Mirror* has found three million new readers, the *Express* a million and a half. Many of them did not read a paper at all before the war; they lacked the means and perhaps the desire to do so. But to catch and preserve the interest of these people it has been necessary to dramatise lighter news more heavily than before. The more serious of the popular dailies, the *Herald* and the *News Chronicle*, have had to follow suit. Even so, they have lost some of their weaker readers, seduced by the bright bubbliness of the *Express* or the passionate black sans of the *Mirror*. The *Mail*, rather remarkably, has gone the other way.'

And the large increase in newspaper copies sold had also ratcheted up the demands of being a leading reporter, no more so than in crime. The Murder Gang reporters were notorious for being the hardest-living in this period, the sheer speed and volume of serious crime and the dark subject matter taking a toll physically, emotionally and mentally in some cases, which needed increased artificial stimulation to just keep going and deliver that ever moving flood of crime news, in that highly competitive elite environment, where advertising revenues, then as now, depended on the paper's circulation.

Those at the top of the Murder Gang felt the pressure the most, the likes of Norman 'Jock' Rae and Harry Procter key examples, although they would continue to deliver scoop after scoop, while men such as Percy Hoskins seemed to thrive on the pressures. Being in the Murder Gang had never been a job for the faint-hearted, but in the years between the late 1940s and early 1960s, the commercial and competitive stresses were at their zenith, caused by the very success of newspapers, to which Murder Gang reporters were very important contributors.

A 1971 study by the criminologist Bob Roshier looked at the percentage of space given to crime news, features and articles in four prominent Fleet Street newspapers, all analysed with the space given to advertisements excluded. It shows that crime coverage in these four newspapers increased substantially between 1938 and 1955 in popular, lighter newspapers, but not in those considered the 'heavy' newspapers.

In September 1938, 5.6 per cent of the *Daily Mirror*'s coverage was taken by crime, by September 1955, it was 7 per cent. On the *Daily Express*, crime had 4.4 per cent of space in September 1938, and 5.6 per cent in the same month of 1955, while the *News of the World*, a very popular 'Sunday', allowed crime to take 17.8 per cent of coverage in September 1938, and by September 1955, this had risen dramatically to 29.1 per cent of space. Whereas the *Daily Telegraph*, a more 'serious' daily, gave 3.5 per cent of its space to crime in September 1938, and this had dropped slightly to 3.4 per cent in September 1955. These percentages would drop on all four newspapers by September 1967, by which time the era of the Murder Gang was over.

Back in the summer of 1954, those hard-bitten hacks were 'at the top of their game', and had to be.

Woman Accused of Killing Her Daughter-In-Law
Daily Mail, Saturday 31 July 1954

That was the headline run by the *Mail*'s Murder Gang reporter Arthur Tietjen two days after the fire in the back garden of 11 South Hill Park, Hampstead. The woman was Styllou Christofi, and in her first court appearance the previous day, she'd 'leaned heavily on the iron bars of the dock as the charge was repeated to her in Greek, and when Detective Superintendent Crawford, the man who had arrested her, gave evidence, Mrs Christofi 'leaned forward on the dock, resting her head on the edge'.

Arthur Tietjen would cover this case more than any other Murder Gang reporter, but it wasn't one which set the crime sheets alight, its interest being in the contrast it allows to a very famous murder case soon after that truly set those crime sheets ablaze.

Tietjen had had an eventful life. Born in 1909, he worked in journalism as a young man, starting at age 16 in 1925, and then he was the press liaison officer at the seminal Nazi Nuremberg and Belsen trials at the close of the Second World War, a very complex job, with the whole world's media wanting information, and his job was to relay it to English-speaking reporters. After the war, he joined the *Daily Mail*, where he worked very closely with his news editor Lindon Laing until Laing's unfortunate death in 1948. Tietjen would build excellent contacts within the police hierarchy and at every level, probably second only to Percy Hoskins of the *Daily Express* in this respect in the Murder Gang.

Tietjen was also an expert on crime around London's West End and Soho, and in 1956, just two years after the Christofi case, he published a book called *Soho: London's Vicious Circle*. In that book, Tietjen spoke of his feelings about the police. 'For a quarter of a century I have worked alongside the police and watched them on duty. I have been their admirer, and at times, if the occasion warranted, their critic. But, all in all, I have never found them wanting. In my opinion, they are the public's finest bargain in this inflationary era.' Tietjen also went on to say that the police force, in mid-1950s Britain, had too much paperwork, and that officers were constantly fighting 'a paper war'.

Tietjen would remain the main Murder Gang man on the *Daily Mail* until his retirement in 1970. He worked closely on that paper with Harry Procter until 1952, when Procter moved to the *Sunday*

Pictorial, and in the remainder of the 1950s and the early 1960s, he'd often work with Hugh Medlicott, a general news and crime reporter. Tietjen retired from the *Daily Mail* in 1970, aged 61. When Tietjen died in December 1990, aged 81, the *Daily Mail* wrote a small obituary, which said, 'In his heyday he was known by every Metropolitan Police Commissioner, as well as many constables.'

In 1954, Arthur Tietjen was in his heyday, in and out of the *Daily Mail* offices at Northcliffe House, telephone number Central 6000, with the acting editor Arthur Wareham overseeing the paper, and news editor Don Todhunter closely overseeing Tietjen, who was usually out and about, at the police and magistrates courts, conferring with a court reporter and coppers, at Scotland Yard's press bureau, chatting to his numerous police contacts, in person at crime scenes and associated sites and by phone, and waiting for the next move in selected Murder Gang pubs and dive bars.

Meanwhile, before being charged with the murder of her daughter-in-law Hella Christofis, Styllou Christofi had been interviewed by the police at length, with a Greek interpreter present to translate both ways. When initially charged at the police station by Det. Superintendent Crawford, Styllou tried to disassociate herself from the burning of Hella's body in the back garden, although she'd been seen doing that by neighbour John Young. Hella was mercifully already dead when she was set on fire.

The pathologist was able to tell that Hella had been bludgeoned on the head from behind in the kitchen, and the police determined that the object used was a heavy ash-plate from the oven. While Hella was unconscious she'd been strangled lying on the floor, before being carried into the back garden and her body soaked with paraffin or petrol. But Styllou was admitting to nothing. 'I did not make use of any petrol, but some few days previously some petrol spilled on the floor. I did not pay any attention to it. I stepped on it and probably the smell was the result of that petrol. From this story I know nothing more.'

The preliminary court appearances followed, and Stavros, grief-stricken by the brutal loss of his wife and the mother of his three children, gave evidence against his mother. A poignant and nasty detail was that Hella's wedding ring had been removed, obviously by Styllou, and could not be found, a symbolic gesture signifying Styllou's hatred of her daughter-in-law and her deep-rooted jealousy at Hella's strong bond with Stavros and the three children. The *Daily Sketch*, possibly written by Owen Summers as Bill Ashenden was now on the *Daily Graphic*, had 'Mother-In-Law Accused of Murder – Husband in Tears over Wife's Ring' on Wednesday 25 August.

Styllou was on remand in Holloway Prison, the female prison in north-east London, and the police file reveals a warder's report on Styllou of 2 September 1954, and what she had done between 7.50 a.m. and 4.50 p.m.. 'In bed most of the day – got up this afternoon for exercise. Laughing and throwing kisses through door this morning. More composed and subdued this afternoon...'

Styllou Christofi went to trial at the Old Bailey on 25 October 1954. Mr Justice Devlin was the judge, and the ubiquitous Christmas Humphreys prosecuting counsel. The evidence against her was overwhelming, and she was found guilty of murder on 28 October, the jury taking less than two hours to reach the verdict. Sam Jackett and his colleagues at the *Evening News* reported on that day's proceedings for the final edition: 'Cypriot Woman Unmoved When Sentenced – GRANDMOTHER TO DIE For Hampstead Murder – Pleads "I Want to Speak"'.

Styllou had shown no emotion when sentenced to death, but asked to re-enter the witness box to say something. Her request was denied. But the police file shows what Styllou was thinking, or at least what she wanted the rest of her family to think.

In a letter to her other son, Nicolas Pantopiou Christofi, on 7 October, less than three weeks before her trial, dictated to and written by an interpreter, and then translated for the Home Office. Styllou said, 'Your brother *(Stavros)* is against me. But I am innocent and I shall not be wronged by justice ... Kiss your children for me ...' Either self-denial, highly manipulative or expressed honestly by a mentally unstable mind, the tone continued in another letter to Nicolas on 4 November after her death sentence was given. 'God is almighty, but I do not hope to see you again. Your brother gave false evidence against me, and found also others to do likewise.'

Then Styllou spoke of there being visitors to 11 South Park Hill on the night of the murder, and that she had left Hella in the kitchen after they had both been cleaning it and gone to bed:

Later two persons called there, who were known to the family because the children got out of bed and went downstairs in their pyjamas, since they know the said persons. Their mother was however angry with them and sent [them] back to bed. Then we went to sleep. I don't know what had happened, and [I] am involved in this myself, your unfortunate mother.

There was no corroboration of these mystery visitors by the children or anyone else. Styllou then continued to feel sorry for herself, 'In London we have many relatives … nobody came to see me, except my solicitor and interpreter.'

The Home Secretary authorised an examination as to Styllou's mental condition on 3 December, as was the rule before any execution could take place. While she was awaiting her fate, Styllou asked for a Greek Orthodox cross to be placed on the wall of her cell, which was granted. She was upset that Stavros didn't visit her, but apart from that she seemed calm. A petition was received by the Home Secretary from Styllou's home village of Rizokarpasso in Cyprus, with thirty-seven signatures, including those of several priests of the Greek Orthodox Church, asking for a reprieve.

Styllou's Appeal was dismissed on 30 November, and the execution was fixed for Wednesday 15 December. Arthur Tietjen reported in the *Daily Mail* that day 'Bid for Woman Killer Fails' referring to the fact that ten MPs had fought for a reprieve late into the previous night, claiming that Styllou was insane. But Styllou Christofi was duly executed at 9 a.m. that day on 'E' Wing of Holloway Prison by Albert Pierrepoint, her body buried as was customary in the prison grounds.

Mrs Christofi: MP's Urge Censure
Daily Mail, Thursday 16 December 1954

The day after Styllou's execution, Tietjen informed his readers on the front page that Sidney Silverman (Labour MP for Nelson & Colne) and Sir Leslie Plummer (Labour MP for Deptford) were leading an attack on the ruling to execute Styllou Christofi. This was indicative of a growing unease with the death penalty amongst the left wing, and one which would continue building throughout the decade and into the early 1960s. Silverman and Plummer were arguing that Styllou had been insane and should never have been executed, and they based this on a medical report written by Dr T. Christie, the senior medical officer at Holloway Prison. The petition, now of course posthumous, had now reached fifty signatures, all Labour MPs.

But on Tuesday 21 December, Tietjen was back with 'Mrs Christofi "Not Insane"'. It was revealed that three doctors had examined Styllou, and reported that the Home Secretary, Major Gwilym Lloyd George, had read a written statement the previous day in the House of Commons about his decision not to reprieve Styllou Christofi. 'The three doctors reported to me that the prisoner was not, in their view, insane. They added that, in their view, she did not suffer from any minor mental abnormality which would justify them in making any recommendation on medical grounds relevant to a question of a reprieve.'

Bizarrely, it would be revealed in a dark twist, much later and not reported by the Murder Gang in 1954, that Styllou had stood trial for murder before – back in Cyprus in 1925, when she was in her early 20s, Styllou had been accused of thrusting a lit torch down her mother-in-law's throat. But Styllou had been acquitted by the Cypriot court, either having been deemed not guilty of murder, or that her mother-in-law had treated her so badly that she'd had reason to react in the murderous way that she apparently had. Just under thirty years later, Styllou killed her daughter-in-law in a different but equally brutal way.

In his memoirs, *Executioner: Pierrepoint*, Albert Pierrepoint made a point of saying that he was surprised by how little press coverage Styllou Christofi provoked, especially compared to the next woman he hanged, very soon after, who would achieve blanket coverage. Indeed, Arthur Tietjen's sparse coverage in the *Daily Mail* was the only sustained Murder Gang reporting on the case, even though it had the primal element of jealous rage and that Hella had suffered a shockingly horrible death and undignified treatment after her death. Styllou Christofi would in fact turn out to be the penultimate woman hanged in Britain.

≣

OUTSIDE THE MAGDALA PUB, 2A SOUTH HILL PARK, HAMPSTEAD, NORTH LONDON, 10 APRIL 1955

It's Easter Sunday, and just two minutes' walk from where Styllou Christofi murdered her daughter-in-law last July, in the very same street, a petite 28-year-old woman waits in the darkened doorway of Henshaw's, the newsagents, her platinum-blonde hair hidden from view, her breathing heavy and her mind mixed-up and emotional, exacerbated by the alcohol she drank a couple of hours ago.

She has spotted the green 1954 HRG Emperor racing car belonging to her ex-lover. It's a stylish car with a custom-built engine, powerful at 1500 CC, and the way it gleams shows how much its owner, an enthusiastic amateur racing driver potentially about to turn professional, loves it. It wouldn't be in London tonight, but instead racing at the Gold Cup motor-racing meet at Aintree, Liverpool, except for the fact that it had an engine problem. So the Emperor and its owner, David Blakely, have had to remain in London.

Blakely has recently taken second place with that car in a race, and is due to drive it again soon in the famous 24 Hours of Le Mans race, for the Bristol motor company. Blakely has treated the Emperor with much greater respect than the woman he has had a tumultuous and passionate relationship with, who now stands in that shop doorway, ominously waiting for him.

It's just after 9.30 p.m. now. Blakely finally comes into view, leaving the Magdala pub, known locally as 'the Magy'. He is 25 years old, tall and handsome. With his dark wavy hair tousled in the wind he looks every inch a dynamic young man. He walks with the confident gait instilled at an expensive school, every centimetre the glamorous up-and-coming racing driver returning to his pride and joy. Next to

David Blakely is his old friend Clive Gunnell. They have just been into the pub to get more cigarettes to take back to the home of their mutual friends, Anthony and Carole Findlater.

The woman, Ruth Ellis, steps out of the shadows. 'Hello David,' she says. He sees her, but ignores her, causing her to yell 'David!' Still no response as David scrambles in his trouser pocket for the keys to the Emperor. Then Ruth pulls out the Smith & Wesson revolver she's carrying in her handbag, and fires at David, misses, and he tries to run. But Ruth follows, shoots again, and this time hits him, and he falls down onto the pavement.

Standing over David, Ruth fires three more shots into him in quick succession, one of them just three centimetres from his back. David has been hit in the aorta, trachea, intestines, liver and a lung. Ruth stands there, seemingly in shock, and then tries to fire the final, sixth, bullet into the ground. But it bounces off the ground and catches a passing woman at the bottom of her thumb. Gladys Kensington Yule was on the way to the pub when hit.

'Will you call the police, Clive?' Ruth says to Gunnell. But an off-duty policeman, Alan Thompson, approaches and takes the gun from Ruth, who says to him, 'I am guilty. I am rather confused.' David Blakely is already dying in the street.

At Hampstead police station in Rosslyn Hill, Ruth Ellis was interviewed by the officer in charge of the case, Chief Inspector Davis, along with Inspector Gill and Inspector Crawford. These officers later stated that she was calm, and that there was no obvious sign that she was drunk, or had been drinking. Ellis didn't ask for a solicitor, and was not given one, and incredibly, this remained the case the next day, 11 April, when she made her first court appearance and was remanded in custody.

Born in Rhyl, Wales, on 9 October 1926, Ruth Ellis was 28 at the time, three years older than David Blakely. But their backgrounds were very different – she was from a poor working-class family, and he from a comfortable upper-middle-class family.

Actually half-Belgian on her mother's side, Ruth's birth surname was Neilson; her Mancunian classical musician father had changed his surname from Hornby at the birth of their first daughter Muriel. The family moved to Basingstoke in England during her childhood. Ruth's first job after leaving school aged 14 was as a waitress and soon after, in 1941, when the German bombs were falling there and many were leaving the beleaguered city, the Neilson family moved to London. Three years later, she became pregnant by a Canadian soldier, and had a son, known by the family as Andy, who would later call himself Andre. The Canadian soldier went back to Canada and only paid maintenance for about a year, and Andy was largely brought up by Ruth's mother, Bertha.

Ruth did what was then known as 'Camera Club' work, basically posing nude for photographs. She'd then become a hostess in a club in Duke Street, the infamous Court Club, where the manager, Morris 'Maury' or 'Morrie' Conley, would 'blackmail' the hostesses into having sex with him, making it very difficult financially for hostesses to say no, or indeed to leave his employ. A frequenter of the Court Club, and many others, was Stephen Ward, the society osteopath who would later, in the early 1960s, be central to the Profumo scandal, which did a great deal to bring down the Conservative government of Harold 'You've never had it so good' Macmillan.

Ruth had also taken up prostitution 'on the side' by the end of the 1940s, and she became pregnant by one regular, having the pregnancy terminated, which was then illegal of course, and performed secretly by dodgy doctors or those 'with the knowledge'. Back at the Court Club, one of the customers was a dentist called George Ellis, and Ruth got to know him, leading to her marrying him on 8 November 1950, when she was 24. The problem was that George Ellis was extremely controlling, subject to violent fits of temper, and also an alcoholic. They would separate and get back together several times, and Ruth gave birth to a daughter named Georgina in 1951. But George refused to accept paternity of the baby girl, and he was convinced that Ruth was having an affair. Soon after, Ruth and Georgina joined Andy back living with Ruth's mother. Ruth reportedly went back to prostitution at this time as a means of income.

But in 1953, Ruth became the manageress of the more upmarket Little Club in exclusive Knightsbridge, where she also lived in a flat above the club. The Little Club had an exciting clientele, and one night Ruth was introduced to David Blakely by the top racing driver Mike Hawthorn.

Mike Hawthorn would win the Le Mans which Blakely had been pegged to race in that June of 1955, before he was shot, but it was actually a race marred by terrible tragedy, when debris from a crashed racing car flew into the crowd, killing eighty-three spectators and the French driver Pierre Bouillin, as well as injuring 180 others. Mike Hawthorn is known to have felt guilty about the crash, as his overtaking manoeuvre to get to a pit stop had caused the driver Lance Macklin to swerve, the collision with Bouillin happening immediately after that, Bouillin's car then being launched into the stands, car parts fragmenting and peppering the crowd. Hawthorn would go on to become Britain's first Formula One World Champion in 1958, retiring on that high, but then being killed in a road accident just six months later. It was later revealed that Hawthorn had been suffering from a terminal illness at the time he was killed.

So Blakely and Ellis were mixing with the 'in' racing crowd, and the 1950s was arguably the most glamorous era of elite motor racing. It wasn't long until Blakely moved in with Ruth above the club. Ruth got pregnant again by David, but she had an abortion as she didn't feel that their relationship was stable enough to have a child together. David undoubtedly treated Ellis very badly, emotionally and physically. When she was pregnant, yet again, he kicked her in the stomach, causing her to miscarry in January 1955. It was just three months before she shot him dead.

Although Ruth also seems to have been a feisty handful, it really was a love–hate relationship. There was a deep connection between them, and Ruth had loved David deeply and obsessively, as he had her. But he became increasingly jealous, as Ruth was seeing at least one other man: Desmond Cussen was an ex-wartime RAF Lancaster bomber pilot, who was wealthy and ran his family's tobacconist business. Cussen was four years older than Ruth, and at first the two reportedly just had a close platonic relationship.

Then Ruth was fired from the Little Club, and as much out of need as anything, she moved into Desmond Cussen's flat near Oxford Street in the West End, at 20 Goodward Court, Devonshire Street, and their relationship became sexual. For a while, Ruth kept the relationships with David Blakely and Desmond Cussen going simultaneously. This can't have been easy for either man, especially the possessive David. When David left Ruth for the final time a few days before the shooting, she was distraught, drinking heavily and taking pills, a spurned lover, spiralling into despair, showing that David Blakely was her real love.

On that Easter Sunday, 10 April, Ruth Ellis was fired up, a woman possessed with a sense of being wronged and treated badly. Her state of mind would be much debated later, as to whether it was a 'crime passionel', a concept invented by the French: a crime of passion, which usually gains more sympathy from a jury. Anyway, Ruth left Cussen's flat in Goodward Court, going in search of David, first going to the home of his friends Anthony and Clare Findlater at 29 Tanza Road, Hampstead. But before she could go up to the second-floor flat, she saw David tear off in his Emperor. She then walked towards the Magdala in South Hill Park, a pub that David often went to when in Hampstead. On arrival there, she saw the Emperor parked outside, and decided to wait for him to come out, standing in that newsagent's doorway.

In the mid 1950s, the biggest-selling daily newspaper in Britain was the *Daily Mirror*. Figures from the Audit Bureau of Circulations show that in 1956, the year after Ruth Ellis pumped those shots into David Blakely, the *Daily Mirror* (Harold 'Jeep' Whittall) had a circulation of 4,649,696. That paper's nearest rivals at that time were the *Daily Express* (Percy Hoskins) with 4,042,334, followed by the *Daily Mail* (Arthur Tietjen) with 2,071,708 readers. Lagging behind were the *Daily Herald* (Bob Traini) with 1,693,997, the *News Chronicle* (Reg 'Fireman' Foster) with 1,442,438 and the *Daily Sketch* (Owen Summers) with 1,123,855 readers. In 1956, the biggest-selling newspaper by far in Britain was a 'Sunday', however – the *News of the World* (Norman 'Jock' Rae) with a readership of 7,493,463, *The People* (Duncan 'Tommy'

Webb) with 4,948,215 and the *Sunday Pictorial* (Harry Procter) with 2,420,159 readers.

Blonde model accused of killing ace car racing driver
Daily Mirror, Thursday 21 April 1955

It was Harold 'Jeep' Whittall who came up with that headline about the shooting of David Blakely by Ruth Ellis for the *Daily Mirror*'s huge readership, under the paper's masthead slogan 'Forward with the People'. Nobody can remember where Whittall got his nickname 'Jeep' from, but it could perhaps be that he had the middle initials of 'G.P.', or that he drove a jeep during military service in the Second World War. Whittall has left little imprint apart from his articles, but he was certainly the main Murder Gang reporter on the *Daily Mirror* from the early 1940s until the late 1950s, and then he would be joined by Tom Tullett, who had equal standing.

Whittall would remain on the paper until about 1970. The veteran journalist John Smith, who started on the *Daily Mirror* in the 1960s, as a reporter and sometimes on the news desk, and later rose to be chief feature writer and assistant editor, remembers little about Harold 'Jeep' Whittall today: 'I can't provide any personal details about Harold as I only met him on a couple of occasions. He rarely came into the *Mirror* office.' Like many of his Murder Gang generation, Whittall was by nature and early training a 'leg man', gathering sources and digging for leads out in the field.

John Smith clearly recalls the *Daily Mirror* of the 1960s, which wasn't too different from the mid-1950s, especially how the crime reporters gathered and sourced information from the police, unless they were lucky enough to have high-level police contacts, as Percy Hoskins and Arthur Tietjen did:

In those days every national newspaper had a reporter permanently based in the Press Bureau in the old Scotland Yard, access to the bureau being a solid, green painted door on The Embankment. Here the reporters would sit around smoking, drinking tea and chatting and, when things were quiet, nipping around to the Red Lion pub near the House of Commons. The duty Press Officers sat in a separate room and whenever there was any information to pass on they would appear in a little hatch set in the wall and deliver the news, normally just verbally rather than in written press release form. Each paper had its own telephone line direct from the Press Bureau to the paper's news desk and the main function of the Scotland Yard reporters was to pass this information on as quickly as possible. This would then be followed up by *Mirror* crime reporters. Very seldom did the Press Bureau reporters venture out on a story themselves. They were seen as the source of info from Scotland Yard and as such they established very good relations with senior detectives who of course could often prove invaluable off-the-record background on police investigations. Incidentally, the Scotland Yard press office was not manned by press officers round the clock and any late night calls from newspapers would be passed to the "back hall inspector", a duty officer who was not usually all that helpful.'

Revel Barker, who was on the *Sunday Mirror* in the 1960s, also remembers how Murder Gang reporters of that generation operated:

Money sometimes changed hands ... 'Buy the kids an Easter Egg/ Christmas present/whatever...' Not a lot: a fiver, which was white until 1961, would buy a decent meal for two in those days. These payments usually appeared on the expenses dockets as 'entertaining special legal contact' – no queries asked. When a reporter had information, he would often try to offer it as 'a swap' for more information in return, from the cops. Sometimes, when the cops hit a stone wall, they would hand it over to a reporter in the hope that he could get more information. Occasionally, senior officers asked reporters to investigate suspected bent cops; the *People* managed this successfully on a few occasions.

Duncan 'Tommy' Webb was the main Murder Gang reporter on *The People* in the 1950s, and Revel Barker recounts how 'Tom Webb allegedly had so many death threats he worked behind a screen of alleged "bulletproof glass". Lots of people, usually day casuals, worked with him as "witnesses". *The People*'s editor Sam Campbell cared more about how bylines looked in type, in the paper. Thus Tom Webb became Duncan Webb.'

But it was the work of Harold 'Jeep' Whittall and his *Daily Mirror* colleagues who would lead the Murder Gang field in reporting on Ruth Ellis, although all papers vigorously chased the story. And in those first weeks after Blakely's shooting, the evidence against Ellis was mounting – not that she'd killed her ex-lover, she freely admitted that and there were of course witnesses – but as to whether the shooting had been premeditated or a crime of passion, done on the spur of the fired-up moment. On 25 April 1955, fifteen days after the shooting, the police file shows that the firearm ballistics report was in, and it stated about the Smith & Wesson revolver, 'The trigger pull is 9.5 to 10Ibs unlocked ... To pull a trigger of 10Ibs requires a definite and deliberate muscular effort.' So those shots were fired wilfully, not that Ruth Ellis ever denied that.

Ruth Ellis went on trial for murder at the Old Bailey on 20 June 1955, before Mr Justice Havers. Christmas Humphreys, who had prosecuted Timothy Evans for the serial killer John Christie's murders of Evans's wife Beryl and baby daughter Geraldine in 1949, and Derek Bentley in 1953, both men hanged and later posthumously pardoned, prosecuted Ruth Ellis too. Ellis pleaded not guilty, but Christmas stated in court that it was 'to all intents and purposes a plea of guilty'. Christmas's own father was the noted and respected barrister and judge Travers Humphreys, and when Christmas was called to the Inner Temple in 1924 it was no surprise. In that same year, Christmas set up the London Buddhist Society, the first of its kind in Britain, and soon the most important in Europe. In the following years, Christmas would become the leading Buddhist light in Britain, publishing many books on the religion.

Ruth Ellis didn't help herself in court, refusing to tone down her platinum blonde hair, insisting on being herself. But it was her reply to Christmas Humphreys's gentle-yet-ruthless cross-examination in the witness box which did the most damage. Asked what she had intended to do when she fired the bullets into David Blakely, Ellis replied, 'It's obvious when I shot him I intended to kill him.' That made short work of it for Humphreys. It was as if Ruth Ellis was ready to die, and put up no resistance.

Ruth Ellis was found guilty of murder and sentenced to death, the jury only going out for twenty minutes. Harold 'Jeep' Whittall took next day's front page.

Model Smiles at Death Sentence
Daily Mirror, Wednesday 22 June 1955

Despite a petition signed by 50,000 people, Ellis herself did not appeal. Going against her was also the fact that Ellis had been lying in wait for Blakely, and especially that she'd taken the revolver with her. But where had she got the gun? On 12 July, just over three months after she gunned Blakely down and on the very eve of the death sentence, Ellis made a statement under the desperate guidance of her solicitor Victor Mishcon as to where she got the gun, which remains in the police file, and is also enlightening as to her state of mind that tragic day of 10 April 1955. As Ruth Ellis had proved – unlike most going to trial accused of murder and facing the death penalty – to be honest, often at her own cost, her words can probably be trusted.

> With the greatest reluctance I have decided to tell how it was that I got the gun with which I shot Blakely. I did not do so before because I felt that I was needlessly getting someone into possible trouble. I had been drinking Pernod (I think that is how it is spelt) in Desmond Cussen's flat and Desmond had been drinking too. This was about 8.30 p.m. We had been drinking for some time. I had been telling Desmond about Blakely's treatment of me. I was in a terribly depressed state. All I remember is that Desmond gave me a loaded gun. Desmond was jealous of Blakely as in fact Blakely was of Desmond. I would say that they hated each other. I was in such a dazed state that I cannot remember what was said. I rushed out as soon as he gave me the gun. He stayed in the flat. I rushed back after a second or two and said, 'Will you drive me to Hampstead?' He did so and left me at the top of Tanza Road [where Blakely's friends the Findlater's lived]. I had never seen that gun before. The only gun I had ever seen there was a small air pistol used as a game with a target.

The Liberal-Conservative Home Secretary Gwilym Lloyd George was not moved by this or the petition to issue a reprieve, and he later wrote that the bullet that hit the passer-by Mrs Gladys Kensington Yule, in the thumb, was a factor in his decision as people couldn't be allowed to go around shooting guns in the street, endangering the public.

Ruth Ellis was hanged at Holloway on Wednesday 13 July 1955, by Albert Pierrepoint, who sometimes had Murder Gang reporters hanging around him like groupies in slow crime news periods, and he was always ready to show them his 'equipment'. The day after Ruth Ellis's execution, Howard Johnson wrote a piece in the *Daily Mirror* entitled 'The Bright Lights Led Her to the Death Cell'. It was a typically emotive piece, on one hand exploiting Ellis, and on the other very sympathetic towards her. The bestselling crime novelist Raymond Chandler, then living temporarily in London and away from his Californian milieu, was moved to write a letter to the *Evening Standard*, calling the execution of Ruth Ellis 'an act of medieval savagery'.

In her very insightful essay, 'Ruth Ellis in the Condemned Cell: Voyeurism and Resistance', the criminologist Dr Lizzie Seal articulates just this point. Referring to the tabloid reporting on Ruth Ellis, it states 'such newspaper coverage reflected both voyeuristic fascination with the incarceration and imminent hanging of a beautiful young woman, and admiration for her strength and forbearance under grimly adverse conditions'. It's also pointed out that the *Daily Express* published photo-stats of Ellis's prison cell letters to Frank Kneale, her friend, which revealed that Ellis wanted to die and that 'the *Woman's Sunday Mirror* ran her ghostwritten life story in four parts, the final instalment appearing the Sunday after her execution'.

In her book *Ruth Ellis: My Sister's Secret Life*, Monica Weller alleges that Ruth's prosecutor Christmas Humphreys manipulated evidence at the trial and changed witness statements. In 1982, just a year before Christmas Humphreys died, Ruth Ellis's son Andre McCallum had a long conversation with Christmas regarding his mother's trial, which he secretly taped. In her book, Monica Weller divulged the conversation, part of which had Christmas saying about the trial, '(Mercy) never came into my mind because, you must understand, how we play parts as if on a stage. I have my part to play. Defending counsel has his. The judge has his. The jury have theirs…mercy never came into it.' Tragically, just weeks later, Ruth Ellis's son Andre committed suicide in a bedsit. Andre had been psychologically damaged since childhood, having been just 10 years old when his mother was hanged. Christmas Humphreys paid for his funeral. Perhaps it was a final twinge of Buddhist conscience.

Back on 14 June 1955, the *Daily Mirror* had a front-page banner headline of 'Should Hanging Be Stopped?' It was a stark contrast to the newspaper's reaction to Styllou Christofi's execution just months earlier, which garnered no newspaper sympathy, even if some socialist MPs fought for Christofi's reprieve. Ruth Ellis had touched a public nerve and would metaphorically become a tragic poster girl for the increasing clamour for the abolition of the death penalty, which would gain real momentum in the late 1950s and early 1960s.

This pity for Ruth Ellis may well have been started by Harold 'Jeep' Whittall's colleague on the *Daily Mirror*, William Neil Connor, better known to his millions of readers as 'Cassandra', the name of his pseudonymous and very popular column. On the day of Ellis's execution, 13 July 1955, Cassandra wrote a powerful column that began:

It's a fine day for haymaking. A fine day for fishing. A fine day for lolling in the sunshine. And if you feel that way – and I mourn to say that millions of you do – it's a fine day for a hanging. IF YOU READ THIS BEFORE NINE O'CLOCK THIS MORNING, the last dreadful and obscene preparations for hanging Ruth Ellis will be moving up to their fierce and sickening climax.'

Styllou Christofi and Ruth Ellis killed people close to them, and nearby in time and place. But they were very different women, and their crimes were very different also. The *Daily Mail* nonetheless drew parallels between them in a 21 July 1955 editorial entitled 'A Jealous Woman'. It reveals how every Fleet Street paper had a different take on events, usually instilled by the newspaper's owner, and to a lesser extent, the editor.

9

THE GOOD DOCTOR?

It's a luxurious flat, just a half-hearted stone's throw from the exclusive Dorchester Hotel, the cars outside only the best, the clothes worn in this neighbourhood reeking effortlessly and fragrantly of real money. It's a grace-and-favour apartment, courtesy of Lord Beaverbrook, known as 'the Beaver', the very hands-on owner and proprietor of the *Daily Express*, *Sunday Express* and the *Evening Standard*, among other titles. The Murder Gang reporter living in this flat has a close relationship with the Beaver. Since 1953, this flat at 55 Park Lane has been the centre of operations for Percy Hoskins, chief crime reporter of the *Daily Express*, where he's worked for almost thirty-two years, since 1924.

Along with being the President of the Crime Reporters' Association and his television and radio work, often in collaboration with the police, Hoskins has been publishing books about the criminal cases he has covered since 1938, the latest, *No Hiding Place!*, coming out in 1951. He also often lectures at police colleges, sharing his wealth of experience of criminals and advising on press guidance, leading to some calling him 'Scotland Yard's Dr Watson'.

Additionally, Hoskins had been touring meetings of Interpol in cities all over the world intermittently in the early 1950s, as Sir Richard

Jackson, then Britain's Interpol representative, is a close personal friend, and is now an Assistant Commissioner at Scotland Yard. Hoskins also has a professional friendship with J. Edgar Hoover, the very powerful Director of the FBI, sometimes visiting Washington DC, and a personal friendship with the film director Alfred Hitchcock, whom Hoskins resembles in physical shape, if not quite in scale, and once posed with in Soho for a 'bookends' photograph.

Another acquaintance is the actress and comedic singer Beatrice Lillie, who also lives at 55 Park Lane. She will reach the populist zenith of her very long career in 1967 with her role in the film *Thoroughly Modern Millie*. It's not unusual for Lillie and other film stars – Gary Cooper is rumoured to have dropped by – to be in attendance at Hoskins's flat, but the main visitors are very high-ranking police officers, for whom he keeps 'open house'. This flat really is Hoskins's base.

Not wishing to keep regular hours at the *Daily Express* offices in Fleet Street, telephone Central 8000, where he purposefully doesn't even have a desk, Hoskins is an independent force at the paper, and this is of course made possible by the esteem in which he is held, particularly by the Beaver, editor Arthur Christiansen and his news editor Morley Richards, with whom Hoskins has worked closely for almost twenty-three years – Richards's milestone of twenty-one years was celebrated at a special dinner at the Criterion Restaurant in Piccadilly, on 16 October 1954, chaired by Christiansen.

But Hoskins's main focus is still his Murder Gang activities – getting scoops for the *Daily Express*. He's the best-connected Murder Gang reporter, and Victor Davis, a veteran reporter who worked with Hoskins, much later called him 'a world-class fixer'. Percy Hoskins is the man when you're in trouble; he knows everyone, and can get things done. But when it comes to scoops, he's as competitive as the rest of them, and when he gets one, he visibly beams and celebrates, although much of his time is spent in good restaurants, especially El Vino, and pubs. A discreet word in a contact's ear, and shrewd listening antennae fine-tuned over decades on the crime reporting frontline, mean that Hoskins doesn't usually have to move very fast.

Always perfectly dressed in an expensive suit and trilby, Percy is happily married to Jeannie. Next year, in September 1957 Hoskins will appear as a panellist on the American game show *To Tell the Truth*, alongside celebrities Ralph Bellamy, Kitty Carlisle, Hy Gardner and Polly Bergen, his West Country accent a novelty to US audiences. But in the months before that, Percy Hoskins will cover the biggest case of his long career, become very closely involved, and take a big risk, one which could end his position as unspoken leader of the Murder Gang, and his relationships with very influential people.

On 23 July 1956, a call was made to the police in Eastbourne, East Sussex, on the south coast of England. The anonymous caller was later found to have been the famous music hall entertainer Leslie Henson, who would die in the following December at his home in Middlesex, aged 66. Henson was concerned about the death of his friend in Eastbourne, Gertrude 'Bobby' Hullett, and especially about the care given to her by her doctor there, Dr John Bodkin Adams.

Eastbourne Police made enquiries, and discovered that Dr Adams had also treated Gertrude's late husband Alfred John Hullett, known as Jack, who had died on 14 March 1956, aged 71. Jack Hullett, an ostentatious self-made man who had bought a large house overlooking Beachy Head with initialled wrought-iron gates, had left Dr Adams the substantial sum of £500 in his will. More sinisterly, it was found that soon after Jack Hullett's death, Dr Adams had gone to an Eastbourne chemist shop and purchased a 10 cc hypodermic morphine solution, in the dead man's name. There was five grains of morphine in the solution, and it was surmised that Dr Adams was 'covering his tracks', by officially accounting for morphine he'd given Jack Hullett from his own personal stock of morphine.

Jack's wife Gertrude, known as 'Bobby', took her husband's death hard and became depressed, and told Dr Adams that she had suicidal thoughts. He prescribed her medication of sodium phenobarbitone, commonly used for treating epilepsy, and sodium barbitone, a hypnotic drug used to aid sleep until the mid–1950s.

Then on 17 July, Bobby Hullett gave Dr Adams a cheque for £1,000, added to the £500 that Adams was receiving from her husband in his will, as Jack Hullett had apparently promised to buy Dr Adams an MG sports car before his death – although Percy Hoskins would later point out that there was nothing sinister about this, and that Bobby Hullett had even instructed a friend in a letter to give Dr Adams the £1,000 from 'Jack's money' if she died, and she was of course then in a suicidal state of mind. The letter hadn't been posted, as Bobby had given the doctor a cheque herself. But in the light of coming events, details such as the fact that Dr Adams asked his bank for the cheque to be expressly cleared the day after he deposited it, as it wasn't due to clear until 21 July seemed inexplicable. This made this incident more potentially worrying to the police, and was seized on by the newspapers the *Daily Sketch* for example running 'Was the £1,000 Widow Murdered?'

On 20 July, Bobby Hullett was found in a coma, having taken an overdose. After examination by another doctor, Dr Harris, Dr Adams had taken over Bobby Hullett's care, consulting a hospital doctor as how to deal with barbiturate poisoning, but not adhering to that doctor's recommendations. Bobby Hullett died in the early morning of 23 July 1956. It later transpired that Dr Adams had called a coroner to organise a private post mortem *before* she had died.

Dr Bodkin Adams was one of the wealthiest 'general practitioner' (GP) or family doctors in the country, with some celebrity residents of East Sussex on his books, and this also obviously made the local police suspicious. Over the following months, investigations by Eastbourne police and Scotland Yard would reveal that Dr John Bodkin Adams had been made bequeaths in 132 patient wills, although Percy Hoskins later maintained that Adams had received just fourteen bequests between 1944 and 1955. In the decade to 1956, many of his patients had died 'in suspicious circumstances', and the eminent Home Office pathologist Dr Francis Camps came to believe that Adams had murdered 163 patients, after reviewing 310 deaths.

Things didn't look good for the bald, rotund and bespectacled, avuncular-looking 57-year-old doctor. Dr John Bodkin Adams was born in County Antrim, (now Northern) Ireland on 21 January 1899. Much like the mainly financially motivated Acid Bath serial killer John George Haigh, Adams was brought up in an extremely conservative, God-fearing and socially repressive Plymouth Brethren family, the son of a preacher and watchmaker, who died when John was 15. John's younger brother William perished in the 1918 Flu epidemic.

After school in Coleraine, John studied medicine at Queen's University, Belfast. He became ill with tuberculosis during his time there, and graduated in 1921, without achieving honours with his degree. He went to work as an assistant doctor at Bristol Royal Infirmary, but he was found to be unsuited to this role, so a year later, on a surgeon's advice, he became a GP, and moved to a practice in Eastbourne in 1922. He began to build up patients, and was known to have a good 'bedside manner', but would also become known as somebody who was very happy to accept free hospitality and gifts, gaining a reputation as something of a scrounger. In 1929, Dr Adams borrowed the very large sum of £2,000 from a patient in order to buy an eighteen-room detached house in Eastbourne. The patient's widow had a low opinion of Adams.

In 1937, Dr Adams even made the pages of the *Daily Express*, when he gave evidence about the suicide of a Professor of Oriental Studies, who had set fire to himself while mentally unstable, ironic as he would be so closely linked to Percy Hoskins of that paper later. But in 1935, there was a report discovered about a disputed will left by a patient, in which Dr Adams had been left the enormous sum of £3,000. This was discovered by the Press Association and Exchange Telegraph Co news agencies in the summer of 1956, and they sent out newsflashes for the Murder Gang and regional newspaper reporters to use. It was the start of the media frenzy over Dr Adams.

The Murder Gang were on to the case the second that Scotland Yard was called to Eastbourne. On 17 August 1956, the Yard's Detective Superintendent Herbert Hannam was sent to Eastbourne to take over the case from the Eastbourne police, and Hannam was assisted by Detective Sergeant Charles Hewett. Percy Hoskins would later tell the journalist Trevor Lancaster that he didn't trust Hannam, and that he'd had 'previous experience of him'. It was now a national, rather than a provincial story, but Dr Adams had yet to be charged with anything, or even arrested.

In his 1984 memoir about the case of Dr Adams, *Two Men Were Acquitted*, Percy Hoskins wrote about the press coverage which was about to unfold that summer and during the trial in 1957, and the resulting negative public opinion of Dr Adams. 'In my many years as a crime reporter I had seldom seen a man so neatly trussed up and ready for the scaffold as Dr John Bodkin Adams. And this was even before he had been accused of murder.'

But Hoskins is particularly if indirectly scathing about the coverage done by the *Daily Mail*, then the Murder Gang domain of Arthur Tietjen and Rodney Hallworth, although Hoskins didn't name the reporters of course, and he didn't have to – he cleverly quoted the future Labour Party leader Michael Foot, then editor of the socialist newspaper *Tribune*, who had written an editorial about the Dr Adams case. Foot had previously been the editor of the *Evening Standard* at the very young age of 28 in 1945, when he also became an MP and remained so until 1955, then returning to Parliament in 1960. So in 1956–57, Foot was solely editor of *Tribune*. Foot wrote on 31 August 1956:

One of the most appalling and shameful examples of newspaper sensationalism and persecution in the history of British journalism has occurred in the past ten days. The result has been that a man charged with no crime and against whom no evidence is available to base any charge, has been made the victim of the wildest gossip and rumour. The worst offender in this ugly competition is the *Daily Mail*. On Wednesday August 22, that newspaper printed across seven columns the following headline: 'YARD PROBE MASS POISONING – 25 DEATHS IN THE GREAT MYSTERY OF EASTBOURNE.' Then came the further headline: 'ENQUIRY INTO 400 WILLS: RICH WOMEN BELIEVED TO HAVE BEEN THE VICTIMS.'

Although Hoskins was retired from frontline journalism by the time he quoted the above in his book, there was probably also an element of long-hewn professional rivalry here, as the *Daily Mail* had been the *Daily Express*'s, and therefore with regard to crime coverage Percy Hoskins's chief rival in terms of place in the market and tone – both Rothermere and Beaverbrook, owners of those two papers, had taken Prime Minister Neville Chamberlain's 'appeasement of Hitler' line in the late 1930s, for instance. In the bitter circulation wars, there was no love lost between the *Express* and the *Mail*, so including Michael Foot attacking the *Daily Mail* would have suited Hoskins very well.

Tietjen and Hallworth at the *Daily Mail* did go in strongly and sensationally on the Dr Adams case, however. It would report details of the inquest into the death of Gertrude 'Bobby' Hullett, under the headline 'Coroner Talks of Careless Treatment. Doctor tells of £1,000 Cheque'. In fact, as Hoskins later pointed out, the inquest verdict on Bobby Hullett was one of suicide, but this conclusion was unreported. The *Daily Express*'s first piece on the case, without a byline, was published on Wednesday 22 August 1956, the day that most national papers entered the fray, headlined 'Drugs Killed Wealthy Widow – Murder Squad Chief Hears the Verdict: Suicide'. So Hoskins's paper was taking a balanced and fair stance, and that meant Hoskins himself, as he was instrumental in working with Morley Richards and higher-ups in directing the crime coverage on the *Daily Express*, even if he didn't write every story himself.

But Hoskins, writing almost thirty years after those events in Eastbourne, was in no doubt that the newspapers had done Dr Adams damage. 'Many newspapers continued to screw the last ounce of sensation from "The Great Eastbourne Mystery", supporting it with lurid tales of samples of earth being taken in cemeteries.' The *Daily Mail* had in fact even reported that Dr Adams, unnamed but referred to as 'the murderer', may have used 'a sinister system of auto-suggestion. Actual hypnosis cannot be ruled out.' There was no evidence of this at all, and of course readers knew that 'the murderer' meant Dr Adams.

Hoskins also commented on the reaction of the police and his own paper to the rush for headlines on the case, and how he steered the *Daily Express* away from sensationalism. 'I had good reason to know that the newspaper stories were causing agitated concern among the most senior officers at Scotland Yard. Equal concern was being expressed among the senior executives of my paper, the *Daily Express*, which on my advice was treading warily. They had agreed, somewhat reluctantly, to adopt a low key while all the rivals were playing a double fortissimo.'

In actual fact, Percy Hoskins had got to know Dr John Bodkin Adams from the beginning. Hoskins himself recalled, 'I first met him in a first class compartment of the 8.30am train from Eastbourne to London on 24 August 1956.' That was two days after the Murder Gang were first reporting on the case in force. But it hadn't been a meeting engineered by Hoskins himself, or a lucky one. Hoskins had been in Eastbourne to help Scotland Yard cool down the media whirlwind and consequent gossip about Dr Adams and alleged murders of his patients. After all, he'd still yet to be arrested.

As part of his 'tread warily' approach to the story on the *Daily Express*, Hoskins had published a piece headlined 'The Truth About Eastbourne', which managed to clarify and debunk some of the wilder claims and gossip flying around in the media and now the streets, particularly in usually quiet Eastbourne. That day, 23 August, Hoskins was summoned to Scotland Yard from 55 Park Lane soon after the paper hit the stands.

Sir Richard Jackson, now an Assistant Commissioner, and whom Hoskins knew well having accompanied him to many international Interpol meetings, wanted to see him, and he was taken through to Jackson by Commander George Hatherill, Head of the CID, another friend. Hoskins being the President of the Crime Reporters Association and his long-forged high-level police contacts, particularly strengthened by his close police–media relations work with the former Metropolitan Police Commissioner Sir Harold Scott, gave him instant access to the inner sanctum. But Sir Richard Jackson needed help.

The Chief Constable of Eastbourne, Richard Walker, was concerned about the press handling of the case, and had asked Scotland Yard for guidance, and after that morning's piece by Hoskins, he was seen as the man to do the job. Hoskins was taken back to his flat to get a bag and a change of clothes, and was on a train straight to Eastbourne, and met at the station there by the Chief Constable's personal car. Hoskins advised Walker to hold an immediate press conference that evening, in which the police should give little away and not fuel the fire – it was a dampening-down damage limitation media exercise, not to give the Murder Gang reporters on the story any fuel to ignite the hot story any further.

The conference duly took place and the Murder Gang got little to report, with Det. Supt Hannam denying the newspaper speculation, and not giving any indication as to where the police investigation was going next. The next morning, Hoskins took the train to London with Dr Adams, who was obviously thankful for Hoskins helping to calm down the press, and for giving him advice on that train journey, even if he didn't realise the true seriousness of his position at that time.

Dr Adams later recalled that train journey with Hoskins: 'I went up to London on the 8.30 train with Mr Hoskins of the *Daily Express*. He warned me that if such adverse publicity continued in the same vein it could endanger my liberty. Perhaps even my life. I must admit now that, at the time, I did not take the warning as seriously as I ought to have done.'

Coverage did quieten down for a time after Hoskins's intervention, but Det. Supt Hannam and Det. Sgt Hewlett had been very busy. Hannam spoke to Dr Adams unofficially, which would be a point of controversy later, Dr Adams's large house was searched, and the police case against him was hardening. On 26 November, the progress of the investigation was finally on the front page of the *Daily Express*.

5 Women are Named in Charges Against Eastbourne Doctor
Daily Express, Monday 26 November 1956

On 28 November, two Labour MPs, Stephen Swingler and Hugh Delargy, tabled two questions to ask the Attorney General, Sir Reginald Manningham-Buller, regarding reports he had apparently sent to the General Medical Council (GMC) about the Dr Adams case, but the Attorney-General denied this, saying that he had only spoken to an officer of the GMC. Then the Attorney-General realised that there had been a leak, and an investigation later found that Det. Supt Hannam had told Rodney Hallworth of the *Daily Mail* about the communications between the Attorney-General and the GMC regarding the case. Hallworth was then something of a star on the *Daily Mail*, along with Tietjen, and would incredibly later move to the *Daily Express*, where he would work in the looming shadow of Percy

Hoskins. Hallworth co-authored a book about the Dr Adams case, which came out in 1983, the year before Hoskins's own.

The case against Dr Adams was building, and on 19 December 1956, he was finally arrested at home in Eastbourne, where he also had his surgery. Dr Adams apparently responded by saying, 'Murder ... Murder ... can you prove it was murder? I didn't think you could prove it was murder. She was dying at any event.' He reportedly also squeezed the hand of his receptionist, and told her, 'I will see you in Heaven.'

It would later be revealed that Gertrude 'Bobby' Hullett had left Dr Adams her Rolls-Royce, worth around £3,000, in her will. Dr Adams had sold it just days before his arrest. But this of course didn't prove that he was a murderer, and Percy Hoskins had already decided that the doctor was no killer.

In a 2016 interview with Thomas Lean, the former journalist Peter Vey, who would go on to work in the oil business, spoke about his start in journalism on the *Surrey Herald* just outside London, before moving in the early 1950s to the *Sunday Express*, the sister paper of the *Daily Express*, both papers, along with the *Evening Standard*, sharing offices in Fleet Street, the heart of Lord Beaverbrook's empire. But Vey luckily had an influential journalist in the family – his uncle Stanley Bishop, a veteran of Fleet Street crime reporting since 1903 – by the time he retired in 1959, Bishop had been working in Fleet Street for fifty-six years.

Stanley Bishop was certainly the longest-serving crime reporter still working in the mid-1950s, and Bishop had worked on many papers, most significantly on the *Daily Herald* (which would become *The Sun* in 1964), the *News Chronicle* (which would be swallowed up by the politically converse *Daily Mail* in October 1960) and the *Daily Express*, on the latter paper working closely under Lord Beaverbrook, and indeed with Percy Hoskins. When Bishop retired, Hoskins became the longest-serving Murder Gang reporter, although in terms of influence, contacts and reach, including being President of the Crime Reporters' Association, he had been the unspoken leader of the Murder Gang for some time.

But Stanley Bishop was hugely respected – he had been reporting crime long before the Murder Gang came into being, knew the old ways of the 'leg man', and had worked at a time when police co-operation with hacks was minimal, and began his career when Victorian values were still very much in force. Proof of his legendary status as an elder statesman of Fleet Street can be understood by the fact that he had been made a Member of the British Empire (MBE) for his services to journalism, and being surprised by the television host Eamonn Andrews outside the BBC Television Theatre on 14 December 1959, where Bishop was the subject of the very popular TV programme *This Is Your Life*.

Bishop was baited to come to the studio by the staging of a pretend robbery, explaining the programme's title 'How Much Have They Got?' Interestingly two of the guests talking about Bishop's life and career were two leading Scotland Yard murder and serious crime detectives, Jack 'Charlie Artful' Capstick and the Flying Squad's Jack Frost, along with Lord (Herbert) Morrison of Lambeth, the leading Labour politician, who had been one of 'the Big Five' of Clement Attlee's radical 1945–51 government. Back in the early 1950s, Stanley Bishop had offered to help his nephew Peter Vey get a reporting job on the *Daily Herald*, but Vey had his heart set on the *Sunday Express*, applied to that paper himself, and after a trial period was offered a job, soon earning a salary of £1,000 a year in the early 1950s, a sizeable amount, when it's considered that the average UK salary in 1950 was £100 a year, but then in the decade 1945–55, over 70% of the British workforce worked in manual labour.

Vey remembered the black marble *Express* building, being shown his desk, the veteran journalists 'educating' him about expenses, the good spirits in the office and not much overt competitiveness – although of course they were working for the same paper. He recalled going for drinks on Friday evenings, the *Express* pub being The Bell nearby. Vey also stressed how important public telephones were for phoning in stories, and the way that the 'Sundays' had to reheat stories used by other papers earlier in the week, making them seem fresh.

Crime stories required greater attention than other news, due to legal restrictions under British law, overseas crime being easier to cover in this respect. Vey reported on crime amongst other stories, including the Ruth Ellis case, revealing that he agreed with her execution at the time. Vey visited crime scenes, like all crime reporters, and said he tried to write about crime in a 'straightforward fashion'. There were the long hours every Saturday – huge deliveries of print rolls, typesetting, proofreading, and finally getting the Sunday edition to press, yelling across the newsroom all the while.

Like the *Daily Express*, the *Sunday Express* was conservative in outlook under Beaverbrook, and Vey spoke about the Beaver once hiring a socialist Labour-supporting journalist purely to force him to write Conservative-supporting articles, and he confirmed that the Beaver took such a close interest in his papers as a way to increase his political influence. Vey also mentioned a juicy tale about how the *Sunday Express* had attempted to pay the IRA for information, and that he had to prepare an envelope to make it 'appear' it was stuffed with money, the 'drop' happening in a branch of WHSmith newsagents in Edgware, north London, with Vey observing from a flat opposite, but that the information left for him did not prove very important.

This was the environment in which Percy Hoskins was working on the *Daily Express* in the mid-1950s, and if anything, the Beaver was more involved in supervising the *Daily* than the *Sunday* paper. The case of Dr John Bodkin Adams would take all of Hoskins's influence with Beaverbrook, who was a very formidable man, and the unpopular stance that Hoskins was about to take, supporting Dr Adams, would prove to be a major test of their friendship.

The Suez Crisis had been all over the news for months, since October 1956, when Percy Hoskins had to go into battle to support his belief that Dr John Bodkin Adams was innocent of murder. As Hoskins later wrote, 'I didn't believe he was a murderer. I was in a very small minority.' The story was on front pages as the committal hearing started in mid-January 1957.

Dr Adams: Man and Wife Named
Daily Express, Wednesday 15 January 1957

At the end of that hearing, which went on for days due to the complexity of the evidence, Dr Adams was committed for trial at the Old Bailey. This would be a charge of murder for the death of Dr Adams's patient Edith Alice Morrell, a wealthy widow who'd had a stroke and died under his care in November 1948, aged 81, leaving him a Rolls Royce and some antique furniture. There was the possibility that a further trial could be held, the charge being the murder of Gertrude 'Bobby' Hullett.

The trial of Dr John Bodkin Adams was delayed, as a key exhibit – the £1,000 cheque made out to Adams by Bobby Hullett had been 'mislaid', and couldn't be found anywhere. Although Adams wasn't facing the court for her murder, her case was part of the prosecution's massive collateral evidence against him. The trial finally began on Monday 18 March 1957 before Mr Justice Devlin at the Old Bailey.

The *Daily Express* coverage of the trial would be extensive, and unusually for Percy Hoskins, he shared joint byline with two other reporters – first Arthur Chesworth, who later became the paper's Beirut correspondent, and then Arnold Latcham, who was the *Daily Express*'s Old Bailey court correspondent, who later reported closely on 1963's Great Train Robbery along with his *Express* colleague Ian Buchan. Latcham died in November 2000.

Whether Hoskins was just being magnanimous in sharing the limelight for a change, or he felt uneasy taking his seemingly neutral stance on Dr Adams alone, compared to the more sensationalist 'Dr Death' angle taken by other Murder Gang reporters on rival papers, is unclear today. But what is known is that Hoskins had never shared bylines before, in the many years since he had been afforded them, and Hoskins by all accounts loved to get full credit for his work.

The trial would last seventeen days, the longest murder trial in British history until that time, later surpassed in 1969 by the gangland murders trial of the Kray Twins and their 'Firm'. Hoskins was with Dr Adams in court every day, and the two certainly passed glances each other's way. It was a fraught time for Hoskins – he had managed to persuade Lord Beaverbrook, and therefore his editor Arthur Christiansen and news editor Morley Richards, all close friends, to hold fire, report the facts, and go easy on Adams.

Although Beaverbrook certainly did not believe in Dr Adams's innocence, and it shows just how much influence Hoskins had that the irrepressible and forceful Beaver was prepared to take Hoskins's lead. But it was a huge risk for Hoskins, the fixer, the man to go to for advice and guidance, the wise man of the Murder Gang. If Adams was convicted, Percy Hoskins would have egg proverbially splattered over his expensive double-breasted suit, let alone his trilby.

But Hoskins's expensive pinstripe was to be saved – on Tuesday 9 April 1957, the jury retired and returned less than forty-five minutes later with a verdict of Not Guilty. There just wasn't enough hard proof of murder to convict beyond a reasonable doubt, but a mountain of circumstantial evidence and suspicion. Of course it took the front pages, and several *Express* reporters spent that evening getting Adams's story from him, it would run all the following week too.

Dr Adams Goes Free – The Daily Express publishes his Picture Diaries – p.6
Why the Daily Express has his own record of what happened
Warning: This serial contains no phoney emotion, no second-hand rhetoric. It is as plain as a piece of evidence …
Daily Express, Wednesday 10 April 1957

Inside that day's paper, there was a signed statement by Dr Adams, 'I feel I owe my rescue from the shadow of the gallows to three men', then thanking Percy Hoskins 'for his courageous stand against what must be the biggest witch-hunt in history', followed by his barrister and his solicitor. In his later book about the case, Hoskins recalled the reaction of the rest of the Murder Gang. 'The *Daily Express* offices were besieged by its Fleet Street rivals. A *Daily Mail* reporter infiltrated the front hall and was detected going up the stairs. The crime reporter of the *Evening Standard*, sister Beaverbrook paper, managed to make it right to the door of the room on the second floor. He was spotted by Richards, who physically closed on him, bellowing with rage, and threatened to throw him downstairs.' The *Evening Standard* reporter was most probably Victor Toddington, and the man who stopped him was of course the *Daily Express*'s news editor, Morley Richards.

The paper was now making the most of the risk it had taken. Hoskins and Dr Adams also went off, by Jaguar, to a flat on the coast in Westgate-on-Sea, where Hoskins would ghost-write Adams's life story over three weeks, Hoskins having the copy driven back to London. Hoskins himself later wrote that 'Naturally, the *Express* squeezed every ounce out of the Doctor's "ghosted" autobiography. And such had been the nature and length of the publicity concerning him that it made compulsive reading.' Dr Adams was paid £10,000 for his story, but he never spent it, although his wealth meant he had little need to use it. On his death in 1983, the cash was found untouched in a bank vault, still in the original envelope.

There would later be claims that there had been political interference in the trial – coming from the Lord Chief Justice Rayner Goddard, the man who had passed sentence of death on Derek Bentley and failed to recommend a reprieve to the Home Secretary back in 1953. Goddard had appointed Mr Justice Devlin as the trial judge, and there have been allegations that Goddard pulled Devlin's strings during the trial, the inference being that Goddard was guiding Devlin to treat Dr Adams favourably.

After the trial, both *Newsweek* magazine and the newsagents WHSmith would be sued for contempt of court for publishing and selling to the public respectively the issue of 1 April 1957, which contained an article entitled 'The Doctor on Trial' that included a list of alleged bequests made to Dr Adams. The writ had been brought by the Attorney-General Sir Reginald Manningham-Buller QC, known in legal circles as 'Bullying-Manner'. Both magazine and newsagent were ordered to pay £50, and share the taxed costs. Dr Adams himself would reportedly successfully sue several newspapers for libel too after his acquittal.

Most of the Murder Gang was shocked: almost everyone thought that Adams would hang. Hoskins was relieved – the journalist Trevor Lancaster later remembered that he'd seen Hoskins out drinking in Fleet Street the night before, having 'a full-scale night out' looking despondent – 'The only time I ever saw him lose his poise, his carefree ruminating manner.' Hoskins was hugely relieved after the acquittal, but Dr Adams was of course thanking God, instilled in him since his Plymouth Brethren childhood.

Dr Adams wouldn't face a second murder trial over the death of Bobby Hullett, due to an abuse of process committed by the prosecution, according to Mr Justice Devlin, and this would lead to questions being asked in Parliament. But Dr Adams was later convicted of thirteen counts of fraud – related to prescriptions and cremation forms, as well as not maintaining a dangerous drugs register and obstructing a police search. He was struck off the Medical Register, but eventually reinstated in 1961, having made two previous unsuccesful applications. He continued to practice in Eastbourne, living in the big house he'd bought in 1929. On his death, Dr Adams left Percy Hoskins £1,000 in his will.

The pressure on Percy Hoskins from Beaverbrook over the case can best be understood by the telephone call that the Beaver made to him on the day of the acquittal. Beaverbrook said, 'Two men have been acquitted today. Adams and Hoskins.'

At 1.15 p.m. on Wednesday 1 May 1957, a special 'subscription lunch' was held in honour of Percy Hoskins by Beaverbrook Newspapers Ltd at the Martinez Restaurant in Swallow Street, just off of the Regent Street end of Piccadilly. It was a Spanish restaurant and General Franco and King Alfonso of Spain had both eaten there. The ten shilling a head subscription for the lunch was to cover 'an unostentatious piece of plate for Mr Hoskins, suitably inscribed to commemorate the Adams case'. One subscriber was the famed *Daily Express* cartoonist Carl Giles, who wrote in reply to the invitation: 'I gladly subscribe towards the "unostentatious piece of plate" and wish to state that anybody responsible for publishing one single word about Dr Adams should be buried in Westminster Abbey.'

The case only cemented Hoskins's reputation further, making him *the* go-to crime man, hugely respected, and no doubt inspiring jealousy in some. But as Michael Foot MP said years later, 'Percy Hoskins was an independent force on the *Daily Express* throughout its most splendid days, when all other journalists would bow before the authority of the real editor in charge, night and day, Lord Beaverbrook.'

In the foreword for Hoskins's memoir of the case, Dr Adams himself wrote, 'I owe a great debt of gratitude to the author for helping to stem the witch-hunt which put me in dire peril, and for his efforts to ensure that I obtained a fair and unprejudiced trial.'

As well as his various journalist and lecturing activities, Hoskins had started the charitable Saints and Sinners' Club in 1947, with the impresario Jack Hylton, and this would contribute to him becoming a Commander of the British Empire (CBE) in 1976. The journalist Victor Davis later remembered that Hoskins's powers were declining in the 1960s, and recalled an occasion when Hoskins stole his byline. But Hoskins would stay on the *Daily Express* until the late 1970s, and then become the paper's 'Crime Consultant'.

But he still kept his hand in. In 1982, his police contacts helped the *Daily Express* and his colleagues Norman Luck and John Warden get the scoop on Michael Fagin, who broke into Buckingham Palace and sat on the Queen's bed, chatting to her. When Hoskins died in February 1989, aged 84, there was a memorial service for him at St. Bride's Church in Fleet Street on 29 March, at which a trumpet fanfare was performed by the Metropolitan Police band and Michael Foot gave the address.

But had Percy Hoskins got it right? Or was Dr John Bodkin Adams really a serial killer?

10

FOOTSTEPS OF A GUNMAN

SOUTH KENSINGTON, LONDON, 3 JULY 1959

It was an affluent area, yet with a feel of excitement. In Rowland Gardens, an American model, Mrs Verne Schiffman, aged 30, was on holiday and staying in a flat. It was 3 July, and while she was out, a man broke in and stole her furs and jewellery, which had a very substantial value, assessed at about £2,000. When Mrs Schiffman returned, she immediately reported the burglary, and that's all it seemed to be.

But four days later on 7 July, Mrs Schiffman received a letter demanding £500, in return for some compromising photographs and tape recordings of her which the writer claimed to have in his possession. Mrs Schiffman knew that no such photos or recordings existed, and so called the police again to report this blackmailing attempt. Five days later, on 12 July, Mrs Schiffman had a telephone call from a Mr Fisher, who had a foreign accent and said that he was a representative of a Mr Levine, and wanted to know if the model was going to pay up for the photos.

On being informed about this, the police arranged with the Post Office to have Mrs Schiffman's telephone tapped, and to immediately tell them if the man called again. They didn't have long to wait, as the very next day just before 3 p.m. a call came through to Chelsea Police Station, a Post Office engineer telling Detective Sergeant Raymond

Purdy that the man was on the phone again, and that he was calling from a public phone in the covered alcove outside South Kensington Underground Station. Det. Sgt Purdy told his colleague Det. Sergeant John Sandford about the situation, and they both rushed to their police car, speeding off towards the tube station before the man could get away.

The man was just leaving as they arrived, and Det. Sgt Purdy calmly introduced himself as he arrested a dark-haired young man with a sallow complexion, causing no commotion at all. The policemen led the man out into the street, but he broke free and ran from them. They pursued him on foot, finally catching him in Roman-pillared Onslow Square. They pulled the man into a block of flats in the square, and placed the man on a large windowsill. The policemen quickly conferred and as the man was so desperate to escape, decided that it would be best to call for another police car to pick them up. Det. Sergeant Sandford went to locate the porter of the block to use a phone, while Det. Sergeant Purdy stayed with the man, who was sitting on the windowsill.

Det. Sergeant Purdy, aged 43, was an experienced police officer with eighteen years of service, and he asked the man to turn out his pockets. The man handed Purdy a notebook, which the policeman placed in his own jacket pocket. Then, before he knew what had happened, the man pulled a semi-automatic pistol from his pocket and fired, shooting Det. Sergeant Raymond Purdy, through the heart. The man then fled again, and Purdy died just minutes later.

Backup was on the scene quickly, and soon Onslow Square was flooded with uniformed policemen and plainclothes CID detectives. It was a cop-killing, and the hunt was on. The newspapers were already on the case, and it was all across the front page the very next day.

17,000 Men Search…Watch at Sea and Airport – Killer Guard at London Model's Flat
Yard Order Goes Out – 'Find Mr J'
Evening News, Tuesday 14 July 1959

The man that the police were searching for, known as 'Mr J' was described as being French-Canadian, aged about 30, and he'd arrived from Montreal about three months earlier. Purdy and Sandford had barely had a chance to speak to the man, but the notebook which the man had given to Purdy was found in the dead policeman's pocket. When his belongings were given to his widow Irene, she noticed that the small notebook didn't belong to her husband, and detectives were soon calling around the phone numbers it contained, and that was how they had this information so quickly, although this wasn't reported yet. There was a photograph of the slain Det. Sergeant Purdy with Irene on that front page, along with the news that Scotland Yard had 'radioed' the Royal Canadian Mounted Police (the Mounties) for more information about the killer.

MOUNTIES SEND KILLER CLUE TO THE YARD – Police Swoop on Liner – London's Underworld Help the Great Manhunt
Evening News, Wednesday 15 July 1959

The case also took the front page again on the next day.

The Mounties had wired information about the man from Ottawa, but no more details were being published yet, apart from the fact that the murder hunt was being led by Det. Superintendent David Hislop, and to report that 'MP's Ask About Police Killers', referring to Sir Jocelyn Lucas, the Conservative MP for Portsmouth South, who was tabled to quiz the Home Secretary, R.A. (Richard Austen, also known as 'Rab') Butler, in the House of Commons.

The crime coverage on the *Evening News* – 'World's Largest Evening Sale' – was being directed by its news editor, Sam Jackett, very much a member of the Murder Gang. Jackett was born in 1910 and started out in journalism in the mid-1930s, working for the Reuters news agency from 1936, marrying Onah in Hendon, Middlesex, in April 1937, before his journalism career was interrupted by the Second World War, for most of which he was stationed in India. After the war, he left Reuters for the *Evening News* of London in 1954, working as a Murder Gang reporter and soon becoming Chief Reporter by 1958, then rising to become news editor in 1959 taking over from Frank Starr, who became assistant editor under acting editor C.R.Willis. Working on an evening paper obviously required quick, reactive filing of stories for that evening's edition, and crime was of course a mainstay of the front and first few pages. Jackett was a very hands-on news editor, and his 'fingerprints' are all over the *Evening News* in this period. Jackett would stay on the paper until 1964.

Jackett divorced and married twice more, in 1949 and 1957. In 1958, Jackett contributed a 'short story' to *Late Extra: A Miscellany by Evening News Writers, Artists & Photographers*, published by the paper's powerful parent company Associated Newspapers. Entitled 'Crime on the Telephone', it was based on a real crime story Jackett had covered back in 1948. It opens, 'When my telephone rings it means – almost invariably – crime, all types of crime. It may be the first news of a murder, an armed hold-up, or a smash-and-grab raid at a West End jewellers', that someone has just seen.' Jackett was especially known for his fast and impressive gathering of crime leads and sources, invaluable on an evening paper such as the *Evening News*, the chief rival of which was the *Evening Standard*, and Victor Toddington's Murder Gang coverage. Jackett's quick news reflex had been honed to perfection at Reuters, and a news agency requires similar quick turnaround and treacherous deadline-chasing as an evening paper.

In his 2004 book *Press Gang: How Newspapers Make Profits from Propaganda*, the seasoned journalist, former newspaper editor and media lecturer and expert Roy Greenslade wrote about the methods used on the *Evening News* to cover crime: 'Topmost of all on the agenda was crime ... Reporters cultivated contacts with the police and also depended on contacts who listened in to police radios ... On at least one occasion, Sam Jackett arrived at a murder scene before the police.' But Jackett was also a great admirer, and like Percy Hoskins and Arthur Tietjen, professional cultivator of the police. In his 1965 book *Heroes of Scotland Yard*, Jackett expressed his feelings about the police, relationships between the police and journalists and the importance of Scotland Yard's Press Bureau, with its entrance of double green doors, and its press officers:

Relations, and co-operation between the Press and the Metropolitan Police, have always in my years of experience, been of a very high order. Each has a healthy respect for the other, and there is a constant flow of information and advice … Officially Metropolitan Police officers are not permitted to impart news directly to a newspaper man – hence the Bureau whose officers give background advice, and do their best to answer questions from the Pressmen who are in direct contact with their newspapers from that office.

Jackett worked out of the *Evening News*'s offices at Carmelite House, and his telephone number for crime tips was Central 6000. On 16 July 1959, Jackett directed the front page of 'Evidence is Taken Off a Plane at London Airport…THE PICTURE HERE'. Photographs of the man who had shot dead Det. Sergeant Raymond Purdy had been flown to Heathrow by the Mounties and picked up from the runway tarmac by Scotland Yard detectives, in that age long before email or fax machines.

The hunt was still very much on for the cop-killer, but that same day, the police got the tip they needed from Mr Paul Carnay, manager of the Claremont House Hotel in Queen's Gate, Kensington, who said that a man had been hiding out in one of his rooms. Detectives and uniformed officers rushed straight down to the hotel and assembled outside of Room 15, and then a burly officer named Det. Sergeant Chambers ran at and smashed open the door. The man inside, obviously listening close to the door, was struck by the impact of the handle and injured, giving him a pronounced black eye. Chambers then leapt on top of the man, who could still have been armed, but he was soon pinned down and handcuffed.

Photographs in the police case file show a very basic hotel room: a bed, a chest of drawers, a wardrobe, a desk and chair in front of a window, an armchair by the side of the period mantelpiece, and a hook on the inside of the door. Another photo shows the man being led from the hotel by four policemen, barefoot and with a blanket draped over his head. The man's name was soon found to be Gunter (sometimes spelt Guenther) Podola, aged 30, who had been born in Berlin, (then West) Germany.

PODOLA OPERATION – Police Guard Him in Ward 5b
Evening News, Friday 17 July 1959

The Home Secretary Rab Butler had personally telephoned Det. Sergeant Chambers and his colleagues who had made the arrest, the front page told readers. The next day, in an echo of post-war British anti-German xenophobia, the front page had 'Fritz – Police Wait – Podola in Hospital for at Least 24 Hours More'. In fact, Podola would remain in hospital for a total of four days.

Podola would then leave the front pages for a while, but on Wednesday 22 July the *Evening News*'s front page was taken by 'THE CRIME BOMB – Alarm over Teenage Hooligans'. The splash by Stanley Dobson was in reaction to the release of the previous year's London crime figures, as the Metropolitan Police Commissioner Sir Joseph Simpson, who would later be seen to have largely turned a blind eye to institutionalised corruption within his force, 'revealed to London his startling report for 1958'. London's 791 CID detectives had an average of 258 cases each to handle in 1958, and the crime figures were the highest ever recorded. The fear of youth violent crime was as palpable at the end of the 1950s as it had been around the Craig and Bentley case earlier in the decade, and this was much fuelled, in public perception, by the knife fights amongst 'Teddy Boys', with their DA's (duck's arse hairstyles), drainpipe trousers, Edwardian jackets and brothel-creeper and winkle-picker shoes.

Gunter Podola, who was unmarried, was born on 8 February 1929, in Tempelhof, Berlin, and a report in the police file, compiled by Det. Superintendent Hislop, states, 'He grew up in a working-class district around Alexander Square, Berlin, and on leaving school did odd jobs. He was too young to join the Army before the war ended, but was known to be a fanatic member of the Hitler Youth Movement.' Podola claimed in police custody that he was a welder by trade, but this was not verified by detectives. In 1952, he had gained an immigrant visa to Canada, and worked there until October 1956 as a labourer, farm labourer and auto mechanic, changing jobs frequently in both Quebec and Montreal.

From October 1956 he was unemployed, and he gained two convictions in Montreal, Canada: on 1 March 1957, he was sentenced to ten days in prison for 'theft by breaking' (burglary), and on 26 March 1957 he got two years for a total of eleven counts of auto-theft, breaking and entering and theft in a dwelling house. He was deported from Canada on 25 July 1958, and was back in Germany by 4 August, where he lived in Gerlingen and Stuttgart, working as an unskilled labourer. On 21 May 1959, Podola flew from Dusseldorf to London. The police file notes, 'Since his arrival in this country he is known to have stayed in various hotels in the South Kensington area, but there is no record of his having been usefully employed.'

Podola had of course been committing burglary, but had upped the ante with attempted blackmail. Now he was a killer, and to great public revulsion, a cop-killer. The fact that Podola had been using pseudonyms since arriving in London perhaps shows his mind-set of 'wannabe gangster', and as well as the 'Mr Fisher' identity he invented for the blackmail attempt on Mrs Schiffman, he was also using the name 'Mike Colato', an alias which could have been pulled straight from the pages of the then very popular American pulp crime novels, featuring hoodlums, molls, police chases, (sometimes sadistic) sex, assault and murder, the lurid content of which the crime historian Donald Thomas has documented. Podola's own life had come to mirror those steamy and violent escapist pages, although there was no record of him having a girlfriend in London.

Podola was deemed to be shaken up and exhausted in his bed at St Stephen's Hospital, and his state – especially his claim and that of his defence team that he had been beaten up by the police, meant that there had to be a medical examination, which would lead to a preliminary nine-day trial at the Old Bailey, delaying the murder trial, the purpose of which was purely to hear contrasting medical opinion as to Podola's fitness to stand trial. Podola claimed that he had amnesia, and that he had no memory of shooting Det. Sergeant Raymond Purdy, so therefore wouldn't be able to enter a plea.

It was 'a first' in a British court for murder – amnesia as a defence. Podola said in court:

> I cannot put forward any defence. The reason for this is that I have lost my memory of all these events. I cannot remember the crime. I do not remember the circumstances leading up to the events or to this shooting. I do not know if I did it or whether it was an accident or an act of self-defence. I do not know if at that time I realised the man was in fact a detective. I do not know in fact whether I was provoked in any way. For these reasons I am unable to admit or deny the charge against me.

Medical opinion was mixed: four doctors evaluating him as suffering from amnesia, with two believing that Podola was faking amnesia. In the end, however, he was passed fit to stand trial, the jury taking three-and-a-half hours to reach this verdict. A new jury was sworn in, as the first one would no longer be objective after hearing so much about the case. Gunter Podola finally went on trial for the murder of Purdy at the Old Bailey on 24 September 1959, before Mr Justice H. Edmund Davies, defended by Mr F.H. Lawton QC and prosecuted by Mr Maxwell Turner QC. It took the jury just over thirty minutes to find Podola guilty of murder, and he was sentenced to death.

In an article entitled 'Verdict on Podola' in the 5 October 1959 issue of *Time* magazine, Podola's reaction to the death sentence was described. 'Before anyone else in the courtroom could move, Gunther Podola turned calmly away and stepped quickly and surely down the steps from the dock to the cells below. Faithful to the last to his profession of emotional shock and indifference, he showed no sign of realizing that he had just been sentenced to die on the gallows.'

But Podola would appeal.

Law Chief Talks about the Onus of Proof to – THE PODOLA FIVE
Evening News, Wednesday 14 October 1959

In the Appeal, the Podola defence team claimed that he had never been fit to plead because of amnesia, and that the defence shouldn't have had to prove this. Sir Reginald Manningham-Buller, the Attorney-General was directing 'the law lords', the High Court of Appeal judges, who had to decide if the onus of providing proof about fitness to plead was on the prosecution or defence. The Appeal would be dismissed.

In other unrelated news, the next day's *Evening News* front page would report the death of the hell-raising actor Errol Flynn. But Podola would soon be back, and this time in the *Daily Express*.

≣

On 23 October, Percy Hoskins and his colleagues on the *Daily Express* had a front-page interview with a Mr Ronald 'Ronny' Starkey, an acquaintance of Podola who had given evidence in his favour at his trial. Starkey lived in Southsea, who described a letter he had sent to Podola in Wandsworth Prison, and a letter he had received back from Podola from the condemned cell, as well as a conversation that Starkey said he'd had with Podola when he visited him in prison.

This prompted the police to immediately interview Ronald Starkey, which he was by Det. Inspector Atkins in Southsea, and the police file reveals in a report regarding concerns about the press coverage, which was unusual for Hoskins and the *Daily Express*, although the concerns were chiefly to do with Podola's different 'versions' about the murder of Det. Sergeant Raymond Purdy. These insights were of course coming from a man who had claimed under oath to have amnesia, and no memory of the fatal shooting, so any revelations could affect and reduce any slim chance of a reprieve, if Ronald Starkey was regarded as a reliable source of information. The report states:

On 23 October, when Starkey was questioned about this newspaper article (*of that same day*) he said he had nothing to add to that article, but pointed out that he had not told them (*Daily Express*) about Podola telephoning him on the night of the murder. He said he had not been paid for the article, but made it perfectly clear that he was going to be paid. Starkey claimed that he gave the story to the Daily Express reporter because he was the most efficient reporter.'

This is highly likely to have been Percy Hoskins, and also shows that Starkey had spoken to other Murder Gang reporters too.

Then Starkey received another letter from Podola, on Saturday 24 October, which appeared on the front page of the next edition of the *Daily Express* on Monday 26 October 1959, under the headline 'Podola Says I Remember', with part of the letter reproduced, the sentence which read, 'Ronny, I know now that it wasn't I who did it.' Podola had written that a man who looked like him, a criminal associate named Bob Levine, who had an American accent, had killed Det. Sergeant Purdy. The police evaluation of Ronald Starkey, his motives and his relationship with the *Daily Express* was as follows in the same report in the police file:

> It is now abundantly clear that Starkey is in the pay of at least one national newspaper and that every word spoken between him and Podola during visits to Wandsworth Prison, and every word written between them as well as photographs of parts of these letters, is appearing in the next edition of the Daily Express. Starkey has in effect become a newspaper reporter, the only one with direct communication to the condemned man. One can only expect that between now and 5 November 1959 *(the date set for Podola's execution)*, the Daily Express will keep its story of Podola going by detailing Starkey to write more letters to Podola to invite more replies from the prisoner, and to arrange further visits to Podola in Wandsworth Prison. While Starkey believes he may be helping Podola, he will do anything if it will prove to his criminal associates that he is not really a Police informer, and if he is to receive payment for this Starkey will be even happier. A man with such motives cannot be regarded as a reliable witness to truth.

But that wasn't all. Another Murder Gang reporter had been sniffing around Ronald Starkey: Ronald Mount, a colleague of Norman 'Jock' Rae on the *News of the World*. Rae was now nearing the end of his very long Fleet Street career, and his paper even ran a series called 'My Front Page Murders by Norman Rae' to celebrate his many crime scoops since Dr Buck Ruxton back in the mid-1930s, in one of which, in 1951, Rae had personally and singlehandedly got a written murder confession from a man called Herbert Mills for the strangulation murder of a woman, Mills later being hanged. Norman 'Jock' Rae himself would drop dead of a heart attack in 1962, aged sixty-five, in his bathroom at home, amphetamines reportedly scattered on the floor around him, leaving a wife and two young sons.

Ronald Maurice Mount was thirty-three years old in late 1959, and had been a crime reporter on the *News of the World* for five-and-a-half years, and lived in Gidea Park, Essex, just outside London. The same police report details the Mount-Starkey relationship too, stating that Mount had first met Ronald Starkey on the day the latter gave evidence for the defence at Podola's trial, and had then 'kept in touch with Starkey in the hope of finding a story concerning Podola'. The police had obviously interviewed Ronald Mount at length.

On 19 October 1959, Mr Mount met Starkey before he visited Podola and waited outside Wandsworth Prison while Starkey went in to make the visit...Before Starkey went into the prison he and Mr Mount drank beer together in the County Arms Public House, Trinity Road, Wandsworth, SW18, which is close to the prison entrance. In the public house Starkey told Mr Mount that the whole thing *(the shooting of Det. Sergeant Raymond Purdy)* had been an accident, and then went on to describe how Podola had telephoned him at his shop at Southsea on the night of the murder and told him what had happened.

This new claim of it having been an accident was vehemently debunked in the report.

The conclusion of the police report pulls together a new claim about Podola's memory, and two 'versions' of the shooting which Podola had allegedly made, to both Ronald Starkey, in the pay of the *Daily Express*, and the *News of the World* Murder Gang reporter Ronald Mount. Firstly, Podola now claimed to have 'partially' regained his memory, allowing him to offer an alibi: he had been breaking into a flat at 121 Chelsea Cloisters, Sloane Avenue, SW3, at the time of Purdy's murder. Secondly, Podola had said that he had 'a double', named Bob Levine who looked like him, and had been involved with him in blackmailing Mrs Schiffman, and that 'Bob' had murdered Purdy. Thirdly, Podola had stated that he had fatally shot Purdy, but that it had been an accident. The report ended with 'The contradiction of these three defences is apparent.'

In a separate memorandum, the police also referred to an anonymous letter received at Scotland Yard on 31 October 1959, postmarked 'Romford & Dagenham, Essex' the day before. In that letter, the writer claimed that he'd seen Podola on the day of the murder, and that Podola hadn't killed Purdy, but a man he knows 'who has a broad American accent and is Podola's double'. The police reaction was that it was clearly a letter written after the publication of the 26 October *Daily Express* front-page article, and that 'No importance can be attached to this letter, which is clearly based on the newspaper article.'

Then on 2 November, just three days before Podola was scheduled to be hanged, a letter was delivered personally to the Governor of Wandsworth Prison, addressed 'Dear Fritzy Boy', which had been sent from Wembley, Middlesex, the same day. The writer claimed to be Podola's double 'Bob Levine', admitting that he was Purdy's real killer, but the police noted that the writer was definitely foreign and not American, as it contained marked grammatical errors: 'When you will read this I will be OK' and 'I wish I can give up myself but can't.' The police dismissed this letter too.

46 Hours To Go … He Hears The Death-Cell News
PODOLA WILL HANG – Butler Decides – No Reprieve
Evening News, Tuesday 3 November 1959

Gunter Podola was to be only the second person hanged since the passing of the Homicide Act in 1957, which had narrowed the types of murder deemed a capital or hanging offence. Hanging offences were now murders committed using firearms or explosives, murders of police or prison officers, murder committed in the furtherance of theft, and murders committed for a second or subsequent time. The first execution since the Act had been that of Ronald Marwood, who had murdered another policeman, Police Constable Summers, outside a north London dance hall.

Extra Police Stand By...Schoolboys In The Crowd
PODOLA IS HANGED – A Lone Woman at Jail Gates
Evening News, Thursday 5 November 1959

Gunter Podola was hanged by Harry Allen at Wandsworth Prison at 8.45 a.m., a crowd of about 100 gathered outside the prison gates, including those schoolboys with their satchels. Podola was buried in the prison grounds later that day. There had been no protests or demonstration against his execution – he was the killer of a policeman, there was post-war anti-German feeling and the fact that it really was a needless murder rendered him no sympathy, apart from that woman in black at the jail gates, who placed some violets there and was never identified. So perhaps Podola did have a lady friend in London?

II

MURDER ON THE MARSHES

At about 10.30 that morning the receptionist of the *Daily Mirror* offices, Mr Frank Butcher, was seated at the reception desk in the entrance lobby when a man walked in and asked to see Mr Tom Tullett. Butcher asked the man if he had an appointment, and the man answered 'No', so Butcher asked him to complete a visitor slip. The man did so, but spelt Mr Tullett's name as 'Thurrock', and Butcher made out another slip for him. Butcher then sent the visitor up to a waiting room to meet Tom Tullett.

Tom Tullett Giving Evidence, the Witness Box, Maidstone Assizes Court, Kent,
21 November 1961
I am the Chief Crime Reporter on the *Daily Mirror* Limited. At about 10.30am on the 11 September, 1961 I went into a waiting room where I saw the Accused. I said, 'What can I do for you?' He replied, 'I want to confess to a double murder.' I said, 'Who have you killed?' and he said, 'A man and a woman, teenagers, I think.' He said it was on the marshes at Gravesend. He then produced from his overcoat pocket a lady's handbag, a man's watch, a girl's watch and a man's wallet. On the table there was a parcel wrapped in newspaper. At that point I left the room, leaving the accused with

Mr Dean, and I arranged for the police at Gravesend to be informed.
I then went back into the waiting room and the Accused then told
me a story of what had happened and I made notes, which I have
with me. Consulting these notes, he said that he had attacked two
people three hundred yards from the Dalton Isolation Hospital on
the Marshes. That he had a sawn off shotgun. He said, 'I held them
up and strangled them. This parcel contains part of their bodies.
I removed skin. The names of the people are in the handbag. They
are Malcolm Johnson, 22 Abbey Road, Gravesend, and Miss Lilian
Edmeades, of 21 Peppercroft Street, Gravesend. I took ten shillings
from each wallet. This happened between 8.30 and 9.30 last night.
I took the skin off with a knife. I toppled the bodies into a ditch.
Then I went home to my mother and my sister and my brother-in-
law. I threw the gun into a drainage ditch alongside the canal. I threw
the shotgun cartridges with it. I stayed at home but could not sleep.
My mother saw I was worried. I went to work taking the parcel and
the handbag with me. I couldn't work so I knocked off and came up
here. I have had the idea of murder for some time and I have walked
round thinking about it. I have had the gun for about four years now.
Last night I walked round and I saw this young couple making up
the canal path. I told them to stop and keep quiet. I told them to lay
face down on the path and put their hands behind their backs and
I tied their wrists up with strong twine. Then I made them stand up
and walk along the canal path. We cut across the marshes under the
sea wall. I made them lay face down and tied their ankles to their
wrists…' At this point Inspector Lloyd of the City Police arrived and
I handed over to him.

When that parcel wrapped in newspaper was unwrapped by Det.
Inspector Cliff Lloyd, it contained a pair of female breasts. The visitor
who had confessed to double murder and brought in that parcel
slumped back in the chair in which he was sitting, asking for a glass
of water. It was a shocking and unprecedented event, even for the
Murder Gang.

When Tom Tullett walked into that waiting room, Room 392 of the *Daily Mirror* offices, that early September morning with his colleague Hugh Saker, he only knew that the man who wanted to see him was called Edwin Sims, that he came from Gravesend, Kent, and that he had assessed his business as 'Confidential'. Tullett had read that on the visitor slip. When he walked in, he saw a well-built man of average height wearing horn-rimmed glasses, sitting in the red armchair. The most noticeable thing about him was that his shirt was open at the front, and he had a large tattoo of an eagle flying on his chest.

Tom Tullett was not a man who was easily shocked. He was unique in the Murder Gang in that he'd been a policeman before becoming a journalist, having been a CID detective at Scotland Yard. Being 'ex-job', Tullett's police contacts were impeccable, and his knowledge of crime, especially the London underworld, was consequently also very strong, all great assets to a Murder Gang reporter.

A good example of Tullett's understanding of who-was-who in the criminal underworld is a piece he ran on page 13 of the *Daily Mirror* on 30 May 1962, the year after Edward Sims walked into the paper's offices. Headlined 'Small Boy Birching for Thug', it concerned Frank Mitchell, aged 33, who was 'birched on his backside fifteen times for making two attacks on Hull prison officers'. Mitchell was a huge man of great physical strength, with a low IQ and violently unstable. He was serving life for robbery with violence, and called himself 'the Big Shot', but he was unknown to the public then. In fact, although a low-level 'heavy' he was connected to serious players in the London underworld. Mitchell had seized a truncheon from a prison warder and hit him hard, breaking his nose, and on another occasion, Mitchell had grabbed a warder by the throat and 'slashed him on the face with a sharpened tin knife'.

Mitchell had escaped from custody in 1957, and terrorised an elderly widow with an axe in the course of robbery, which led to him being dubbed 'the Mad Axeman' in criminal and Murder Gang circles. Sent to Broadmoor Hospital for the Criminally Insane, Mitchell escaped again in 1958 for two days and with another escapee threatened and terrified an elderly couple, again in the pursuit of robbery, leading to his life sentence in 1958. Four years after Tullett wrote this article in

1966, Frank Mitchell was sprung from prison by the infamous London gangsters the Kray Twins, hidden in a flat with hired female company. But when Mitchell became restless and agitated and made threats towards the Krays, they had him shot to death in the back of a van, and his body has never been found. The whole of Britain would come to know about 'the Mad Axeman' when the Kray Twins and their 'Firm' went on trial in 1969, but Tom Tullett was watching him back in 1962.

Born Eric Vivian Tullett in 1915, he changed his name to Tom when he started on the hectic news desk, and 'Tom Tullett' was also a snappy byline. Bylines were all important, and the journalist John Edwards of *The People*, later a columnist on the *Daily Mail*, was inexplicably bylined early in his career as 'Kay Windsor'.

Tom Tullett had become Chief of the *Mirror* Crime Bureau by the start of the 1960s, and would work alongside fellow crime reporters Harold 'Jeep' Whittall and Ed Vale. Revel Barker remembers Ed Vale returning from a crime scene in the late 1960s, and regaling him with the story that when he'd got there, a man was lying dead at the bottom of a fifteen-storey block of flats with his hands and feet tied behind him with piano wire and mouth gagged. When Vale approached the police to see what their theory was of the case, the detective in charge said, 'We have not yet ruled out the possibility of foul play'.

Tom Tullett was a big man, a 16-stone ex-rugby player, well-spoken and very articulate. He would stay on the *Daily Mirror* into the 1980s. Younger reporters were in awe of him and Percy Hoskins particularly in the 1960s and 1970s because of their influence and reputation. Along the way, he wrote and co-wrote eight true crime books. When he died in December 1991, aged 76, the *Daily Mirror* published a tribute piece entitled 'Goodbye to Tom'. At his memorial service at St. Bride's Church in Fleet Street, dozens of journalists and police officers, including the Deputy Assistant Commissioner Walter Boreham of the Metropolitan Police, attended.

Back in 1961, Tom Tullett was just approaching his peak, and the appearance of Edwin Sims in the offices was certainly a landmark in his Murder Gang career, and he and the *Daily Mirror* certainly got mileage out of the macabre situation, splashing it in banner headlines across the next day's front page.

MAN VISITS THE MIRROR – THEN A MURDER CHARGE
– Girl dead in a dyke
Daily Mirror, Tuesday 12 September 1961

Bylined 'By Tom Tullett', there was a large photo under the headline which had been taken by a *Mirror* photographer as Edwin Sims was led away from the newspaper's offices, sandwiched between Det. Inspector Cliff Lloyd and Det. Sergeant Reg Newdick, who was captured carrying the parcel wrapped in newspaper, with Tom Tullett snapped from behind, looking on at Sims. On the centre pages that day, there was an in-depth story, headlined 'Horror on the Marshes'.

Sims had only been charged with the murder of Lilian Edmeades, aged just 16, at this point. Her tragic companion, Malcolm Johnson, was also only 16, and they had been on the way to church when Sims attacked them and murdered them on Denton Marshes. Sims's statement to police was very close to what he had told Tom Tullett, but he said that he hadn't set out to murder anybody that night, despite having the sawn-off shotgun – he planned to dispose of that and the cartridges by throwing them in the river. He claimed his intention after that had been to rob a premises, he hadn't decided which one, 'to clear my financial difficulties'. For this purpose, he also had rubber gloves, four lengths of cord, two modelling knives, and two four-inch nails with which to break in somewhere.

But he hadn't thrown away the gun and cartridges, as 'After proceeding along the towpath for 200 or 300 yards I saw this couple in front of me. I pulled out the gun, which I was carrying inside my raincoat, which in the meantime I had loaded intending to frighten the couple. I had no other thoughts in mind except to frighten them.' Sims was saying that the brutal double murder had been committed on impulse, and not premeditated before he left home at 7 p.m. on 10 September 1961.

Edwin David Sims was 28 years old, and lived at 136 Hampton Crescent, Gravesend, Kent with his mother, sister and brother-in-law, as he told Tom Tullett. He was a carpenter's mate, and very much a loner. When his bedroom was searched, 'obscene' books and photos, showing sadomasochism, were found in a trunk. Sims would also tell doctors that he had visited prostitutes in London.

Police divers searched the dyke where Sims said he'd tossed the bodies of poor Lilian and Malcolm, and Lilian was found first and Malcolm a little later. The Home Office pathologist Dr Francis Camps, then also a Reader in Forensic Medicine at the London Hospital Medical College, performed the autopsies. Both had been strangled with a piece of cord, both mutilated, with Lilian's injuries being worse. It was soon confirmed that the breasts belonged to her.

It was a terrible double murder, but for once there was no hunt for the killer.

Burial of the Sweethearts
Daily Mirror, Tuesday 19 September 1961

Lilian Edmeades and Malcolm Johnson, childhood sweethearts, had been buried in the same grave the previous day, after a funeral service at the Methodist Church, Gravesend, attended by 600 people, flowers were laid out with the word 'Sweethearts' spelled out in silver across them. About another 1,000 people, mainly women and children, some in prams, lined the streets. It was also reported that Malcolm had been a member of the Methodist Boys' Brigade, and Lilian a member of the Methodist Girls' Life Brigade.

But was Edwin Sims mentally sane? Doctors examined him while on remand in Canterbury Prison, Kent, where he was held from 12 September to 16 October, when he was moved to Brixton Prison in south London.

A medical report in the police file, written on 13 November by Dr James Leonard Brown, the Senior Medical Officer of Brixton Prison, stated 'His experience of abnormal sexual conduct dates from the age of thirteen and he appears to have read extensively about the subject in recent years and become incapable of normal sexual activity. He has worn female underclothes and pierced his penis and his breasts, as scars show. He joined a Nudist Club before doing this, and it is obvious that he is a sexual psychopath of some standing. Later, violence and mutilation entered his sexual phantasies. He has shown no remorse, but lately some apprehension. He is of good intelligence, and I find no evidence of mental illness.'

The Director of Public Prosecutions (DPP) judged Sims as 'a psychopathic personality', but 'sane and responsible for his actions'. The trial of Edwin Sims opened on 20 November 1961 at Maidstone Assizes Court in Kent. Sims was defended by Mr S. Rees QC, and prosecuted by Mr Tristram Beresford QC. He was facing charges of the two murders of Lilian Edmeades and Malcolm Johnson 'in the course or furtherance of theft', which meant that he would be eligible for the death sentence under the 1957 Homicide Act if found guilty.

But on 29 November 1961, Edwin Sims was found not guilty on both counts of murder, but guilty of two counts of manslaughter on the grounds of diminished responsibility, the jury finding that Sims was mentally ill.

Monster of the Marshes gets 21 Years
A KILLER CALLED AT THE MIRROR By Peter Harris
MY 28 MINUTES WITH STRANGLER – The horror in his parcel By Tom Tullett
Daily Mirror, Thursday 30 November 1961

Bookending the arrest and sentencing, the *Daily Mirror* gave all of page 3 over to the Sims case, it had been closely involved after all. After about eighteen months in prison, Sims's mental health was obviously deteriorating, and he was transferred to Broadmoor Hospital for the Criminally Insane in 1963, and then to Ashworth Hospital near Liverpool, which would also later hold the Moors Murderer Ian Brady. Edwin Sims died there at the age of fifty-seven in 1990.

DARKNESS AT DEADMAN'S HILL

A CORNFIELD, DORNEY REACH, BUCKINGHAMSHIRE, TUESDAY 22 AUGUST 1961

The registration of the car parked in that lonely field that late summer was 847 BHN, a grey Morris Minor with four doors, the 1956 model. It was just before 9.30 p.m., and darkness was descending. Inside the car were a man and a woman, Michael Gregsten, aged 37, a scientist who worked at the Road Research Laboratory in Slough, Berkshire, and Valerie Storie, aged 22, who was a junior lab assistant there. Gregsten was married, but separated from his wife Janet, their two children living with their mother. Gregsten was now having an affair with Storie, and this quiet – silent apart from passing cars on the nearest road and the natural sounds of the English countryside – after-work evening rendezvous was a lovers' tryst.

Suddenly, the peace was shattered. There was a knock on the driver's window on Gregsten's side of the car. Gregsten lowered the window by winding it down, and then a man pushed a gun into his face, saying in a London Cockney accent, 'This is a hold-up. I'm a desperate man. I've been on the run for four months. If you do as I tell you, you'll be all right.' The intruder then climbed into the back seat and ordered Michael Gregsten to drive deeper inside the cornfield, before telling him to stop. Valerie Storie looked on at her older lover, in anxious silence.

For about two hours the three sat in the Morris Minor, the man, dressed in a smart dark suit with waistcoat and with polished shoes, was talking non-stop in a conversational way, full of nervous energy, almost manic at times, Gregsten and Storie trying to placate him by responding when necessary. Finally, at about 11.30 p.m., the man complained that he was hungry, ordering Gregsten to drive out of the field and onto the road. After a while, the man told Gregsten to buy some milk from a machine and buy cigarettes from a nearby shop, before stopping at a petrol station to fill up the car.

The two kidnap victims were now becoming more alarmed, and Gregsten offered to give the man his car, and both of them all the money they had. When the man ignored this and just seemed to want to go for a drive with them, the dread deepened in Gregsten and Storie. The man's motive obviously wasn't just robbery. They were soon on the outskirts of London, and then towards St Albans in Hertfordshire, north of London, and then onto the A6 road, going south.

It was now the following morning, 23 August, and at just after 1.30 a.m. – the man had now been with them for around four hours – he said that he wanted to sleep for a while, telling Gregsten to pull off the road, changed his mind, and then did the same again. The man seemed unsure about what he wanted to do. When Gregsten asked him what he wanted to do, the man said, 'Be quiet will you? I'm thinking?' Like most with a true cockney accent, the tongue-between-front teeth pronunciation of the 'th' was lacking, meaning it sounded like 'I'm finking'.

As they approached a place called Deadman's Hill, Gregsten was told to stop the car in a lay-by, a slip off the road. Gregsten sensed danger and said no, the first time that Gregsten or Storie hadn't complied. This made the man agitated, and for the first time since getting in the car he actively used the gun as a threat. Then the man said that as he needed to sleep – in the man's Cockney parlance 'have a kip' – he would have to tie them up. The helpless Gregsten and Storie begged him not to kill them.

The man then told Gregsten to take off and give him his tie, and then bound Storie's hands tightly behind her back with it. The man then spotted a bag in the car, which actually contained a change of clothes. The man ordered Gregsten to give him the bag, and as Gregsten moved to retrieve it and turned around, the man fired the gun twice, Gregsten taking both shots in the head. Gregsten died instantaneously.

Valerie Storie was now hysterical, and screamed, 'You bastard! You shot him! Why did you shoot him?' The man, also agitated, said in response that Gregsten had moved too fast and panicked him. Storie then begged the man to let her get help for Michael Gregsten, or, in a rage, to shoot her too, but the man just told her to kiss him. Storie said no and then tried to grab the gun from the man, but she was easily overpowered, and had to kiss the man, who had intense blue eyes. It was now obvious that there was a sexual motive, even though it had started as if it were a robbery.

The man got a piece of clothing from the bag and put it around Gregsten's head, then told Storie to get into the back of the car with him, but she said no again, and the man got out of the car, pointed the gun at her and made her get out too, then told her to remove her knickers and loosen her bra. The man then raped Valerie Storie.

In her highly distressed state, Storie was next told to pull Michael Gregsten's dead body to the side of the lay-by, which she did with a struggle. Next the man ordered her back into the car, and made her show him how to operate the gears and controls of the car – he seemed to have little idea how to drive it. Storie was then told to exit the car and sit next to Gregsten's body. The man also got out of the car and approached her. She took a £1 note from her pocket and waved it at him, yelling, 'Here, take this, take the car and go!'

The man seemed to have decided to do this as he turned his back on her towards the car, but then he spun round and fired the gun four times at Storie, before reloading and firing three more bullets. Five of the seven shots hit Storie – four times in the left shoulder, and once in the neck. She slumped to the ground next to Gregsten. She miraculously wasn't dead, but pretended to be. It worked; the gunman got back into the Morris Minor and then drove it away, south, towards Luton in Bedfordshire, having some trouble with the gears.

The man had driven off at about 3 a.m., so when John Kerr, a university student doing a traffic census, found Valerie Storie still semi-conscious next to Michael Gregsten's corpse, she had been lying there in the lay-by at Deadman's Hill for three hours and forty-five minutes. Kerr got the attention of a passing farm labourer named Sydney Barton, who in turn got two cars to stop, who called for an ambulance.

Valerie Storie would survive, but be paralysed from the shoulders down until her death, almost fifty-four years later, on 26 March 2016. The above account of events is taken from Valerie Storie's sworn testimony.

The Morris Minor, which had actually belonged to Michael Gregsten's mother and aunt, was found left at Redbridge Underground Station in Essex, just outside London, that very evening of 23 August 1961.

The needless and cold-blooded slaying of Michael Gregsten and attempted murder and rape of Valerie Storie caused widespread outrage, public revulsion and fear that late August and September of 1961. In more everyday news terms, betting shops had been made legal on 1 May that year, the Liverpool record shop manager Brian Epstein was about to meet the four members of the Beatles on 9 November, and the contraceptive pill would be introduced on 4 December.

The Murder Gang coverage immediately after what became known as 'The A6 Lay-by Murder' was extensive and front page, and the mystery of who the killer and rapist was would fuel reporting until the late spring of 1962, and sporadically, for decades to come.

The focus would be on the police investigation after the initial shock had subsided. Led by the seasoned Det. Superintendent Bob Acott, it moved quickly. Firstly, the murder weapon – as later proved by ballistics analysis – a .38 revolver, was found on the next evening, 24 August. It was wrapped in a handkerchief under the seat at the back of a No.36A London bus. It contained no fingerprints so had been cleaned, and was still loaded.

A first suspect was then pulled in and interviewed. Realising from experience that the killer may well have booked into a cheap bed-and-breakfast or hotel, the police made an appeal to all managers and owners to report any guests 'acting suspiciously' to them. The manager of the Alexandra Court Hotel in London informed the police team that a man named Frederick Durrant had been locked in his room for five days after the murder. It was a false name, and the man was actually called Peter Louis Alphon, ironically the son of a man in a senior position at Scotland Yard, who was living modestly on an inheritance and by gambling.

Alphon's alibi was that he had been with his mother on the evening and night of the murder, 22/23 August, and that he'd spent the following night of 24 August at another hotel, the Vienna in Maida Vale, west London. Both alibis checked out, and Alphon was released without charge, but he would soon be back on police radar and keep reappearing in the case for years, mostly because of his own doing and seeking of publicity.

At this time, an Identikit picture of the killer was being made with Valerie Storie, who was recovering from surgery, and also with the help of Edward Blackhall, who'd seen the man driving the Morris Minor after he'd left Valerie Storie for dead. This was released to the newspapers on 29 August, but on 31 August Storie told police that she now remembered different details about the man.

Then on 7 September, in Richmond, Surrey, south-west of London, a woman named Meike Dalal was attacked at home. The man had threatened her and told her that he was 'the A6 murderer'. Four days later, two cartridge cases were discovered in a guest bedroom in the basement of the Vienna Hotel in Maida Vale, the same hotel where Peter Louis Alphon had stayed on 24 August. But the manager of the Vienna, William Nudds, told the police that the last occupant of the room had been called James Ryan.

Nudds – who had a criminal record, including for fraud – would later reveal in a change of story that although Alphon had stayed in the hotel, he was in the basement, with the other man called James Ryan in Room 6, but strangely they had swapped rooms in the middle of the night, and that when Ryan left the hotel, he'd asked the way to the 36A bus stop, on which bus the gun had of course been found. Who was James Ryan, and why had he swapped rooms with Alphon? Then, on 23 September it got more confusing when Meike Dalal picked out none other than Peter Alphon from an ID parade as her Richmond attacker. Was Peter Alphon the killer?

Det. Superintendent Acott then took the brave step of naming Peter Alphon to the press as an A6 murder suspect, and with the publicity, the eccentric Alphon soon handed himself in to the police. He was aggressively interviewed at length, but when put on an ID parade before Valerie Storie she failed to pick him out. Alphon was released after four days. Acott and his team then turned their attentions to 'James Ryan' and intensive enquiries led to him being identified as James Hanratty, a 25 year-old petty criminal.

James Hanratty was born in Farnborough, Kent, on 4 October 1936, the eldest of four sons. The family moved to Wembley, Middlesex, where he attended the St James Catholic High School, leaving at the age of fifteen, after which he did a series of unskilled jobs. In July 1952, Hanratty fell off his bike and injured his head, and it was later put forward that he may have suffered either post-concussion syndrome or epilepsy – though never diagnosed – which could have adversely affected his personality. Hanratty was a compulsive liar.

Hanratty had four criminal convictions, for theft, larceny and car theft. The most serious occurred in October 1955, aged 18, when he was sentenced to two concurrent terms of two years imprisonment for house-breaking (burglary) and stealing property. He was placed in the junior wing of London's Wormwood Scrubs Prison, where he attempted suicide by slashing his wrists. There he was labelled 'a potential psychopath' – but he was not yet diagnosed *as* a psychopath, as the youthful multiple killer Donald Hume had been, for instance.

On release, his father, in an effort to keep his eldest son clear of the law, resigned his job as a council dustman and began a window-cleaning business with James. But it was not to be. Just five months later, aged 20, James was sentenced to six months' imprisonment for car theft and driving without a license, actually serving four months at Walton Prison in Liverpool. This time James Hanratty was labelled a psychopath, the 'potential' no longer applicable.

Now 21 years old, Hanratty was sentenced to three years of corrective training at Wandsworth Prison, then being transferred to Maidstone Prison in Kent. But he tried to escape from there, and was moved to Camp Hill Prison on the Isle of Wight, isolated from mainland Britain. Another escape attempt forced his transfer to the formidable Strangeways Prison in Manchester, and then on to Durham Prison, and finally back to Strangeways. So while he had only committed relatively minor offences, James Hanratty had done a tour of British prisons by the time he was released in March 1961, five months prior to the 'A6 Lay-by Murder'.

James Hanratty went on the run when the police put it out publicly that he was wanted for questioning regarding the murder of Michael Gregsten and the attempted murder and rape of Valerie Storie. But while he was hiding out, Hanratty did phone Scotland Yard a few times to tell the police that he had not been involved in any way with the crimes, but that he had 'gone on his toes' as he had no alibi for 22–23 August.

On Wednesday 11 October, Hanratty was arrested in the seaside town of Blackpool, Lancashire, at a café called the Stevonia. Three days later on Saturday 14 October, Valerie Storie picked out James Hanratty from an ID parade. As she had failed to pick out Peter Alphon before, this time, the men lined up were asked to say the line the killer had spoken, 'Be quiet, will you? I'm thinking?'

James Hanratty was charged with the murder of Michael Gregsten that day.

In The Shadow of the A6 – A Mother and Father Walk Alone
Daily Express, Monday 16 October 1961

The photograph on the front page of the *Daily Express* that day, with extra 'photo-news' about the A6 murder case on page 5, showed that Percy Hoskins and his colleagues were cultivating Hanratty's parents for an inside story. That large photo, artistic and haunting by tabloid standards, showed Hanratty's mother and father, Mary Ann and James Francis Hanratty, aged 54 and 45 respectively, walking forlornly in a wood, the photo taken from behind in an emotional and forlorn scene.

But Tom Tullett and Harold 'Jeep' Whittall and their colleagues on the *Daily Mirror* were not to be outdone with their front page five days later:

Day-and-night guard on Valerie – THREAT TO ATTACK A6 GIRL
Daily Mirror, Saturday 21 October

Somebody had called the *Daily Mirror* news desk back on 1 October, threatening to harm Valerie Storie, and then again on Friday 21 October, at which point the newspaper immediately called the police. Throughout November 1961, the *Daily Mirror* would keep the story bubbling away, publishing a photo of Michael Gregsten on Wednesday, 22 November, and with pieces by the journalist Howard Johnson, with headlines such as 'Valerie Saw Man's Icy, Saucy Eyes' in a two-page spread across pages 16 and 17 on Thursday 23 November, and Storie recalling 'Face I Saw In Car Kept Me Awake' by Howard Johnson and Arthur Smith on Friday 24 November.

On Tuesday 5 December 1961, the *Daily Express* had 'Yard Man and A6 Counsel In 140-Minute Duel', referring to an intense and extended exchange between Det. Superintendent Bob Acott and Hanratty's defence counsel, Mr. Michael Sherrard QC. But it was still the preliminary hearings, and Hanratty's main murder trial hadn't even started yet.

The trial of James Hanratty for the murder of Michael Gregsten opened at Bedfordshire Assizes on 22 January 1962. Michael Sherrard QC for the defence had argued that it should be held at the Old Bailey, but this had been denied, and it went ahead in Bedford, a factor in this decision may have been its proximity to Stoke Mandeville Hospital, where Valerie Storie, the key prosecution witness, was receiving specialist treatment for her traumatic injuries.

The trial would last for twenty-one days. Hanratty had two alibi defences: that he had been in Liverpool at the time of Gregsten's murder, and that he'd been in Rhyl, a seaside town in North Wales at that time. It was the latter which gained him more traction, especially when a woman came forward to give evidence that she had seen him in Rhyl at that time: Mrs Grace Jones, aged 58, landlady of a Rhyl bed-and-breakfast. This prompted the *Daily Mirror* front-page headline of Saturday 10 February 1962: 'Landlady at the A6 Trial – I FEEL I SAW THIS MAN'. In fact, the prosecution at the trial attacked Mrs Jones in cross-examination, and made her look like an unreliable witness. It didn't bode well for Hanratty.

The jury went out, but returned after six hours of deliberation to ask the Judge to define the true meaning of 'Reasonable Doubt'. It took the jury just three more hours to come back with a Guilty verdict. It was a unanimous decision. James Hanratty was sentenced to death.

OUR SON'S TWO LIVES
By Hanratty's Father, as told to Express Reporter Ian Brodie
Daily Express, Monday 19 February 1962

Hanratty's father, James Francis Hanratty, gave a front-page interview about his anguish over his son. 'I could never figure out why he became the black sheep because he was so good in so many ways. And it's not sympathy I'm seeking. I'm numb with shock.' The paper had got the scoop it wanted, and had obviously kept in close touch with Hanratty's parents since running that first front-page posed photo of them back on 16 October the previous year. On page 5 there was 'Photo-news – My Ordeal by Valerie Storie'.

James Hanratty's appeal was dismissed on Tuesday 13 March 1962, and the next day the *Daily Mirror* ran on page 11, 'Appeal Judges reject the A6 Killer's plea – HANRATTY TO HANG? – It's up to Mr. Butler' – a reference to the Home Secretary, Hanratty's last chance of a reprieve.

Three days later, on Saturday 17 March, the same paper had a piece by Howard Johnson entitled 'A6 WITNESS DEATH RIDDLE', all over page 1. Charles France, aka 'Dixie', a former West End nightclub manager, who had given evidence for the defence at Hanratty's trial, having known James Hanratty before the murder, had gassed himself in a rented room in Acton, west London, after disappearing from his family home in St John's Wood, north-west London, on the previous Thursday. His wife and daughter had also given evidence for Hanratty, and Mrs France said that Charles had been ill since the trial.

A petition for a reprieve reached 23,000 signatures, but no reprieve was given. James Hanratty was hanged by Harry Allen at Bedford Prison at 8 a.m. on Wednesday 5 April 1962. The next day, Thursday 5 April, page 13 of the *Daily Express* had 'Wreath Left at Jail for A6 Killer'. It had been left there by Mr Raymond Miles, who had helped to organise the petition for a reprieve. The note on the wreath compared Hanratty to Timothy Evans and Derek Bentley, who were both considered to have been wrongfully hanged, and both of those men would receive posthumous pardons.

There were many supporters for Hanratty's innocence. Three official inquiries into the case would take place, in 1967, 1975 and 1996, but no conclusive proof of his innocence was found. Many believed that Peter Alphon, who died in 2000, was the real A6 killer. Campaigning journalists such as Paul Foot, Bob Woffinden and Ludovic Kennedy wrote important books and articles about Hanratty's case.

But in 2002, advanced DNA analysis of the handkerchief in which the .38 revolver had been wrapped, and on the knickers worn by Valerie Storie when she was raped, found DNA in both mucus and semen respectively. After comparing the DNA with Hanratty family DNA, there was a high chance that it was Hanratty, and the Lord Chief Justice ordered the exhumation of Hanratty's body. When compared, it matched perfectly with James Hanratty's DNA. This was seen as 'certain proof of guilt'. But some of his supporters, including Paul Foot and Bob Woffinden – Ludovic Kennedy accepted the DNA result – still felt that the poor exhibit handling techniques at the time and the handkercheif's fifty years in storage could have led to DNA contamination. Still, there would be no posthumous pardon for James Hanratty.

One of the reporters chasing the A6 Lay-by Murder story was James 'Jimmy' Nicolson, later to become known as 'the Prince of Darkness'.

Reporting on Hanratty was Nicolson's first big case, and he would remain in Fleet Street into the 1990s, becoming a legend. In the words of the veteran Revel Barker, Nicolson was 'possibly the last of the breed' of old-school Murder Gang reporters. Larger-than-life, with an unforgettable aura and personality, Nicolson left an impression on every other journalist he encountered, including the seasoned journalist Duncan Campbell, a former chairman of the Crime Reporters' Association himself, who in February 2017 gave a speech at a London Freelance Branch meeting of the National Union of Journalists about his long career in national crime reporting, in which he remembered Nicolson fondly.

Nicolson got his nickname 'The Prince of Darkness' while covering the Spaghetti House Siege in Knightsbridge in September 1975, when three gunmen attempted to rob the restaurant, which had a large amount of cash to pay wages on site, and when police were alerted, nine hostages were taken and there was a long-stand-off.

Nicolson had a sartorial habit of wearing a cape rather than a coat, and at 3 a.m. during that tense siege, when journalists were getting inebriated while waiting for a development, Nicolson walked out on to that Knightsbridge balcony in his cape and was silhouetted against the sky. John Edwards (formerly bylined Kay Windsor) of the *Daily Mail* turned to the BBC correspondent Keith Graves, and said, 'He looked like Dracula, the Prince of Darkness.' This then became Nicolson's nickname in crime reporting circles, and one which he enjoyed. That night would also help prompt one of Nicolson's great lines, 'I've been at every siege since Troy', and another, which Revel Barker remembers, 'I've been on more doorsteps than a milk bottle.'

Jimmy Nicolson worked for the *Daily Express*, *The Star* and the *Daily Mail*, amongst others, in a long and fascinating career, covering some seminal crime stories, and he was an exemplary reporter too, with a vast knowledge and contact-list in the police and underworld. He was also very generous and relaxed with younger journalists. He died in his late 80s in June 2016.

CODA

The A6 Lay-by Murder of 1961–62 was the last big crime story covered by the Murder Gang on a large scale. Times were changing: many of the key Murder Gang reporters had retired or died, and while veterans such as Percy Hoskins, Arthur Tietjen, Tom Tullett and Harold 'Jeep' Whittall would continue in Fleet Street for some time, and fresh blood such as Ed Vale and Jimmy 'the Prince of Darkness' Nicolson were coming through, the atmosphere and environment of Fleet Street, and consequently the way that crime scoops were chased and reported was altering.

By the early 1960s, the national newspaper world based in and around Fleet Street was shifting. Circulations were falling from their late 1940s to mid-1950s peak, with the rise of television news hitting sales, just as the internet and social media news sites would hit circulations again in the early twenty-first century. Newspapers are businesses, and they adapt to market conditions, so many newspapers disappeared, or were swallowed up by other newspapers and groups. Titles in this book such as the *Daily Herald*, *Daily Sketch*, *News Chronicle*, *Daily Graphic*, *Evening News*, *Sunday Graphic*, *Sunday Pictorial* and *Sunday Dispatch* didn't exist by 1970.

Additionally, ways of covering cases were moving on too: very slowly, there was less out-there reporting except when necessary, crime reporters using pubs as an outside base between stories was becoming less frequent, and the old pack mentality was beginning to wane, and then began to disappear, as did the trench-coat and trilby. Britain was also changing – the Beatles and 'Swinging London' brought about a shift in social attitudes, and the so-called 'permissive society'. The old cliché that the culture turned from black-and-white to colour in the early–mid-1960s is certainly true of the Murder Gang – its day was done.

Shock was becoming harder to manufacture by reporters, although crime was still happening every day, and in many ways becoming worse, especially in scale. There were big cases, such as the child serial killers Moors Murderers Ian Brady and Myra Hindley in 1965–66, the case of the little girl killer Mary Bell, who killed two toddlers in 1968, and so on and so on. Murder was still big news, but the Murder Gang, a loose fraternity and a shared experience, was no more.

The Murder Gang was very much of its time, and the practices of some of its members were not suited to the modern era, although the phone-hacking scandal that closed the *News of the World* and implicated several other national papers in 2011 reminded us that every generation of journalist will use dubious practices to get a story, if the pressure is great enough within their newspaper and the wider competitive culture to do so.

But by far the biggest factor in the demise of the Murder Gang was the abolition of the Death Penalty in Britain, with the last executions, of two men, Gwynne Evans and Peter Allen, in separate prisons on 13 August 1964, for the brutal murder of Alan John West, 'in the furtherance of theft' in Cumberland, raised almost no interest from crime reporters. Nobody knew then that they would be the last executions of course, and crimes which are particularly cold-blooded or where the guilt of the defendants is not in doubt have always tended to get less coverage, unless the murder(s) had an extra shock factor. Between the execution of Hanratty in April 1962 and those of Evans and Allen in August 1964, there had been several other executions, with no media whirlwind.

Were crime reporters just mirroring the changing tastes of the British public, as they became more civilised and less morbidly fascinated by that drop from the scaffold? Perhaps just a little bit, but not to a great extent – just look at the shocking and graphic coverage of later crimes in the 1960s and 1970s. Fleet Street crime reporters were still producing that shock factor when the case warranted, but it had to be a huge case, not like in the old Murder Gang days when a different murder could often dominate front pages every week for months at a stretch.

It was the removal of the ultimate penalty, the death sentence, which took away that primal fear and shock amongst readers. Ironically, moves had been being made since the late 1940s to abolish hanging, and the Homicide Act of 1957 greatly reduced the number of executable murders. Ironically, Percy Hoskins of the *Daily Express* had been pro-hanging for his whole career until 1957, when the man who he thought innocent, Dr John Bodkin Adams, was almost executed, and then he changed his mind. But abolition would mean the end of Hoskins and his Murder Gang ilk as they knew it within six or seven years, although the death penalty wouldn't be officially abolished until five years after the last hangings, in 1969.

The former journalist Victor Davis, who worked in Fleet Street in the late 1950s and 1960s, wrote in his article *Murder We Wrote*, 'When hanging was abolished in 1969, much of the buzz went out of crime reporting. The Swinging Sixties swung a little less. No more judge's black cap, no more execution date planted squarely on the home secretary's desk as a reminder that there is a yes–or–no decision to take, no more Albert Pierrepoint and Harry Allen, the deadly duo, overnighting with the prison governor while they tested the trap, rigged the rope and ate a dinner always described as hearty – just like the condemned man's breakfast. Parliament had spoken. That particular life and death drama became grim history and the legend faded of the Yard's star killer-hunters, such as Fabian and Charlie Artful and The Count. It was their dashing careers that were so colourfully chronicled by those other casualties of abolition, the crime reporters.'

The frisson of danger had gone. There was just less at stake. Readers knew that convicted murderers would get a long stretch in prison or perhaps for the rest of their lives if they were particularly dangerous or crime(s) especially heinous, but they would be alive. The macabre fascination of the state ending the life of a mortal miscreant – with even the likes of the often sanctimonious George Orwell admitting that he liked to read about a good murder after Sunday lunch – was what drew many readers to the Murder Gang crime sheets. It was 'an eye for an eye', and often the story of the murder was very interesting too – Orwell too bemoaned the decline in ingenuity of murder, but for him, writing that in the 1940s, the golden era was the 1920s, pre-Murder Gang.

So it was at about the time that the future Nobel Laureate was writing 'The Times They Are A-Changing', in the early-mid-1960s, that Fleet Street crime reporting was changing too. The old ways didn't disappear overnight, but as old hands exited the scene, so did Murder Gang mores. It was left to the likes of Percy Hoskins or Tom Tullett to regale younger journalists in El Vino or their newspaper's pub, about the time when murder reigned, and the elite crime reporters were kings. In the late 1960s and 1970s the first women were entering crime reporting – another sign of the cultural shift. It would have been impossible for women to have got into the Murder Gang; but then those were different times, and perhaps it was for the best that the hard-drinking, chain-smoking, pill-popping, lack of sleeping lifestyles of those old reporters died with them.

It was a hard world in which the Murder Gang operated, especially post-war, when the British public were greatly deprived, many living in bombed-out surroundings, some of them having lost loved ones or friends. The crime coverage offered up by the Murder Gang gave them an escape: Did he or she really do that? Oh, that poor man or woman… Human empathy, mixed with a dash of 'I'm-all-right-Jack' relief, as they contemplate another week with rationing, their children playing where dead bodies are still sometimes dragged from. The Murder Gang speak to them, inform them, use the language they understand, often with a slightly moral tone, even if some slightly immoral machinations had gone on behind the scenes to make that day's crime story appear.

Most wouldn't want to go back to those times. Life is easier now, with so many comforts. On the other hand, some would say that life was simpler then – you knew where you were. Above all, though, the characters were more colourful, a stark contrast to today's increased homogeneity. And nowhere were there more interesting characters than in the Murder Gang you might think.

But if you close your eyes, use a little imagination and enjoy a look into how things used to be done, you will see the reporters drinking in that pub, being tipped off by a colleague fresh from the Crime Bureau at Scotland Yard, rushing off to the scene, getting their stories for that evening's, the next day's or Sunday's edition. That little envelope you saw change hands? 'You didn't see a dickie bird', they would say in their parlance. But also remember as you watch them that they are great professionals, great reporters, who know their subject and their jobs and can make things happen. Press releases for them are just a police tip, it's up to them to find and build the story, and, within reason, not be told what to write. Amen to that.

BIBLIOGRAPHY

FILES

The following Metropolitan Police, Home Office and Assizes files concerning key murder cases were accessed at the National Archives, Kew, London. Thanks to the staff:

Dr Buck Ruxton: MEPO 3/793
Frederick Field: CRIM 1/662; HO 144/20123
Harry Dobkin: MEPO 3/2235
Marian Grondkowski & Henryk Malinowski: MEPO 3/2316
Jenkins, Rolt & Geraghty: MEPO 3/2849
Donald Hume: MEPO 3/3144
Craig & Bentley: MEPO 2/9401/1
Styllou Christofi: PCOM 9/1721
Dr John Bodkin Adams: MEPO 2/9752
Guenther Podola: DPP 2/2979
Edwin Sims: ASSI 36/334
James Hanratty: CRIM 1/3814; HO 291/2184

Files containing information about Percy Hoskins and Montague Lacey of the *Daily Express* were accessed from the Carl Giles Archive at the British Cartoon Archive, Templeman Library, University of Kent in late March 2017. Thanks to the staff.

NEWSPAPERS

The following newspapers were accessed between the years of 1934 and 1964. All dates, editions, headlines, and bylines where given, are acknowledged in the text. A few later editions of these newspapers were also accessed, and again these are all acknowledged in the text. All were accessed on microfilm and digitally at the Newsroom, British Library, London. Thanks to the staff:

Daily Express, Daily Sketch, Daily Mirror, Daily Mail, Daily Graphic, Daily Herald, News Chronicle, Evening News (London), *News Chronicle, Evening Standard* (London), *News of the World, Sunday Pictorial, Sunday Dispatch*.

Two editions of *Time* magazine were also consulted and quoted, the issues and articles referenced in the text.

INTERVIEWS

Revel Barker interviewed by the author in June and July 2017
John Smith interviewed by the author in June 2017
Peter Vey interviewed by Thomas Lean, January–May 2016, accessed at the British Library

BOOKS

Campbell, Duncan, *We'll All be Murdered In Our Beds: The Shocking History of Crime Reporting in Britain*, Elliott and Thompson, London, 2016

Chibnall, Steve, *Law-and-Order News: An Analysis of Crime Reporting in the British Press*, Tavistock Publishing, London, 1977

Firmin, Stanley, *Crime Man*, Hutchinson, London, 1950

Greenslade, Roy, *Press Gang: How Newspapers Make Profits from Propaganda*, Pan, London, 2004

Hoskins, Percy, *No Hiding Place! The Full Authentic Story of Scotland Yard in Action*, Daily Express Books, London, 1951

Hoskins, Percy, *The Sound of Murder*, John Long, London, 1973

Hoskins, Percy, *Two Men Were Acquitted: The trial and acquittal of Doctor John Bodkin Adams*, Secker & Warburg, London, 1984

Jackett, Sam, *Heroes of Scotland Yard*, Robert Hale, London, 1965

Late Extra: A Miscellany by Evening News Writers, Artists & Photographers, Associated Newspapers, London, 1958

Maclaren-Ross, Julian, *Bitten by the Tarantula and other writing*, Black Spring Press, London, 2005

McCrery, Nigel, *Silent Witnesses: The Story of Forensic Science*, Arrow (Random House), London, 2013

Read, Simon, *Dark City: Crime in Wartime London*, Ian Allan Publishing, Surrey, 2010

Ritchie, Jean, *150 Years of True Crime: Stories from the News of the World*, Michael O'Mara Books, London, 1993

Root, Neil, *Frenzy! Heath, Haigh & Christie: How the Tabloid Press Turned Three Evil Serial Killers into Celebrities*, Preface, 2011 and Arrow 2012 (both Random House)

Thomas, Donald, *An Underworld At War: Spivs, Deserters & Civilians in the Second World War*, John Murray, London, 2003

Thomas, Donald, *Villain's Paradise: A History of Britain's Post-War Underworld from the Spivs to the Krays*, John Murray, 2006

Tietjen, Arthur, *Soho: London's Vicious Circle*, Allan Wingate, London, 1956

Tullett, Tom, *Murder Squad*, Triad Granada, London, 1981

Webb, Duncan, *Crime Reporter*, Fleetway Colourback, London, 1963

World's Press News & Advertisers' Review, World's Press News Publishing Ltd, London, 1954–1968

ARTICLES

Beavan, John, Fleet Street 1954, *Spectator*, 5 November 1954

Davis, Victor, Murder We Wrote, *British Journalism Review* Vol. 15 no.1, 2004

Hoskins, Percy, The Press and the Administration of Justice, *Medico Legal Journal*, 1 December 1958

Hoskins, Percy, Crime Reporting and the Police, *Police Journal* Vol. 41 No.8, 1 August 1968

Marchant, Hilde (words) and Hardy, Bert (photos), Fleet Street's Murder Gang, *Picture Post* May 17 1947

Seal, Dr Lizzie (Durham University), Ruth Ellis in the Condemned Cell: Voyeurism and Resistance, *Prison Service Journal*, Issue 199

WEBSITES

www.gentlemenranters.com
www.scoop-database.com
www.britishnewspaperarchive.co.uk

VIDEO

Every Day is Like Sunday (a documentary about the *Mirror* group newspapers post-war) www.youtube.com/watch?v=cicunsmUnas

ACKNOWLEDGEMENTS

Many thanks go to Mark Beynon and the team at the The History Press for commissioning and publishing this book.

Thank you to the veteran crime journalist and gentleman Duncan Campbell, for writing the Foreword to this book.

Thanks also go to veteran journalists Revel Barker and John Smith for generously sharing their memories of Fleet Street and the *Mirror* group newspapers.

Huge thanks to my brother Matthew, Andrea, Ellie, Ollie, Abbie, and Lorna and Len.

Above all, love and thanks to Tracy and Shana for their love and support, and for tolerating me living in the past for a while.

INDEX

The History Press

The destination for history
www.thehistorypress.co.uk